THE TRUTH ABOUT FREUD'S TECHNIQUE

PSYCHOANALYTIC CROSSCURRENTS
General Editor: Leo Goldberger

THE DEATH OF DESIRE: A STUDY IN PSYCHOPATHOLOGY
by M. Guy Thompson

THE TALKING CURE: LITERARY REPRESENTATIONS OF
PSYCHOANALYSIS
by Jeffrey Berman

NARCISSISM AND THE TEXT: STUDIES IN LITERATURE AND
THE PSYCHOLOGY OF THE SELF
Edited by Lynne Layton and Barbara Ann Schapiro

THE LANGUAGE OF PSYCHOSIS
by Bent Rosenbaum and Harly Sonne

SEXUALITY AND MIND: THE ROLE OF THE FATHER AND THE
MOTHER IN THE PSYCHE
by Janine Chasseguet-Smirgel

ART AND LIFE: ASPECTS OF MICHELANGELO
by Nathan Leites

PATHOLOGIES OF THE MODERN SELF: POSTMODERN STUDIES
ON NARCISSISM, SCHIZOPHRENIA, AND DEPRESSION
Edited by David Michael Levin

FREUD'S THEORY OF PSYCHOANALYSIS
by Ole Andkjaer Olsen and Simo Køppe

THE UNCONSCIOUS AND THE THEORY OF PSYCHONEUROSES
by Zvi Giora

CHANGING MIND-SETS: THE POTENTIAL UNCONSCIOUS
by Maria Carmen Gear, Ernesto Cesar Liendo, and Lila Lee Scott

LANGUAGE AND THE DISTORTION OF MEANING
by Patrick de Gramont

THE NEUROTIC FOUNDATIONS OF SOCIAL ORDER:
PSYCHOANALYTIC ROOTS OF PATRIARCHY
by J. C. Smith

SELF AND OTHER: OBJECT RELATIONS IN PSYCHOANALYSIS
AND LITERATURE
by Robert Rogers

THE IDEA OF THE PAST: HISTORY, SCIENCE, AND PRACTICE IN
AMERICAN PSYCHOANALYSIS
by Leonard Jonathan Lamm

SUBJECT AND AGENCY IN PSYCHOANALYSIS: WHICH IS
TO BE MASTER?
by Frances M. Moran

JACQUES LACAN'S RETURN TO FREUD: THE REAL, THE
SYMBOLIC, AND THE IMAGINARY
by Phillippe Julien

THE TRUTH ABOUT FREUD'S TECHNIQUE: THE ENCOUNTER
WITH THE REAL
by M. Guy Thompson

THE TRUTH ABOUT FREUD'S TECHNIQUE

The Encounter with the Real

M. Guy Thompson

NEW YORK UNIVERSITY PRESS
New York and London

NEW YORK UNIVERSITY PRESS
New York and London

Library of Congress Cataloging-in-Publication Data
Thompson, M. Guy, 1947–
The truth about Freud's technique : the encounter with the real / M. Guy Thompson.
p.   cm.—(Psychoanalytic crosscurrents)
Includes bibliographical references and index.
ISBN 0-8147-8206-X (alk. paper)
1. Psychoanalysis and philosophy.   2. Freud, Sigmund, 1856–1939.
3. Heidegger, Martin, 1889–1976.   I. Title.   II. Series.
[DNLM: 1. Freud, Sigmund, 1856–1939.   2. Heidegger, Martin,
1889–1976.   3. Psychoanalytic Theory.   WM 460 T474f   1994]
BF175.4.P45T56   1994
150.19'52'092—dc20   94-2933
CIP

New York University Press books are printed on acid-free paper
and their binding materials are chosen for strength and durability.

Manufactured in the United States of America

10 9 8 7 6 5 4 3 2 1

For Sharada

During my whole life I have endeavored to uncover truths. I had no other intention and everything else was completely a matter of indifference to me. My single motive was the love of truth.

—Sigmund Freud

Whoever, like Freud, eschews philosophy, reveals a truly philosophic mind.

—Lou Andreas-Salomé

Contents

Foreword by Leo Goldberger   xiii

Preface by Stanley A. Leavy, M.D.   xvii

Introduction   xxi

I. The True and the Real in Freud   1

1. Psychical and External Reality   7
2. Realistic and Neurotic Anxiety   12
3. Realistic and Wishful Thinking   21
4. The Neurotic and the Psychotic Experience of Reality   27
5. Real Love and Transference-Love   37

II. The True and the Real in Heidegger   51

6. Heidegger's Conception of Truth   57
7. Heidegger's Conception of Un-truth   64
8. Truth and Science   69
9. Truth and Technology   78
10. Truth and Psychoanalysis   88

III. The Truth about Dora   93

11. The Paradox of Neurosis   97

12. A Case of Secrecy   101

13. Dreams of Vengeance and Farewell   110

14. Freud's Last Word   115

15. Love and Reality   122

IV. The Truth about Freud's Technique   133

16. The Employment of Dream Interpretation ("The Handling of
    Dream-Interpretation in Psycho-analysis," 1911)   141

17. Freud's "Recommendations to Physicians Practising Psycho-
    analysis" (1912)   145

18. On Beginning the Treatment (1913)   155

19. The Concept of Transference ("The Dynamics of Transference,"
    1912, and "Observations on Transference-Love," 1915)   175

20. Working-Through ("Remembering, Repeating, and Working-
    Through" 1914)   192

V. The Rat Mystery   205

21. The Cruel Captain   213

22. The Rat Mystery   219

23. Guilt and Truth   224

24. "Classical" Technique—and Freud's   230

VI. The End of Analysis   241

25. Psychoanalysis, Terminable—or Impossible?   247

26. The End of Analysis   264

References   275

Index   281

Foreword

The *Psychoanalytic Crosscurrents* series presents selected books and monographs that reveal the growing intellectual ferment within and across the boundaries of psychoanalysis.

Freud's theories and grand-scale speculative leaps have been found wanting, if not disturbing, from the very beginning and have led to a succession of derisive attacks, shifts in emphasis, revisions, modifications, and extensions. Despite the chronic and, at times, fierce debate that has characterized psychoanalysis, not only as a movement but also as a science, Freud's genius and transformational impact on the twentieth century have never been seriously questioned. Recent psychoanalytic thought has been subjected to dramatic reassessments under the sway of contemporary currents in the history of ideas, philosophy of science, epistemology, structuralism, critical theory, semantics, and semiology as well as in sociobiology, theology, and neurocognitive science. Not only is Freud's place in intellectual history being meticulously scrutinized; his texts, too, are being carefully read, explicated, and debated within a variety of conceptual frameworks and sociopolitical contexts.

The legacy of Freud is perhaps most notably evident within the narrow confines of psychoanalysis itself, the "impossible profession" that has served as the central platform for the promulgation of official orthodoxy. But Freud's contributions—his original radical thrust—reach far beyond the parochial concerns of the clinician psychoanalyst as clinician. His writings touch on a wealth of issues, crossing traditional boundaries—be they situated in the biological, social, or humanistic spheres—that have profoundly altered our conception of the individual and society.

A rich and flowering literature, falling under the rubric of "applied psychoanalysis," came into being, reached its zenith many decades ago, and then almost vanished. Early contributors to this literature, in addition to Freud himself, came from a wide range of backgrounds both within and outside the medical/psychiatric field, many later becoming psychoanalysts themselves. These early efforts were characteristically reductionistic in their attempt to extrapolate from psychoanalytic theory (often the purely clinical theory) to explanations of phenomena lying at some distance from the clinical. Over the years, academic psychologists, educators, anthropologists, sociologists, political scientists, philosophers, jurists, literary critics, art historians, artists, and writers, among others (with or without formal psychoanalytic training), have joined in the proliferation of this literature.

The intent of the *Psychoanalytic Crosscurrents* series is to apply psychoanalytic ideas to topics that may lie beyond the narrowly clinical, but its essential conception and scope are quite different. The present series eschews the reductionistic tendency to be found in much traditional "applied psychoanalysis." It acknowledges not only the complexity of psychological phenomena but also the way in which they are embedded in social and scientific contexts that are constantly changing. It calls for a dialectical relationship to earlier theoretical views and conceptions rather than a mechanical repetition of Freud's dated thoughts. The series affirms the fact that contributions to and about psychoanalysis have come from many directions. It is designed as a forum for the multidisciplinary studies that intersect with psychoanalytic thought but without the requirement that psychoanalysis necessarily be the starting point or, indeed, the center focus. The criteria for inclusion in the series are that the work be significantly informed by psychoanalytic thought or that it be aimed at furthering our understanding of psychoanalysis in its broadest meaning as theory, practice, and sociocultural phenomenon; that it be of current topical interest and that it provide the critical reader with contemporary insights; and, above all, that it be high-quality scholarship, free of absolute dogma, banalization, and empty jargon. The author's professional identity and particular theoretical orientation matter only to the extent that such facts may serve to frame the work for the reader, alerting him or her to inevitable biases of the author.

The *Psychoanalytic Crosscurrents* series presents an array of works from the multidisciplinary domain in an attempt to capture the ferment of scholarly activities at the core as well as at the boundaries of psychoanalysis. The books and monographs are from a variety of sources: authors will be psychoanalysts—traditional, neo- and post-Freudian, existential, object relational, Kohutian, Lacanian, etc.—social scientists with quantitative or qualitative orientations to psychoanalytic data, and scholars from the vast diversity of approaches and interests that make up the humanities. The series entertains works on critical comparisons of psychoanalytic theories and concepts as well as philosophical examinations of fundamental assumptions and epistemic claims that furnish the base for psychoanalytic hypotheses. It includes studies of psychoanalysis as literature (discourse and narrative theory) as well as the application of psychoanalytic studies of creativity and the arts. Works in the cognitive and neurosciences will be included to the extent that they address some fundamental psychoanalytic tenet, such as the role of dreaming and other forms of unconscious mental processes.

It should be obvious that an exhaustive enumeration of the types of works that might fit into the *Psychoanalytic Crosscurrents* series is pointless. The studies comprise a lively and growing literature as a unique domain; books of this sort are frequently difficult to classify or catalog. Suffice it to say that the overriding aim of the editor of this series is to serve as a conduit for the identification of the outstanding yield of that emergent literature and to foster its further unhampered growth.

LEO GOLDBERGER
New York University

Preface

Nothing persuades us more fully of the vitality of psychoanalysis as a supreme intellectual achievement than the fresh insights into Freud's writings gained by successive generations of students. In them Freud offered far more than he could himself have been aware of. In this way he resembles, for example, Shakespeare and Goethe. For all the massive changes in life and culture that have taken place over the centuries—and perhaps especially during the dark century that has passed since Freud began to write—these writers appear to have anticipated the questions we moderns have to put to them. They speak out of a timeless wisdom, cast in the language of particular times and places, from which new epochs derive nourishment and inspiration. In large measure their greatness resides in their perpetual novelty.

Freud differs from other creative geniuses in a respect we should never lose sight of: he was not only a literary and philosophic creator, but also the founder and chief exponent of a therapeutic method, a method of caring for troubled humans through understanding, with the intention of the alleviation of suffering. As we see in Michael Thompson's exposition, it is necessary to be very clear to what extent this kind of therapy is analogous to medical care, and to what extent the psychoanalyst must depart from his or her disposition to think medically, for the very purpose of offering help. A similar distinction, to which Thompson has also devoted his thinking, rests in the question whether psychoanalysis is a science. Were it not for the prevailing dogma that equates scientific truth with objective validation, this would not be a question worth pursuing. However, in the constant state of attack by the uncomprehending that has been the fate of psychoanalysis since its inception, such questions and distinctions need to be faced again and again.

It is here that Thompson's understanding of Freud brings to light Freud's own largely implicit replies. We are shown how Freud, ever the biological scientist attempting to look to his patients for substantiation of hypotheses established on biological models, was simultaneously engaged in the pursuit of the inner personal truth that defies objectification. For example, he came to recognize the phenomenon of transference—which is the foundation of all modern psychoanalytic theory and therapy, and to which Thompson directs our attention extensively—in the unexpected ways in which patients entered into their converse with him. In the cliché of our own day, the analyst becomes "a part of the problem," and the interaction and dialogue between analyst and patient become the arena in which the hidden truths of the patient's soul are disclosed. This lived transference cannot be grasped in the language of impersonal causality.

Unburdened by the requirement to make psychoanalysis sound like traditional science, Thompson reads Freud in the light of a philosophy of *existence* that was alive in Freud's time, but out of direct contact with his thought or that of his followers. Indeed, as we have been taught, Freud rather disdained philosophy, although with bursts of admiration for a few philosophers. Like many natural scientists, he did not usually consider that scientific method itself was grounded in philosophic proportions. The philosophy of existence, of being, found its most eloquent voice in Martin Heidegger. Thompson's subtitle, "The Encounter with the Real," summarizes an important aspect of Heidegger's philosophy in a nutshell, but fortunately Thompson does not leave us modestly equipped, and he expounds it in relevant detail. I must parenthetically remind those who would write off anything connected with Heidegger—Hitler's unrepentant if ambivalent follower—that the fundamental principles of the philosophy of existence were developed independently by among others Karl Jaspers, a man of uncompromised character, although not nearly as exciting a writer.

Heidegger's influence on psychoanalysis appeared in the important work of Jacques Lacan, and Thompson is also indebted to that eccentric innovator, as he has shown more fully in his earlier book *The Death of Desire*. Lacan too took exception early in his career to the aspirations of psychoanalysts towards affiliation with biological science. One may also see in Lacan's therapeutic approaches, including his highly controversial sessions of variable length, ways of putting into practice the idea of psychoanalysis as a human encounter in pursuit of "the real." The ultimate blunder of organized psychoanalysis in its quest for purity of doctrine occurred in 1963, when the International Psychoanalytical Association pronounced its anathema on Lacan—admittedly not without provocation—thereby helping to sequestrate his school into a cult barely tangential to the mainstream. Happily, Thompson has not followed Lacan in employing mystification as a presumed way of exposing the mysteries of the unconscious; he presents his insights in an exceptionally lively and accessible language.

Thompson persistently questions the technological stratification that has in too many hands deadened psychoanalytic theory and practice since Freud. Freud's own disposition toward systematizing was there all the time, but it was literally concretized in the English translation, the *Standard Edition* of his works, as Darius Ornston and others have amply demonstrated. Thompson does not offer a new language or a new all-encompassing system as a substitute. He does not dispute essential Freudian theory of the unconscious. Rather the other side of Freud comes into focus here: the side that was implied from the start in Freud's greatest technical invention, the fundamental rule of free association. If the rest of Freud's teachings were lost through some misguided censorship of psychoanalytic instruction, we could still reconstruct all that we needed for a great rediscovery, so long as we were permitted to listen to the unguarded discourses of our patients, and to respond to them out of the parallel mental processes of our own minds. For, as Thompson insists, this unique form of discourse moves of its own momentum toward the revelation of personal truth, which is the reality of one's own being.

In this regard, Thompson has done us a service in pointing out the affiliation—direct or not—of Michel de Montaigne with Freud. The sixteenth-century essayist had discovered that allowing his thoughts to run on would bring him to insight into motivations as unexpected to himself as to his readers, and at a long remove from his ostensible subject. We need not assume that Montaigne's essays were spontaneous products of his free associations, knowing that they were subjected to his careful editing, but we remain astonished and delighted at this candor and conscientiousness in allowing so many unorthodox expressions to persist, and so doing to produce, as Didier Anzieu noted, "an awareness of universal mental processes."

Thompson tells us that some of the implications of Heidegger's philosophy for psychoanalysis were developed by the late Hans Loewald, who was in his youth a student of Heidegger's. Being reminded of that, I want to put in a word here in the defense of traditional psychoanalytic institutes and their training programs. It is true that the often excessive length of both training analyses and training programs may inhibit independent thought among young analysts, and that years of confinement to the teachings of a faculty limited in numbers, if not in talent, may narrow openness to new ideas. Nevertheless, I was a colleague of Loewald's in one of those schools for over twenty years, where his influential presence attested to a latitude of psychoanalytic theory that has been not only permitted but encouraged. Anyone with an ear to hear with could discern that Loewald's traditional psychoanalytic vocabulary, and his close follow-ing of Freud, delivered a message profoundly different from the mecha-nistic or "behavioral" prejudices of other formulations. In my career as a training and supervising psychoanalyst, I did not find that the sometimes oppressive structure of the training program kept down native ingenuity, spontaneity or personal responsiveness among candidates who possessed those qualities. Psychoanalysis, despite sometimes heavy-handed theoriz-ing in the institutes, still liberates and enlightens. The ironist Karl Kraus wrote, with malice aforethought, that psychoanalysis cures the neuroses that it creates; we might paraphrase the aphorism to say that the psycho-analytic experience ought to make us impatient with the theories sup-posed to explain it.

Michael Thompson has earned our thanks in producing a book that qualifies as what Heidegger called a "Lichtung," that is, a "clearing" in the woods that opens the way for further exploration.

STANLEY A. LEAVY, M.D.
New Haven, Connecticut

Introduction

We speak of psychoanalytic "schools" in a rough and ready way. In the early days its schools were identified with the cities where they were located. Over time, some of Freud's followers introduced ideas that competed with his (Adler, Jung, Rank, Klein). Subsequently, analytic schools became identified with the work of specific analysts and only vaguely with the city where they resided. Yet, even now psychoanalysis is essentially identified with Freud. How far can analysts stray from the Master and still call themselves a "psychoanalyst"?

Increasingly, analytic schools are recognizable in the ways that they disagree with Freud. Some schools still emulate him (New York, Vienna) and others are critical (Kleinian, Kohutian). The vast array of schools and the respective theories they promote are so complicated that one's position in relation to the others isn't so easy to determine. For example, one needs to distinguish between the American Freudians, on the one hand, and the French, on the other; or between the British object relationists and the Latin Americans. There is so much to choose from, one envisions the possibility of "menus" comprised of endless variations and nuance, selecting what one likes and rejecting the rest: a little bit of this, a dash of that, a spoonful of the other.

When we invoke Freud, to which Freud do we refer? We talk about "the Freudians" as though they're apart from the rest; as though they agree amongst themselves; as though we could spot one if we saw one. We typically say there isn't one Freud, but many. There's the Freud of Hartmann and Arlow and Brenner, and the Freud of Rappaport, Gill, and Schafer. And then there's the Freud of George Klein, Hans Loewald, and Stan Leavy. And those are only some of the Americans. What about the Freud of Jones, Strachey, and Freud's own daughter? And that of

Lacan, Mannoni (Octave), or Brown (Norman O.)? Or the Freud of Laing, Binswanger, and Sartre? Then there's Freud himself and his output: all twenty-three volumes. Who has read them all? There's the Freud of the structural model, which many believe is the "best," and the Freud of the "technical papers," who analyzed Dora and the Rat Man. The earlier Freud was wild and in his prime, humanistic and personal. He made all the "mistakes." He talked—and acted—like an outlaw, a "*conquistador* of the mind.*"

Later he gave us the "death drive," a theory about life's enigma, existential to the core. It's been rejected by almost every one of the Freudians I just mentioned. In fact, this brief inventory of Freud's interpreters shows how extensively his influence has transcended the self-enclosed boundaries of conventional analytic institutions. His reach is legion. The impact is still too immediate, too close to our age to assess. It's too much to take in. When we speak of the school of Freud, we speak of a "university"—a *universe* even—of possibilities. He is the source of a point of view so basic to our era and culture that we grasp at the wind to contain it. How does one go about separating it from the other schools of analysis when they, in turn, are a part of it?

Will the real Freud please stand up? Is there a true Freud? If so, is he good or rotten? Of all the Freuds that are said to exist, is there an essential Freud that they all share in common? Or was Freud hopelessly eclectic, a tinkerer whose thoughts were too restless to pin down? The fact is, there was only one Freud. He was the man who wrote all those works, who lived his life and gave us psychoanalysis. We meet him on every page that we read. He was, and still is, just human. We love him—and hate him—for the person he was. We talk about the man and his ideas. We aspire to separate the two. Surely, if we want to understand his ideas we should come to terms with the man.

The Freud I want to discuss is no stranger. We all know him. You accept him or reject him for who he is, but *who* he is isn't in dispute. He's the one, with increasing frequency, we disparage and attack. We say he was too personal with his patients. He was "excessively involved" and out of control. He never understood countertransference—a concept he invented. This was the Freud who, for many, was too real. Yet, this is the same Freud we continue to hold up as the primogenitor—in fact, the epitome—of "classical" technique, a term whose implied definition is as far from his behavior as the moon. What explains this contradiction? How can the same man embody the two views we have of him: the exemplar of neutrality, on the one hand, and the most brazen psychoanalyst ever, on the other?

The Freud I am going to discuss in these pages may come as a shock to those who have reduced him to the epitome of the aloof, controlled, inscrutable depth behind a mask of implacability; the man who introduced neutrality so he could keep his thoughts to himself. Freud never acted that way and we know it. They say that Freud should have been neutral but wasn't. Freud was involved. There's no denying that. His views are classical, but not because they're recognizable in the style of analysis that has evolved since his death. His views are classical because they're his. There's so much confusion about this issue that it is now impossible to depict Freud's clinical behavior as at all "classical." For this reason I prefer to call it existential. In this book I explain why.

About this issue—Freud's classical status and his alleged betrayal of it—there are some who claim there are two Freuds: the one who wrote the technical papers (between 1911 and 1915), where the technique of classical analysis was established, and the Freud of his famous cases (Dora, the Rat Man, the Wolf Man), the clinician we accuse of disregarding his recommendations and who failed to apply them correctly. This is a picture of a Freud who said one thing and did another, who failed to practice what he preached. Yet, when I read Freud I see no contradiction. I see a man who did what he set out to do; a man who was true to his word, whose behavior was the measure of his words. When I read Freud, I see a man whose rules are not etched in stone. His recommendations about the practice of analysis were uncommonly flexible by today's standards. Many of his rules simply reflected his personality, and he told us why. We, in turn, are invited to do the same. But at the same time, we are admonished to use our heads. To whatever degree we do so, however successfully or not, we're on our own. Ultimately, we're the measure of what we are and who. At the end of each day, we answer to ourselves.

The very nature of analytic "rules" requires that they be flexible. We mold them to our personalities, as Freud molded them to his. Those who take rules too literally deny the spontaneous nature of analysis and its purpose: the freedom to be oneself and become oneself in the presence of another human being. In fact, it's only in the presence of another that we can be ourselves and find ourselves when we're lost. According to Freud, analysis seeks no other purpose than to allow two human beings to meet, in privacy and in truth. Yet, being honest isn't so easy. That's why Freud believed that the only rule that was indispensable—in fact, fundamental—was the one about candor: say what you must and don't hide it.

Freud's ideas about the rules for analysis and the way he treated them himself were profoundly personal. The relationship between the two participants is personal too. That's why his conception of technique was essentially existential. The situation they encounter together is real. How could its technique be anything else? His rules were elastic. Their application with each of his patients were adapted accordingly. He was prudent. Those who wish to refine rules, who seek the "right" rule for every occasion—to be applied en masse—don't understand this. They perceive Freud's flexibility as his downfall and his humanity as a failure.

The Freud I want to talk about was concerned about the nature of truth and its accomplice—the secrets we endeavor to conceal. The truth about Freud's technique is that it is essentially about truth. Freud was only peripherally concerned about mechanisms and psychology. He recognized the enormous ambiguity contained in the phenomenon of phantasy, its latent truths, and its potential for denying reality. Freud realized that our denial of reality inspires every form of psychopathology, that the only way of overcoming the suffering we conspire to evade is to know the reality we deny, and face it. This task is not as abstract—as "intellectual"—as we sometimes make it out to be. It is inherently practical, in the Socratic sense: Know your own mind and be your own person, and the truth will make you free.

We're not that accustomed to thinking about psychoanalysis, in general, and Freud, in particular, in terms of truth, so I have decided to risk including a section in this book on Heidegger's conception of truth and showing its facility for Freud's thoughts about the nature of repression and the unconscious. It's risky because the vast majority of people who are involved in psychoanalysis aren't interested in philosophy. I don't blame them. Most of what passes for philosophy today is so alienated it's of practical use to no one. Freud felt the same way about philosophers in his day. Yet, there are philosophers who are the exception. Freud knew some and was influenced by them. Had Heidegger been older, perhaps their paths might have crossed. As it was, they didn't. I think, however, that the risk is worth taking because Heidegger's thinking is so compatible with Freud's that I'm surprised this book wasn't written much earlier, by someone else. You will have to judge for yourselves if I am right and whether including this section (Part Two) is helpful. If not, disregard it. The rest stands on its own.

I am primarily concerned with Freud's work from the time he analyzed Dora (1900) to the completion of his technical papers on psychoanalysis (1915). A section is devoted to each of these events and a third explores Freud's treatment of the Rat Man. My aim is to show how his analysis of these two patients—a hysteric and an obsessional—is entirely consistent with the recommendations he explicated in his technical papers, written subsequent to their respective analyses. I include another section—Part One—devoted to examining some of Freud's references to the nature of reality throughout his writings, the principal thesis of this work. Freud's views about truth and reality are intertwined, and sometimes only hazily distinguished. Yet, his thoughts on the matter pervade the technique he had crystallized, once and for all, when the technical papers were completed. Finally, I include in Part Six a discussion of Freud's paper on termination, published in 1937, to show its fidelity—at this advanced age—to the papers he had written more than twenty years earlier.

I hope the final result is a Freud who, despite the enormous diversity of his output and the ambiguous nature of his conclusions, was consistent to the end. This is a Freud we have systematically rejected and are in danger of losing. Though some would claim that he is merely a historical figure, I believe that Freud's contribution to analysis is more radical now than ever before. His ideas are no less controversial today than they were in 1900, and for the same reasons. If I have succeeded in encouraging anyone to take a second look at Freud before dismissing him, to really look at him for himself despite the bias against him, then my purpose in writing this book will have been achieved.

Over the last two years I have discussed portions of this book with a number of colleagues and friends. Although I cannot list them all, I would like to thank in particular my colleagues in London, Dr. John Heaton, Mr. Chris Oakley, and Dr. Steven Gans; and, in the United States, Dr. Robert Westfall, Dr. Murray Bilmes, Prof. Wilfried Ver Eecke, Dr. Julius Heuscher, Dr. Randall Weingarten, Prof. Walter Menrath, and Dr. Kirk Schneider. I especially want to thank Dr. Stanley Leavy, who

xxvi *Introduction*

contributed many invaluable suggestions; and Dr. Otto Allen Will, Jr., for whose encouragement and support I am eternally grateful. Both have had a profound impact on my thinking. Of course, none of the people who helped me are accountable for the ideas expressed here for which I, alone, am responsible.

THE TRUTH ABOUT FREUD'S TECHNIQUE

I

THE TRUE AND THE REAL
IN FREUD

Despite Freud's insistence about his relationship with truth, confessed at an old age on reflection of his life, nowhere in his writings about psychoanalysis is the concept of truth discussed. It isn't even a basic term in his theory. When Freud admitted his "single motive was the love of truth" and that during his whole life he only "endeavored to uncover truths," was he talking about his personal relationship with truth, or his professional one? If the search for truth encompassed the entirety of his life, why is its nature neglected in his analytic theories? Why did Freud never talk about truth, as such? The nature of truth is a philosophical question. It isn't now nor has it ever been a medical or psychological *problem*. Freud refused to couch psychoanalysis in specifically philosophical terms. Even ethics and epistemology, so central to psychoanalytic aims, were systematically avoided. He condemned philosophers, almost all of whom generally dismissed his work. Instead, Freud identified with science as it was then understood (and even now). Science, in and of itself, isn't concerned with the question of truth, a speculative meditation concerning one's *experience*. The nature of truth is far more encompassing than what we are able to "observe" about it. It is profoundly personal. Instead, science is concerned with—grant me this generalization—reality, a reality however, which, when defined by scientific method, is strictly measurable and observable. Yet, Freud rejected this definition of reality. The object of his explorations—the mind—isn't measurable or observable. It can only be known according to a person's capacity for thinking. The scientific method—in the social as well as the hard sciences—investigates behavior and the laws in nature that are presumed to govern it. Psychoanalysis is concerned with the mind. Though our minds aren't specifically observable, it is possible to become aware of our thoughts through consciousness. Psychoanalysis also aspires to gain access to a so-called unconscious mind, a form of thought that is not only unobservable but is even inaccessible to consciousness.

Freud's insistence on reporting his findings in scientific terms was one of history's supreme juggling acts, one that has left everyone (scientists and psychoanalysts alike) dissatisfied, spawning endless arguments about whether or not psychoanalysis is a science and, if so, what kind of science it might be if it doesn't (and we know it doesn't) meet its traditional standards. Recall the apparent discrepancy between Freud's statement about truth, on the one hand, and its absence in his "scientific" papers on the other. In fact, Freud's writings reveal a relentless effort to explore the nature of reality, including his remarkable conception of a so-called psychical reality. Even phantasy enjoyed the status of reality in Freud's depiction of it. The manner in which Freud explored the nature of reality shows varied meanings in multiple contexts—only occasionally explicitly acknowledged—many of which bear little, if any, resemblance to science. In spite of Freud's insistence on making his new science appear scientific, he never compromised his avowed endeavor of searching for truth—not fact.

When Freud proposed that psychoanalysis deserved to be accepted as a science, the science that he specifically favored was psychology, one of the most dubious branches of science. The psychological school of behaviorism is probably the only one that has succeeded in gaining at least some amount of credence from the scientific community. Psychology as a whole, because it is increasingly influenced by behaviorism, claims for itself a capacity to engage in scientific research and the ability to interpret the data from its "findings" into general "laws" of behavior. Yet, what relevance can such an endeavor possibly have for a method of investigation—psychoanalysis—that is only minimally concerned with behavior?

Freud's principal concern throughout his writings revolved around the problem of determining what was real in the world and in oneself, and distinguishing what was real from what, unbeknownst to us, wasn't. This is a philosophical proposition and not, strictly speaking, psychological. This question only becomes psychological when it begins to concern the ways in which self-deception may occasion states of confusion that we bring on ourselves in order to avoid a reality we don't wish to accept. Yet, the degree of anguish that prompts us to deceive ourselves in the first place isn't strictly psychological either. Aristotle examined these questions in his book on ethics. There he explored the nature of pleasure, happiness, misery, deception, and honesty—all major themes in Freud's work.

Historically, questions concerning the nature of reality have always been associated with metaphysics, the branch of philosophy that seeks to determine what is real in the world and in the universe. Metaphysics looks at the nature of a "thing," whether it actually exists, whether it's tangible or consists of matter. If it lacks those qualities we're probably imagining it. It becomes an "idea." It isn't real. But the reality or realness of something can't always be equated with its actuality. One of the questions that has always preoccupied metaphysics is the scope and nature of the universe. Another is the existence of God. Proofs of God's existence have been offered, but none of them has ever been based on His actuality. These "proofs," however elegant, never led to any certainty that He exists, though many believe that He does. Consequently, certainty has never been an essential criterion for determining whether something is real (Leavy 1990).

Questions concerning what is or isn't real are ultimately existential in nature. A thing's existence always presupposes, in one way or another, something tangible. That doesn't mean, however, that we can necessarily touch it. Some philosophers—rationalists like Descartes and idealists such as Berkeley—doubted tangible existence and suggested the only thing we could know for sure are mental phenomena. The reality of the world can't, in their minds, be proven, so we can't really know that it's real. Fortunately, philosophers today don't tend to depend on proofs in order to determine if something exists. Generally speaking, we all share a degree of confidence—based essentially on faith—that the world is real and does, indeed, exist in a commonsense sort of way. Freud wasn't especially concerned with such abstract questions. He was deeply preoccupied with the problems that many of his neurotic patients had with what was going on in their lives, in the world around them, and in their thoughts and feelings. They couldn't seem to determine what was going on. They didn't know. Knowledge about something—what is and isn't so—isn't specifically metaphysical. It concerns epistemology, the philosophy of knowledge.

Many of Freud's questions concerned the nature of knowing. How do we know, for example, what is true or false? Freud said this was the question that guided his entire life. What it means to know something—whether or not such and such a thing is true—isn't exactly the same thing as determining whether something is real. But obviously the two are related and at a certain point overlap. Questions about what we can know for sure tend to rely on statements we make about the thing we're questioning. "Is it true that I'm feeling sad?", for example, is a statement that may lead to the nature of sadness, or it may suggest how out of touch I am with my feelings. This is why false statements can be construed as lies if the person says them knowingly, or error if the person says them unknowingly. Freud believed that people who make false statements could do so unknowingly while having a purposeful, ulterior motive for doing so. He referred to this as an *unconscious* act, but he was raising epistemological, not psychological questions: How can I know what I deny and not know that I deny it? Knowledge always implies a truth about whatever it is I'm supposed to know. This is what epistemology is concerned with: How do I know what I know?

 Freud wasn't formally schooled in philosophy in the academic sense, but he was concerned with philosophical questions. He tried to couch them in the terminology of science and psychology. This has led to accusations that he reduced some of these questions to "psychologistic" and "scientistic" explanations. For example, psychologism assumes that all philosophical questions can be reduced to mental criteria. This borders on the rationalist idea that the totality of existence is based on rational constructs. But it's obvious that Freud didn't really believe this. He was a profoundly practical person who insisted that neurotics weren't sufficiently practical themselves. The accusations of "scientism" follow a similar fate. Scientism insists anything that doesn't conform to empirical or rational rules of evidence isn't valid. In other words, it has no truth value. Freud's theory of the unconscious defies scientific norms to such a degree that psychoanalysis is still rejected by the scientific community as anything remotely scientific.

Despite Freud's identification with science, it isn't true that he ignored philosophers or that he rejected philosophy out of hand. One of the problems in recognizing the pervasive philosophical concerns in Freud's thinking is that the philosophers who influenced him weren't conventional, modern philosophers. He was principally influenced by the Greeks—Socrates, Plato, and Aristotle. He was profoundly indebted to Greek myths, to such a degree that he adopted the Greek attitude about human emotion as universally valid. His ideas about passion, tragedy, and deception reveal a predominantly Greek view of life. It permeates everything he came to believe about the origins and nature of *psychopathology,* a psychological term that fails to grasp the devious and melodramatic underpinnings of human passion.

Freud alluded to the problem of truth and reality in both literal and philosophical contexts. He used these two concepts interchangeably and often metaphorically. But when he tried to modernize these ancient questions by insisting they were psychological in nature, he obscured the inherently ethical principles that underpinned what eventually became *psychoanalysis.* Psychoanalysis—to the degree that it's used to help people get well—is an ethic, in Aristotle's sense. This form of ethic, however, goes further than the "Hippocratic Code" because it is essentially concerned with our manner of living and what's wrong—or right—with it. This is what every person who enters analysis comes to explore. It concerns the matter that troubles our souls, the tangible, concrete preoccupations that psychoanalysis was invented to address.

Freud held that the aim of psychoanalysis was to make the unconscious conscious. The nature of the psychoanalytic cure—how to define and how to effect it—was, nonetheless, problematical. Is the process of expanding one's consciousness over and above the unconscious repressions the necessary path to cure? Or is it cure itself? What's more, what does the expression, "making the unconscious conscious," really mean? Psychoanalysis, as Freud conceived it, is essentially concerned with helping us determine what is going on in our lives. It tries to disclose the secrets we hide from awareness, secrets we deny exist. Paradoxically, it's these secrets that evoke our deepest fears about reality, whatever we imagine reality to be. We may be right about reality or we may be wrong. But whatever we are convinced is the case invariably prompts those frustrations we endeavor to conceal. This isn't particularly viable because the things we hide come back to haunt us in indirect ways. We eventually suffer from the secrets we harbor, the same secrets that alert us to the things we fear about reality. These secrets contain a truth, not because they necessarily reveal the nature of reality, but because the things we conceal seem too real to accept.

Psychoanalysis is concerned with revealing the truth about a reality we're predisposed against. The analytic cure, as Freud conceived it, is based on the premise that it's better to know where we stand than to avoid reality, however painful that reality is. Freud didn't talk about truths, per se, but he talked at length about the nature of secrecy, hidden wishes, repressed desires, unconscious motives, displaced libido, and avoided realities. He was a philosopher of truth who never included this term as an integral part of his theory. If we want to determine the place truth enjoyed in Freud's conception of psychoanalysis, we will have to extract it from the context in which he alluded to it. Ultimately, we will find it contained in his many references to our inherent difficulty with reality, and the significance he believed that reality assumes in our lives.

Freud discussed his conception of reality in at least five contexts: (a) inner (psychical) reality versus outer (external) reality; (b) realistic versus neurotic anxiety; (c) realistic (secondary thought process) versus wishful (primary thought process) thinking; (d) the neurotic versus psychotic experience of reality; and (e) real love versus transference-love. I would like to examine each of these contexts in turn to show how Freud tried to formulate a program of psychoanalytic enquiry based on a search for truth—essentially, a philosophical endeavor —while his objective was to get to the "facts" of observable behavior. However scientific his argument appeared, there's no doubt Freud was searching for the truth—whatever he thought about the facts he discovered.

1

Psychical and External Reality

Freud rather reluctantly reached the conclusion that neurosis could neither be explained by nor limited to traumatic events. It wasn't until his "On the History of the Psychoanalytic Movement," published in 1914, that he confessed his despair over the discovery that his seduction theory (that hysteria was the consequence of having been seduced by one's parent) could not explain, in every case, the genesis of hysterical neurosis:

> The firm ground of reality was gone. . . . If hysterical subjects trace back their symptoms to traumas that are fictitious, then the new fact which emerges is precisely that they create such scenes in *phantasy,* and this psychical reality requires to be taken into account alongside practical reality. (1957b, 17–18)

In a recent study of psychoanalysis, Marshall Edelson suggests that "Freud's discovery of psychic reality is described reluctantly in relatively few passages throughout his writings; yet, it is the foundation of all his major achievements. Rarely has any discovery been made so contrary to the intentions and predilections of its discoverer" (1988, 3). Freud arrived at the concept of psychical or "thought" reality as early as 1895 in his "Project for a Scientific Psychology," when he was seeking a foundation for psychology in empirical terms. He believed even then that "indications of discharge through speech are also in a sense indications of reality—but of thought-reality not of external reality" (1966b, 373). Freud was shaken by this discovery and only reluctantly abandoned his seduction theory because of it. Edelson believes that "Freud's despair and even antipathy were not simply a rejection of the sexual context of psychical reality. . . . His anguish is that of the utilitarian rationalist who, wishing the cause of psychopathology to be 'out there,' is confronted by the obdurately non-

rational and subjective" (4). Later, in his *Introductory Lectures,* Freud
lamented the problems this discovery presented in terms reminiscent of a
man who has learned that his wife was unfaithful, as though his patients
had been "lying" to him. Edelson observes that, in Freud's *Lectures,* "the
psychoanalyst is perplexed by the 'low valuation of reality, the neglect of
the distinction between it and phantasy,' and is 'tempted to feel offended
at the patient's having taken up . . . time with invented stories' " (5).

Freud's foreboding at the implications of this discovery is understandable. In fact, he never abandoned the search for confirmation of his
theories in empirical, scientific terms. Even when his discoveries were
taking him further and further away from such confirmation—indeed,
these discoveries comprise psychoanalysis—Freud continued to couch his
discoveries in "scientific" garb. He was afraid that his patients would
refuse to accept his interpretations of their phantasy and imaginative life
unless they were told their experiences were real:

> It will be a long time before he can take in our proposal that we should
> equate phantasy and reality and not bother to begin with whether the
> childhood experiences under examination are the one or the other. . . . It
> remains *a fact* that the patient has *created* these phantasies for himself and
> *this fact* is of scarcely less importance than if he had *really experienced* what
> the phantasies contain. (1963, 367–68; emphasis added)

Freud assumed that his patients would feel insulted if he told them
what they thought was real was only phantasy. They, Freud believed,
wanted—like Freud himself—the truth. All human beings, including
neurotics, want to be taken seriously and resent being told their experiences and recollections are merely products of their imagination. They
feel—and want—these phantasies to be true. Freud knew these phantasies seemed real to the person having them. He even says they are real—
in a way. But how could these phantasies be real if they aren't, unless
they're *experienced* as such by the person who has them? In *Totem and
Taboo,* Freud added that

> what lie behind the sense of guilt of neurotics are always *psychical* realities
> and never *factual* ones. What characterizes neurotics is that they prefer
> psychical to factual reality and react just as seriously to thoughts as normal
> people do to realities. (1958i, 159; emphasis in original)

Freud's depiction of psychical reality isn't the sort of factual reality or
material reality that is supported by empirical science. Freud even defines

this so-called reality in terms of phantasy and hallucination. In what sense can one describe these phantasies as realities when they aren't actually real? Freud sometimes uses the term *reality* metaphorically. He thought that phantasies might be real in the same way that reality may be—but often isn't—"real." In other words, Freud recognized that phantasies, though not literally correct depictions of the past, convey meaning. And this meaning tells us more about our patients' histories than might otherwise be learned. By interpreting phantasies and their symptoms, Freud was able to obtain what was truly meant by them. His use of the term *psychical* reality, which was opposed to *external* reality, actually juxtaposed a *truthful* (psychical) reality with a *literal* (external) one. This isn't to say that literal—or external—reality is false, but it was Freud's genius to see that the truth about one's history—and, by extension, one's existence—can be obtained linguistically by interpreting phantasies and symptoms as disguised messages. The recognition that these phantasies were also messages suggested there was something truthful about them that the patient couldn't simply say. Freud's insight that these phantasies were in some way real was a truth he discovered about the nature of phantasy.

Herbert Marcuse, in a famous study of Freud from a philosophical perspective, discussed the link between Freud's conception of phantasy and the latent truths—if correctly understood—they potentially disclose:

> As a fundamental, independent mental process, phantasy has a truth value of its own—namely, the surmounting of the antagonistic human reality. Imagination envisions the reconciliation of the individual with the whole, of desire with realization, of happiness with reason. While this harmony has been removed into utopia by the established reality principle, phantasy insists that it must and can become real, that behind the illusion lies *knowledge*. (1955, 220)

In other words, phantasy serves a purpose: It reveals the intentional structure of the individual's deepest longings and aspirations. But Freud lacked a conception of "intentionality"—though he talked about intentions and meanings all the time—which would have explained *how* his patients were able to convey in disguised and indirect ways truths they "knew" but couldn't bring themselves to admit. In other words, his neurotic patients unconsciously intended their symptoms and phantasies, they weren't simply "caused" by their unconscious. Freud apparently suspected the existence of an unconscious form of subjectivity that was capable of intending symptoms when he invoked the term *counter-will*, early in his development. In a philosophical study of psychoanalysis, Stanley Leavy notes Freud's difficulty in grappling with the notion of an "unconscious subject":

> One of Freud's earliest ways of presenting the idea of unconscious motivation was as "counter-will" *(Gegenwille)*, a word that is worth keeping in mind whenever we say "the unconscious." Will, so rich in philosophical overtones, has been played down by psychoanalysis. Being a verb as well as a noun, the word *will* always implies a subject. When I do something that I claim I didn't want to do . . . it does no good to plead that blind, impersonal, unconscious forces "did" the act: they are me. (1988, 8)

Leavy's use of the term *will* does not, of course, refer to the conventional usage of conscious will, any more than Freud's expression *counterwill*. Will refers to an "intentional act" and alludes to prereflective, or unconscious, sources of motivation and behavior. Freud first used the term *counter-will* in 1892 in his "Case of Successful Treatment by Hypnotism" (Freud: 1966a). He used it to depict an idea that the patient was unaware of while awake, but became manifest under hypnosis. He continued to use the term here and there in a variety of contexts for some twenty more years. Quoting from Leavy:

> This concept helped Freud to come to an understanding of hysterical attacks. In "The Mechanism of Hysterical Phenomena" [1962] (*Standard Edition*, vol. 3, 32), he said that a patient's "fear that she might make a noise turned into actually making one—an instance of 'hysterical counterwill.'" Freud turned to counter-will in his 1901 [1960] *Psychopathology of Everyday Life* (*Standard Edition*, vol. 6, 158n) to explain the mistakes and delays that often occur in making payments; elsewhere in the same work, Freud attributes many kinds of errors and omissions to the same origin. (12n.)

And later, in a paper on love and sexual impotence, Freud turned to the concept of counter-will again. "He [the patient] now becomes aware that it is some feature of the sexual object which gives rise to the inhibition of his male potency, and sometimes he reports that he has a feeling of an obstacle inside him, the sensation of a counter-will which successfully interferes with his conscious intention" (1957d, 179).

Leavy adds that the term seems to disappear thereafter. "Probably the generalization fell apart into concepts like resistance, repression, unconscious conflict, and ultimately, drive. But the gain in specificity was accompanied by the loss of the implication of a personal 'will'" (1988,

12n.). In other words, as Freud pursued his aim of establishing the empirical "causes" of symptoms, the notion of the unconscious as a subtle agent, anonymous ego, or counter-will, receded into the background. This tendency to depersonalize the unconscious into impersonal drives, forces, and instincts has not met with universal acceptance, even within psychoanalytic circles. The term *instinct*, or *drive*, was scarcely used before 1905, though the concept was there under other guises. Yet, expressions like *affective ideas* and *wishful impulses* clearly convey more subjective nuances than do *instinct*, *drive* or *excitations*. With all the current debate over Strachey's translation of Freud into English, especially regarding the translation of *trieb* into drive or instinct, neither *trieb* nor drive manage to alter Freud's use of the concept itself. Strachey himself went to some lengths to explain the ambiguous way in which Freud used the term *trieb*, but it basically refers to a nonsubjective, impersonal edition of "unconscious will." Whichever term one prefers, *drive* or *instinct*, psychoanalysts, with few exceptions, find it agreeable to use a term—any term— in which the impersonal aspect of the unconscious prevails.

One of those exceptions—in addition to Leavy—is Hans Loewald, who takes pains to explain how his use of *instinct* conveys a human quality. "When I speak of instinctual forces and of instincts or instinctual drives, I define them as *motivational,* i.e., both *motivated* and *motivating.* . . . Instincts remain *relational phenomena,* rather than being considered energies within a closed system" (1980, 152–53; emphasis added).

Terms such as *motive* and *relational* convey a clearly personal use of the term *instinct,* and even the word *phenomena* sounds more personal than *forces,* for example. Freud's shift from counter-will to instinct lent credence to his claim that psychoanalysis—at least in appearance—deserved the status of a science, but a science more similar to that of academic psychologists who "study" rats or physicists who "measure" energies. However much some analysts may strive to measure the psychoanalytic investigation of truth in specifically scientific terms, the legitimacy of phantasy can only be grasped metaphorically, in essentially personal terms.

2

Realistic and Neurotic Anxiety

In a paper read before the Baltimore Psychoanalytic Society in 1949, Hans Loewald addressed a central aspect of Freud's conception of reality, focusing on Freud's insistence that "external" reality—that is, the world—is essentially hostile and antagonistic.

> In psychoanalytic theory we are accustomed to think of the relationship between ego and reality as one of adjustment or adaptation. The so-called mature ego has renounced the pleasure principle and has substituted for it the reality principle. It does not follow the direct path of instinctual gratification, without regard to consequences, to the demands of reality, does not indulge in hallucinatory wish fulfillment, but tests external reality . . . adapting its thoughts and actions to the demands of reality. This conception of the relationship between ego and reality presupposes a fundamental antagonism that has to be bridged or overcome in order to make life in this reality possible. (1980, 3)

Two years after he delivered "Ego and Reality," Loewald returned to this theme again in "The Problem of Defense and the Neurotic Interpretation of Reality."

> The relationship between organism and environment, between individual and reality, in general has been understood in psychoanalytic theory as basically antagonistic. It is Freud's "biological assumption" that a stimulus is something hostile to the organism and to the nervous system. Ultimately, instinct itself is understood as a need or compulsion to abolish stimuli. Any stimulus, as stimulus, represents a threat, a disturbance. On the psychological level, Freud comes to the conclusion that at the stage of the original reality ego, "at the very beginning, it seems, the external world, objects, and what is hated are identical." (1980, 28)

Yet, what is this "reality" that poses such a threat to us? Is this a reality of our own making, as Freud hypothesized so enigmatically as "psychical reality," or is it a reality completely independent of ourselves, impervious to our whims and indifferent to our needs—unheeding, barren, cold? Even Marshall Edelson, no friend of philosophical or hermeneutical interpretations of psychoanalysis, had to admit Freud's problems with this concept.

> We have seen that Freud had trouble with "psychic reality." But judging from the variety of adjectives preceding "reality"—external, factual, material, practical—we may conclude that the conceptual status of "external reality" offered as much difficulty. Freud avoided philosophical questions as much as possible in his work in the interest of creating an empirical science, but here an ontological specter seems impossible to evade. (1988, 7)

Freud was too subtle and complex a thinker to be accused of adopting a superficial attitude toward the nature of reality, especially because it plays such an important role in his theories of psychopathology and psychoanalysis. Edelson points out that Freud "thought about such questions. That he knew and admired the work of Kant and was aware that our knowledge of external reality was shaped by the character of our minds is evident from Jones' biography" (7). Freud explicitly refers to Kant in his paper "The Unconscious":

> Just as Kant warned us not to overlook the fact that our perceptions are subjectively conditioned and must not be regarded as identical with what is perceived though unknowable, so psycho-analysis warns us not to equate perceptions by means of consciousness with the unconscious mental processes which are their object. Like the physical, the psychical is not necessarily in reality what it appears to be. *We shall be glad to learn, however, that the correction of internal perception will turn out not to offer such great difficulties as the correction of external perception—that internal objects are less unknowable than the external world.* (1957e, 171; emphasis added)

What an amazing thing to say. As difficult and imperfect as our knowledge of our own minds is—and Freud is alluding to unconscious mental processes when he refers to "internal perception"—he says that "external" reality is even more unknowable than that! What is the ego's relationship with this unknowable and hostile reality like? How does that relationship generate anxiety and what, in turn, does that tell us about the nature of reality, as Freud conceived it?

It was due to anxiety, in Freud's view, that the ego developed out of the id in the first place, what Freud once referred to as "a frontier creature," whose purpose was to "mediate between the world and the id

... and to make the world fall in with the wishes of the id" (1961d, 56). As I argued in *The Death of Desire* (Thompson 1985, 1–23), Freud's initial conception of the ego was that of a defensive, repressive agency. Even when he modified this view to include a synthetic function, the synthetic function itself continued to be perceived in terms of defense. Freud never abandoned his conception of *Das Ich* as basically defensive, partially because he never entirely abandoned his view of reality as predominantly hostile. Freud viewed the individual as essentially opposed to the world and culture. Culture and reality are repressive, thus they present a threat to every human being. But isn't this how neurotics typically perceive reality, as essentially hostile, ungratifying, threatening? Isn't the nature of "transference" such that the patient in psychoanalysis anticipates—and, indeed, experiences—the analytic relationship in such terms? Loewald proposes that

> on three levels, then, the biological, psychological, and cultural, psychoanalysis has taken for granted the neurotically distorted experience of reality. It has taken for granted the concept of a reality as it is experienced in a predominantly defensive integration of it. Stimulus, external world, and culture, all three, on different levels of scientific approach, representative of what is called, reality, have been understood unquestioningly as they are thought, felt, experienced within the framework of a hostile-defensive (that is, regressive-reactive) ego-reality integration. It is a concept of reality as it is most typically encountered in the obsessive character neurosis, a neurosis so common in our culture that it has been called the normal neurosis. (1980, 30)

Loewald concludes that "psychoanalytic theory has unwittingly taken over much of the obsessive neurotic's experience and conception of reality and has taken it for granted as the 'objective reality' " (30). Of course, Loewald is referring to Freud's conception of reality, and that conception, generally accepted by contemporary analysts, is based on Freud's understanding of anxiety and fear. Freud discussed anxiety throughout his lifetime and revised his thoughts about it periodically. He returned to the subject in 1933 in the *New Introductory Lectures on Psychoanalysis* in his lecture "Anxiety and Instinctual Life" (1964c, 81–111). Here Freud reviews his earlier paper on anxiety in the *Introductory Lectures,* while incorporating more recent thoughts from his "Inhibitions, Symptoms, and Anxiety" (1959a).

Freud initially believed that anxiety was the consequence of sexual repression. Accordingly, when an idea is repressed, "it's quota of affect is regularly transformed into anxiety" (1964c, 83). Anxiety was conceived in terms of a transformation of libido and, so, served an unconscious purpose. The symptom of anxiety was a displacement of the repressed wish that was incapable of being fulfilled. Anxiety was thus unconsciously exciting. Freud eventually came to the conclusion, however, that this theory was untenable. Certain symptoms and conditions, such as phobias, showed that neurotics went to great lengths to avoid anxiety, so the view that anxiety was unconsciously experienced as pleasure wasn't necessarily universal. Freud conjectured that at least some "symptoms are created in order to avoid the outbreak of the anxiety state. This is confirmed too by the fact that the first neuroses of childhood are phobias" (84). Earlier, Freud had defined real anxiety as a signal elicited from an external threat or danger. Neurotic anxiety, on the other hand, was a derivative of the economics of sexual life. This suggested there was an ulterior motive in the neurotic experience of anxiety, similar, for example, to conversion hysteria. But Freud began to suspect that there was a real fear in neurotic anxiety as well. Yet, this fear was presumably located on the "inside" rather than "outside." In other words, "what he is afraid of is evidently his own libido. The difference between this situation and that of realistic anxiety lies in two points: that the danger is an internal instead of an external one and that it is not consciously recognized" (84). Freud concludes that "anxiety, it seems, in so far as it is an affective state, is the reproduction of an old event which brought a threat of danger; anxiety serves the purposes of self-preservation and is a signal of a new danger; it arises from libido that has in some way become unemployable and . . . is replaced by the formation of a symptom" (84).

Freud subsequently incorporated his formulation of the structural model into his new conception of anxiety. The ego is increasingly conceived as the seat of anxiety, whereas the id is the source of passion (85). Freud concluded that "it was not the repression that created anxiety; the anxiety was there earlier; it was the anxiety that made the repression" (86). Whereas neurotic anxiety was previously interpreted in terms of the (id's) unconscious demand for pleasure, it is now understood—in the same way as normal anxiety—as a response to "a threatening external danger." Freud resolves his apparent dilemma by proposing "castration" as the external danger, the inevitable consequence of the boy's lust for his mother.

But we have not made any mention at all so far of what the real danger is that the child is afraid of as a result of being in love with his mother. "The danger is the punishment of being castrated, of losing his genital organ. You will of course object that after all that is not a real danger. Our boys are not castrated because they are in love with their mothers during the phase of the Oedipus complex. But the matter cannot be dismissed so simply. Above all, *it is not a question of whether castration is really carried out; what is decisive is that* the danger is one that threatens from outside and that *the child believes in it*" (86; emphasis added).

Castration—which is to say, the threat of castration—now becomes the source of all our (male) neurotic fears. This threat is "perceived" as a real danger, coming from outside. Yet, as Freud acknowledges, castration doesn't ever really occur, so in what sense is it real? Keep in mind that what we're talking about—the threat of castration—is a concept, not an event. Yet, children are said to experience, in phantasy, the possibility of danger, not because they perceive it, but because they believe it. But isn't this how Freud characterized "internal" (i.e., hallucinatory) reality, as something we believe is so, in contrast to something that is actually the case? This presumably external, real threat is, fundamentally, a belief that is apparently derived from (a) noticing that girls lack a penis and (b) threats from adults to cut off one's hands or penis for playing with oneself. In what sense, however, are threats and discoveries of this kind real, rather than a product of the imagination?

What about the situation with girls? Freud observes that "fear of castration is not, of course, the only motive for repression: indeed, it finds no place in women, for *though they have a castration complex they cannot have a fear of being castrated*. Its place is taken in their sex by a fear of loss of love, which is evidently a later prolongation of the infant's anxiety if it finds the mother absent. *You will realize how real a situation of danger is indicated by this anxiety*" (87; emphasis added). We can see what these two forms of "castration" share in common: loss of penis for the boy; loss of mother for the girl. The penis and the mother are real, and their loss would truly prove catastrophic. But these losses are anticipated, not actually experienced, so in what sense can they be said to be real, unless we employ the "real" in a purely subjective, impressionistic way of speaking? In spite of this theoretical ambiguity, Freud insisted that reality was an outside, hostile force, represented by the father's interference in his child's libidinal strivings toward his (or her?) mother. Yet this position apparently conflicts with Freud's observation in *Civilization and Its Discontents* that "I cannot think of any need in childhood as strong as the need for a father's protection" (1961a, 72). Loewald said that this apparently positive view of the father "harks back to *Totem and Taboo* where the longing for the father is described as 'the root of every religion' " (1980, 8). Also, in *Civilization and Its Discontents,* Freud suggested that "the origins of the religious attitude can be traced back in clear outlines as far as the feeling of infantile helplessness" (1961a, 72). Loewald concludes that "religious feelings, thus, are understood as originating in an attempt to cope with *hostile reality forces.* . . . The longing for the father, seeking his help and protection, is a *defensive* compromise in order to come to terms with this superior, *hostile power*" (9; emphasis added).

Understand that "castration"—a concept—is supposed to symbolize in some concrete way the child's encounter with reality, implemented by the fear of a threatening father. According to Freud, the ego was initially formed out of the infant's experience of frustration. The ego is supposed to protect the infant from (a) its own wishes and (b) the reality of the world's potential opposition. After Freud's adoption of the structural model, the ego was conceived as the seat of identity that comes under assault from three sides: (a) the id (that is, the ego's libidinal yearnings), (b) the superego (its—that is, its parents'—morality, right and wrong, conscience and ideals) and (c) the outside world, in other words—other people—what Freud calls "external reality." Where is the rest or sanctuary for an existence so essentially at sea, at war with its environment and with itself, when even a son's longing and positive regard for his father is merely a way of protecting himself from that very father? Freud was so confident that anxiety is always provoked by an *external* threat that he came to view our wishes as "external" also. In *The Ego and the Id,* he observed that "all the experiences of life that originate from without enrich the ego; *the id, however, is its second external world,* which it strives to bring into subjection to itself" (1961d, 55; emphasis added). And again, "Psychoanalysis is an instrument to enable the ego to achieve a progressive *conquest* of the id" (56; emphasis added). But, in what way can the id be conceived as real unless (a) reality is not objective or external, but rather experienced as such; and (b) reality is a metaphor? And why was Freud so insistent that (a) reality is always external; (b) that this reality, external or no, is always dangerous; and (c) that the prototypical embodiment of this reality is the father? Loewald summarizes Freud's view:

Reality, then, is represented by the father who as an alien, hostile, jealous force interferes with the intimate ties between mother and child, forces the child into submission, so that he seeks the father's protection. The threat of the hostile reality is met by unavoidable, if temporary, submission to its demands, namely to renounce the mother as a libidinal object, and to acknowledge and submit to paternal authority. (1980, 7)

How did Freud become convinced that reality accounts for neurotic conflict? What did he actually mean by reality? Remember the impact, the near-crippling effect, on Freud when he discovered that his patients' accounts of seduction weren't "real," after all. Yet, when Freud, years later, was continuing his search for the cause of repression, he was still looking for something that really happens, something that concretely threatens the child in an actual way. Freud's conception of castration, in its specifically anatomical context, is insupportable, and every psychoanalyst knows that. It becomes even more untenable as a universal symbol of anxiety when we search for castration fears in girls, who, after all, haven't a penis to lose. Sometimes Freud characterizes her anxiety as essentially envious; and sometimes he attributes her anxiety to the "loss of her mother." In fact, Freud could never finally determine the nature of anxiety in girls because he never determined its source in boys, the standard by which he continued to compare and contrast the nature of feminine anxiety.

What is it about castration anxiety that can be said to be real? Does the father actually threaten to cut off his son's penis because he covets his mother? Does the father ever, directly and unequivocally, confront his son about their "rivalry"? Freud says the answer to these questions is "no." The boy, he suggests, more or less puts it together. He takes this piece of evidence ("Don't play with your penis") and that ("That's naughty!"), and another ("Why don't girls have penises?") and interprets these (presumed) experiences and (possible) observations and, in his imagination, concludes he is at risk because the world, his father, forbids him from enacting his sexual phantasies. But if the experience of this prohibition isn't actually conveyed to him, then on what is the child's intuition founded?

Freud hoped to couch his theories in scientific terms, seeking to prove his "findings" through a scientific—in the main empirical—definition of reality. We can see the problem he faced when trying to define his notion of reality logistically, as though situating it "outside" settles the matter.

The distinction between "internal" and "external" may be valid in scientific experiments concerned with physics or mechanics, or even chemistry. But it falls short when applied to a specifically human reality, because for us there is no way of *existing* "outside," strictly speaking. That which exists beyond our imagination is social, not "external." They aren't the same thing. Although there is an inside and outside to a house, there is no inside and outside to a *person*. This is only apt in terms of anatomy or physiology, but not in terms of experience. The social world isn't "outside" of me. In fact, I am in a social world. I inhabit that world. Freud's depiction of an external reality that presumably causes castration anxiety in boys is actually the social world to which boys belong. It isn't dangerous because it poses an "external threat"—it's threatening because boys are involved in a setting that includes fathers, a situation that interferes with—and to that degree endangers—what they want to be to their mothers, that is, the object of unrealizable phantasy. Trying to distinguish between internal and external aspects of reality only confuses the actual sources of anxiety: the world to which one belongs.

Reality, in essence, is social. It is life. This conceptual problem eluded Freud because he insisted on couching his observations about human nature in scientific terms. This problem was only compounded later by object relations theorists such as Melanie Klein (1937), who based her conception of anxiety on the notion of internal and external "objects." How is one to reconcile the difference if the one is always "invading" the other? When human experience is conceived as a mere reflection of "internal" phantasies, is it any wonder that some analysts reject the concept of reality entirely, replaced with "operations" that purportedly determine our experiences for us? These developments are a far cry from Freud's efforts to determine what is real and why we're so afraid of it.

The world to which we belong includes our thoughts, feelings, and beliefs about it. When Freud finally traced the source of castration anxieties to the beliefs that children have about their fathers, he was describing a social—actually, an existential—conception of reality, not a "scientific" one. This is a conception of reality that science has no access to. It has to be thought, experienced, and eventually realized. What threatens children most are the limitations society imposes on them. Transformed into phantasies, their unbridled wishes become treasures they are afraid they'll lose if discovered. The reality they encounter doesn't merely conflict with their desires—it threatens to displace them. Reality challenges them to accept the limits to what is obtainable through their experience of frustration. Reality isn't inherently ominous; it entices and threatens at the same time. Its blows can be harsh, but they also transform. Freud discovered that children haphazardly experience these disappointments through anticipation and belief. If his term for this experience—castration—seems so literal, we should remember that our most tangible experience of reality is contained in that moment of knowing that something precious—however much we may want it—eludes us.

3

Realistic and Wishful Thinking

Once Freud formulated his theory of the structural model in 1923, his earlier allusions to the unconscious as a "second subject," depicted by "counter-will," gradually disappeared. The precedent for this revision was probably determined earlier still, however, by Freud's distinction between "primary" and "secondary" thought processes. In fact, the publication in 1911 of "Formulations on the Two Principles of Mental Functioning" (1958b) roughly coincided with his final reference to the unconscious as "counter-will" in 1912.

Freud believed that the primary thought processes were essentially unconscious. They were presumed to account for displacement, condensation, and the ability to symbolize. This type of thinking is supposed to apprehend time and syntax and gives rise to dreaming. Freud felt these processes were governed by the pleasure principle and so, "strive toward gaining pleasure" and draw back from "any event which might arouse unpleasure. . . . Our dreams at night and our waking tendency to tear ourselves away from distressing impressions are remnants of the dominance of this principle and proofs of its power" (1958b, 219). Freud also believed that unconscious processes were "the older, primary processes, the residues of a phase of development in which they were the only kind of mental process" (219). Originally, whatever the infant wished for "was simply presented in a hallucinatory manner, just as still happens today with our dream-thoughts every night" (219).

Yet, this state of bliss is soon awakened by the "real world":

It was only the non-occurence of the expected satisfaction, the disappointment experienced, that led to the abandonment of this attempt at satisfaction by means of hallucination. Instead of it, the psychical apparatus had to decide to form a conception of the real circumstances in the external world and to endeavor to make a real alteration in them. A new principle of mental functioning was thus introduced; what was presented in the mind was no longer what was agreeable but what was real, even if it happened to be disagreeable. This setting up of the reality principle proved to be a momentous step. (219)

Freud's theory of the unconscious—especially after the introduction of the structural model—rests on the distinction between these two principles and related styles of thinking. The secondary thought processes, ruled by the reality principle, characterize the ego's concern about the outer world. Secondary process thinking "binds" the free energy of the unbound primary processes and is responsible for rationality, logic, grammar, and verbalization. However, if the primary processes are only capable of striving toward pleasure and avoiding unpleasure, and the secondary processes are essential for delaying gratification and forming plans in pursuit of pleasurable goals, to what does Freud refer when he suggests that it's the psychical apparatus that "decides to form a conception of the real circumstances" and "endeavors to make a real alteration in them" (219)? Is this psychical apparatus the primary or the secondary process? It can't be the secondary process, because Freud just explained that the psychical apparatus decided to bring these processes into being. On the other hand, he justified the need for "realistic" modes of thinking because the primary processes are presumably incapable of them. If, after all, the primary processes were capable of the kind of judgment and rationality needed to decide to create the secondary processes, wouldn't the latter prove redundant?

Charles Rycroft, the British psychoanalyst, questions Freud's conception of the "two types" of thinking in "Beyond the Reality Principle" (Rycroft 1968, 102–13). He questions, for example, whether it makes sense to argue that the primary processes actually precede the ones that are said to be secondary. Rycroft suggests that even Freud doubted it, because according to a footnote in "Two Principles of Mental Functioning," Freud himself admitted that

it will rightly be objected that an organization which was a slave to the pleasure-principle and neglected the reality of the external world could not maintain itself alive for the shortest time, so that it could not come into existence at all. The employment of a fiction like this is, however, justified when one considers that the infant—provided that one includes with it the care it receives from its mother—does almost realize a psychical system of this kind. (quoted in Rycroft 1968, 102–3)

Freud might have added to this "fiction" the notion that the infant is virtually helpless before it enjoys the "protection" of its developing ego. Rycroft observes that "Freud's notion that the primary processes precede the secondary in individual development was dependent on . . . the help-lessness of the infant and his having therefore assumed that the mother-infant relationship . . . was one in which the mother was in touch with reality while the infant only had wishes" (103). Again, we are struck by the notion, Freud's notion, that the infant needs somebody else (in this case, the mother) or, later, an ego, to grapple with reality on its behalf. Rycroft believes that infants aren't as helpless as they seem: "If one starts from the assumption that the mother is the infant's external reality and that the mother-infant relationship is from the very beginning a process of mental adaptation, to which the infant contributes by actions such as crying, clinging, and sucking, which evoke maternal responses in the mother, one is forced to conclude that the infant engages in realistic and adaptive behavior." (103)

Rycroft concludes that the secondary thought processes probably oper-ate earlier than Freud had supposed, that they even coincide with primary process thinking. Did Freud accurately depict the responsibilities of the two (hypothesized) thought processes in question? Even if he was right in proposing that infants are ruled by the ones he presumed were primary, what if those processes happen to include those very qualities he attrib-uted to the secondary, such as rationality, judgment, and decision mak-ing; even an awareness of reality? Wouldn't such a scenario negate the utility of the ego's "synthetic" powers? If Freud's original formulation of the ego is retained—that it is essentially defensive in nature—then the so-called unconscious id, governed by primary thought processes, might be conceived as a form of consciousness. Freud's wish to distinguish between two types of thinking could be retained, but only after remod-elling their capacities and functions. Paradoxically, what I'm suggesting would in many ways reverse Freud's scheme. The primary thought pro-cesses—which I believe are "conscious" but prereflective—enjoy a spon-taneous relationship with the world (i.e., reality), whereas the secondary thought processes—those employing the tasks of reflective conscious-ness—determine the individual's relationship with *himself.*

Rycroft reminds us that, by Freud's definition, the primary processes aren't necessarily unconscious, which is to say, without awareness or intentional forethought. He adds that "(a) dreams are conscious; (b) the conscious operation of the primary processes can be observed in (i) various pathological phenomena, notably hysterical dissociated states and fetishistic activity, and (ii) imaginative activity such as play in children and artistic creation in adults" (104).

The line between the conscious and unconscious is ambiguously blurred in Freud's characterization of primary and secondary thought process. The idea that children require an intermediary to grapple with reality posed insurmountable logical difficulties that Freud's increasing reliance on "metapsychological" theories couldn't resolve. Freud's characterization of the ego as an agency at odds with three sources of "danger"—the id, the superego, external reality—is consistent with a depiction of secondary processes that are subjected to the demands of reality on the one side and the urges of the id on the other. An ego that has no desires of its own, but that "pop out," as it were, from the depths of an anonymous otherness could never be truly reconciled with those desires but, as Freud says, could only hope to serve, at best, as "a submissive slave who courts his master's love. *Whenever possible,* it tries to remain on good terms with the id" (1961d, 56; emphasis added). Consequently, this hen-pecked and near-helpless ego resigns itself to a position somewhere between the id and reality, whereby "it only too often yields to the temptation to become sycophantic, opportunistic and lying, like a politician who sees the truth but wants to keep his place in popular favor" (56). The "reality principle," derived from these assumptions, is naturally preoccupied with self-preservation. Given the defensive nature of the ego, even the primary processes pose a threat because after all, it is the primary processes that are thrusting one's ego into the world.

Another paradox posed by Freud's efforts to distinguish between primary and secondary thought process concerns the nature of the so-called irrational and nonsensical thoughts verbalized in the analytic session. If they're so irrational, how can they be comprehended in terms of egoistic, rational, and scientific ways of thinking? If Freud's conception of the rational was rooted in causal, scientific explanation, then why did he insist on seeking the unconscious meaning of the neurotic's dreams and symptoms, rather than their "causes"? By relying on interpretation as his epistemological framework, Freud abandoned science for semantics. This has been noted by others, including Rycroft. If, in fact, we are creatures of semantics and it is language that manifests our symptoms and desires, psychoanalysis no longer relies on scientific rationality to justify its aims — at least not in the way Freud understood science. Rycroft believes that Freud's insistence on couching psychoanalysis in scientific terms resulted in

> the tendency of classical analytical theory to conceptualize primary process mentation, phantasy, and often even emotion, in terms which suggest that they have an intrinsic tendency to be experienced as alien and intrusive to the self, to describe the primary processes as primitive, archaic, unrealistic, etc., and to treat artistic and religious phenomena as analogues of neurosis. . . . [The ego] has been cast in the mould of the scientist at work, and the normal man implied by theory has been modeled on the rationalist ideal. (1968, 106)

Perhaps nowhere is the presumed split between desires on the one hand and the capacity to act on them on the other more evocatively described than in Freud's analogy of the rider on a horse:

> The horse provides the locomotive energy, and the rider has the prerogative of determining the goal and of guiding the movements of his powerful mount towards it. But all too often in the relations between the ego and the id we find a picture of the less ideal situation in which the rider is obliged to guide his horse in the direction in which it itself wants to go. (1964c, 77)

Freud's depiction of the normal state of affairs would seem to characterize, instead, the sort of splitting we might ordinarily characterize as pathological, even paranoid. Instead of assigning to the individual a necessary and inevitable fear of the external world that reduces one's relationships to a capacity for adaptation, why not envision the human infant, as Rycroft suggests, as a creature who starts life in a state of primary integration, by which the infant's expectations, phantasies, and capacity to perceive are epitomized by something akin to Hartmann's notion of an "average expectable environment" and Winnicott's "ordinary devoted mother"? Insofar as the child's "expectations are fulfilled, primary integration continues . . . and he feels at home in the world" (Rycroft 1968, 111–12). On the other hand, when expectations are thwarted and the child experiences disappointment, the child's capacities for wishful thinking and adjusting to the environment split off into different realms, or "types," of thinking. This doesn't mean, however, that the one type of thinking doesn't "know" what the other is doing, or that ignorance, however pleasing, reigns supreme.

The nature of subjectivity has always puzzled philosophers and psychologists alike. Freud's depiction of an "unconscious" agency whose purpose requires interpretation was his singular contribution to our age. But his theories could never explain what his intuition could actually see. Freud hypothesized some sort of self, or agency, prior to the formation of the ego. This was supported by his theory of primary thought processes and, in another context, by his conception of a primary form of narcissism (see chapter 5). We know that the id is capable of thought because, after all, it "decided" to form an extension of itself—the ego—to insulate itself against the anxiety of being in the world.

In practical terms, the division between the id and the ego is a false one. As Freud himself emphasized, the ego is merely an "outer layer" of the id—it was never conceived as a separate entity. If we want to be consistent with the ego's origins, then that ego—following Freud's reasoning—is nothing more than a "reservoir" of anxiety; in fact, the experience of anxiety itself. That is why "realistic" thinking, however else we conceive it, could never be divorced from one's intentions, however unconscious they seem.

4

The Neurotic and the Psychotic Experience of Reality

Perhaps nowhere did Freud demonstrate more persuasively his conception of reality than when he sought to distinguish between the neurotic and psychotic experience of it. After having introduced the structural model in 1923 in *The Ego and the Id* (1961d), Freud wrote two papers in 1924 on the nature of neurosis and psychosis from this new perspective. The first paper, simply titled, "Neurosis and Psychosis" (1961g), contained a formula for "the most important genetic difference between a neurosis and a psychosis: *neurosis is the result of a conflict between the ego and its id, whereas psychosis is the analogous outcome of a similar disturbance in the relations between the ego and the external world*" (149; emphasis in original). Freud depicts the nature of neurosis, now described in accordance with the structural model, accordingly:

> Our analyses go to show that the transference neuroses originate from the ego's refusing to accept a powerful instinctual impulse in the id . . . or from the ego's forbidding that impulse the object at which it is aiming. In such a case the ego defends itself against the instinctual impulse by the mechanism of repression. The repressed material struggles against this fate. It creates for itself, along paths over which the ego has no power, a substitutive representation . . . the symptom. The ego . . . threatened and impaired by this intruder, continues to struggle against the symptom, just as it fended off the original instinctual impulse. All this produces the picture of a neurosis. (1961g, 149–50)

Typically, the ego obeys and even follows the commands of its superego—its "conscience"—which, in turn, "originates from influences in the external world" (150). In its effort to accommodate reality the ego may feel compelled to "take sides" with it. When this happens, "the ego has come into conflict with the id in the service of the super-ego and of reality; and this is the state of affairs in every transference neurosis" (150). On the other hand, when it becomes psychotic "the ego creates, autocratically, a new external and internal world; and there can be no doubt of two facts—that this new world is constructed in accordance with the id's wishful impulses, and that the motive for this dissociation from the external world is some very serious frustration by reality of a wish—a frustration which seems intolerable" (151).

Freud suggests, however, that despite these differences, neurosis and psychosis share the same aetiological factors. "The aetiology common to the onset of a psychoneurosis and of a psychosis always remain the same. It consists in a frustration, a non-fulfillment, of one of those childhood wishes which are forever undefeated and which are so deeply rooted in our phylogenetically determined organization. *This frustration is in the last resort always an external one*" (151; emphasis added). What, then, accounts for the divergence between a neurosis and a psychosis? According to Freud, whether "the ego remains true to its dependence on the external world and attempts to silence the id, or whether it lets itself be overcome by the id and *thus torn away from reality*" (151; emphasis added).

In other words, the ego's relationship with reality governs, (a) the onset of a neurosis and a psychosis and, (b) whether we eventually succumb to a neurosis or a psychosis. Neurosis, generally speaking, is a result of complying with an unacceptable reality, whereas psychosis is a consequence of rebelling against reality by denying it. Because of the ego's incessant "conflicts with its various ruling agencies," it is always striving for a fragile "reconciliation between its various dependent relationships" (152).

Soon after the publication of "Neurosis and Psychosis," Freud published another paper focusing specifically on "The Loss of Reality in Neurosis and Psychosis" (1961f). Now his preoccupation with reality itself comes closer to the fore. While continuing to distinguish between neurosis and psychosis, Freud emphasizes even more emphatically their similarities, specifically their respective relationships with the "real world." Highlighting the difference, he reiterates that "neurosis is the result of a conflict between the ego and its id," whereas psychosis is the result of an analogous conflict "between the ego and the external world." However, he quickly adds that "*every neurosis* disturbs the patient's relation to reality in some way, that it serves him [her] as a means of withdrawing from reality, and that, *in its severe forms, it actually signifies a flight from real life*" (1961f, 183; emphasis added).

Freud's distinction between these two forms of psychopathology—the neurotic's compliance with reality on the one hand and the psychotic's disregard for reality on the other—appears to be compromised by the observation that the neurotic, too, is capable of "taking flight from real life." But Freud resolves this seeming contradiction by qualifying the two steps that are essential in the formation of every neurosis. Step one entails the ego's repression of its (id's) desire. This step, however, isn't specifically neurotic. Neurosis, rather, consists in step two. As a consequence of repression and its failure, the ego tries to compensate for the damage to the id that resulted from its efforts to repress it in the first place. Hence, the loosening of the ego's relationship "to reality is a consequence of this second step in the formation of a neurosis" (183).

Of course, there isn't anything new in Freud's characterization of neurosis "as the result of a repression that has failed" (183). That the return of the repressed—rather than the act of repression itself—constituted neurosis was noted in his correspondence to Fliess in 1896. Later, his increasing interest in the ego and its relationship with reality led him to look at this problem from a fresh angle. At the same time that he wrote these two papers, Freud wrote a third dealing with "The Dissolution of the Oedipus Complex" (1961b). In that study he distinguished between two types of repression in the context of the Oedipus complex.

> After its [the Oedipus complex] dissolution takes place, it succumbs to repression, as we say, and is followed by the latency period. It has not yet become clear, however, what it is that brings about its destruction. Analyses seem to show that it is the *experience* of painful disappointment. (173; emphasis added)

Freud's use of the term *repression* is ambiguous. It is used to characterize a total, or "successful," repression on the one hand, as well as those acts of repression that are only partial, or unsuccessful, on the other. The expression, "dissolution of the Oedipus complex" refers to the successful type, whereas, if the complex isn't actually "dissolved," it is destined to return in the form of a neurotic symptom. Anticipating our objections to this ambiguity, Freud defends his use of this term as synonymous with the more radical dissolution of the original complex:

> I see no reason for denying the name of a "repression" to the ego's turning away from the Oedipus complex. . . . But the process we have described is more than a repression. It is equivalent, if it is ideally carried out, to a destruction and an abolition of the complex. We may plausibly assume that we have here come upon the borderline—never a very sharply drawn one—between the normal and the pathological. If the ego has in fact not achieved much more than a *repression* of the complex, the latter persists in an unconscious state in the id and will later manifest its pathogenic effect. (177; emphasis in original)

If we assume, however, that the origin of all neuroses lies in the failure to "dissolve" our (Oedipal) demands for satisfaction, surely the resolution of future, adult neuroses rests on the same principle, which is to say, the ability to "dissolve" that demand when it arises. How, then, does Freud conceptualize the difference between merely repressing libidinal urges on the one hand, and dissolving them on the other? The preconditions for onset of neurosis are determined by (a) failure of the ego to fully repress (i.e., dissolve) the id's demands, so it displaces them instead onto symptoms, or (b) the relative strength between the id's demands and the ego's repressive forces though, according to Freud, an inordinately powerful id is consistent with the onset of psychosis. How does Freud imagine resolving these conflicting forces in terms other than the ego's success at repression itself? As we shall see, this question suggests no clear answer.

Having suggested that the neurotic, like the psychotic, is capable of losing his grip on reality, Freud examines more closely the psychotic's relationship with frustration. He gives the example of a former patient, a young woman who, at the time, was in love with her sister's husband. "Standing beside her sister's death-bed, she was horrified at having the thought: 'Now he is free and can marry me' " (1961f, 184). She became so guilt-ridden by this sudden eruption of passion that she developed an amnesia of the incident. The repression of her wish, consequently, led to a conversion hysteria. The specifically neurotic component of this resolution to her distress, according to Freud, is that "it took away from the value of the change that had occurred in reality, by repressing the instinctual demand which had emerged—that is, her love for her brother-in-law" (184). On the other hand, had she developed a psychotic response to her anguish, her "reaction would have been a *disavowal of the fact of her sister's death*" (184; emphasis added).

Just as two steps are necessary to generate a neurosis, two steps are also required for the development of a psychosis. Whereas repression of the id entails the first step in a neurosis, psychosis follows a disavowal of reality. And just as the second step in a neurosis—in fact, the neurosis itself—establishes a compensation toward the damage done to the id by displacing the repressed desire onto a symptom, one would expect the second-stage movement in the psychosis to "make good" the damage done to reality. "The second step of the psychosis is indeed intended to make good the loss of reality, not, however, at the expense of a restriction of the id—as happens in neurosis at the expense of the relation to reality—but in another, more autocratic manner, by the creation of a new reality which no longer raises the same objections as the old one that has been given up" (184–85).

The apparent differences between neurosis and psychosis diminish in their respective second stages. Each is supported by the same trends. The second stage in both neurosis and psychosis is designed to aid the id in its aversion to reality. Both represent "a rebellion on the part of the id against the external world, of its unwillingness—or, if one prefers, its incapacity—to adapt itself to the exigencies of reality, to *Avayxn* [Necessity]" (185). But now the distinctions become more complicated. Having suggested that neurosis and psychosis differ more in their first reaction to reality than in the second, "reparative," response, Freud attempts to separate their respective outcomes. "In neurosis a piece of reality is avoided by a sort of flight, whereas in psychosis it is remodelled. Or we might say: in psychosis, the initial flight is succeeded by an active phase of remodelling; in neurosis, the initial obedience is succeeded by a deferred attempt at flight. Or again, expressed in yet another way: neurosis does not disavow the reality; it only ignores it; psychosis disavows it and tries to replace it" (185). The basic difference seems to revolve around what he means by *avoid* or *flight* on the one hand, and the terms *remodel* and *disavow* on the other. Obviously, the key to these distinctions should ultimately rest on what Freud means by reality, because his argument rests on the proposition that (a) the neurotic merely ignores reality and takes flight from it, whereas (b) the psychotic disavows reality and attempts to remodel it. Freud suggested that, ideally, the healthy individual combines aspects of both the neurotic and psychotic, when his behavior "disavows the reality as little as does a neurosis, but [if] it then exerts itself, as does a psychosis, to effect an alteration of that reality" (185).

What, however, is the nature of this reality that we seek to disavow while striving to alter it? Freud suggests that reality is essentially perceptual. In fact, the psychotics' wish to alter it is potentially healthy, if only they didn't need to "disavow" it beforehand. Their decision to reject reality in the first place leads them to alter their perceptions of what is real by way of hallucinations, so they become "faced with the task of procuring for [themselves] perceptions of a kind which shall correspond to the new reality" (186). Freud suggested earlier (see chapter 2) that our original and most startling experience of reality is a perceptual one, the so-called perception of the absence of a penis in girls. In "The Infantile Genital Organization" (1961e), Freud said, "We know how children react to their first impressions of the absence of a penis. They disavow the fact and believe that they *do* see a penis, all the same. They gloss over the contradiction between observation and preconception by telling themselves that the penis is still small and will grow bigger" (143–44). Of course, in order for a hallucination of this kind to occur, the child—or, as the case may be, the psychotic—must, as Freud confirms, believe in it. In other words, the psychotic loss of reality is the consequence of (a) denial of an intolerable reality, and (b) adopting a delusional belief in its place. The denial of reality—the first step to psychosis—doesn't in and of itself occasion psychotic symptoms. Step two—the subsequent delusion that attempts to "repair" the impact of step one—is actually the psychotic symptom, comprising a phantasy that, according to Freud, is inherently distressing, even persecutory. The delusion, then, is the key to psychosis. What is its ostensible purpose? Freud says that, "In regard to the genesis of delusions, a fair number of analyses have taught us that the delusion is found applied like a patch over the place where originally a rent had appeared in the ego's relation to the external world" (1961g, 151).

The denial of reality—such as the hypothetical disavowal of her sister's death, in the example Freud used—creates a "rent," a hole, in the situation that the person is in. This hole, however, becomes intolerable. Although the neurotic is able to survive "gaps" in his memory, a world can't so easily be maintained if the holes we inflict in it remain empty. They need to be replaced with something. But what? According to Freud, with a delusion, a "false belief" that becomes fixed—like a brick in a wall—in the place it becomes inserted, to insure that the "banished" reality stays banished. This is the step—the crucial step, it turns out— that Freud neglected to elaborate in his analogy of the woman whose sister was dying. Had she, as Freud speculated, disavowed her sister's death as a way of avoiding a morally compromising attraction to her brother-in-law, she would have needed to follow this step with another in order to effect a psychosis, in order to insure that her denial would be safe from the encroachments of reality. For example, she might have adopted the delusion that her brother-in-law, the man whom she secretly loved, was conspiring to murder her sister. This type of delusion is consistent with the persecutory phantasies we frequently encounter in paranoia. In fact, Freud believed that the object of paranoid phantasies is the original object of one's love. In his famous book on Judge Schreber, Freud's only case study of psychosis, written in 1911, he said:

> It appears that the person to whom the delusion ascribes so much power and influence, in whose hands all the threads of the conspiracy converge, is, if he [she] is definitely named, either identical with some one who played an equally important part in the patient's emotional life before his illness, or is easily recognizable as a substitute for him. (1958f, 41)

This is why denial of reality, in and of itself, doesn't comprise a psychosis. After all, denial isn't an infrequent occurrence in neurosis. But if denial isn't "supported" by a delusional accomplice, its survival is fragile. It remains open to refutation, in life as well as in treatment. In order to enter the domain of the truly "psychotic," the piece of denied reality has to be "patched" with a delusion. But why is this delusion frequently—indeed, always—distressing? Freud proposed that

> this fact is without doubt a sign that the whole process of remodelling is carried through against forces which oppose it violently. . . . On the model of a neurosis . . . we see that a reaction of anxiety sets in whenever the repressed instinct makes a thrust forward, and that the outcome of the conflict is only a compromise and does not provide complete satisfaction. Probably in a psychosis the rejected piece of reality constantly forces itself upon the mind, just as the repressed instinct does in a neurosis. (1961g, 186)

In other words, the neurotic and psychotic share similar aims and employ similar methods. Neurotics seek to protect their relationship with reality—epitomized by the object of their desire—by repressing their desire for that object. Psychotics, however, seek to protect their desire by remodelling the reality—either the object of desire or whoever assumes its place—which frustrates them. Either method—the neurotics' or the psychotics'—keeps the conflict alive because, in fact, neither neurotics nor psychotics are prepared to "dissolve" their desire when they meet insurmountable frustration, by allowing themselves, according to Freud, to *experience* it. The (neurotics') "repressed" desire returns in the form of a symptom because it's never been wholeheartedly abandoned. Likewise, the psychotics' "disavowed" reality persists in spite of having been remodelled, because the original object of desire—now rendered unconscious— wasn't abandoned either. This "new" reality, in the form of a delusional phantasy, effectively replaces the original (internal) conflict with one that is "outside" of themselves, against which they are now embroiled. They become convinced, and need to *feel* convinced, that they're being persecuted by someone to whom they're attached.

This is best epitomized by delusional jealousy. The object of desire is protected from the aggression that jealousy always occasions by displacing it (the aggression) onto an intruder. Freud recognized that beneath this aggression was an attraction—but the object of that attraction has been repressed. Though the line between neurotic and psychotic jealousy is ambiguous, it can be understood in terms of the degree to which delusional jealousy is directed at someone who torments them, whether they are neurotic or psychotic. Whereas neurotics feel persecuted by their desire, psychotics feel persecuted by the object of their desire. In their *experience,* their relationship with that object is essentially tormenting. Recall how Freud accounted for our capacity to successfully "dissolve" the Oedipal complex, how "analyses seem to show that it is the experience of painful disappointment" (1961c, 173). In other words, our unwillingness to submit to the experience of disappointment arouses pathological defenses against it, whether these defenses are neurotic or psychotic. The acceptance of that disappointment—through one's experience of it— enables us to accept the reality that we're confronted with. While neurotics suppress a bit of "themselves" in their avoidance of disappointment, psychotics seek to disavow reality itself, "altering" it in elegant, though inevitably tormenting, symmetry.

As we saw in chapter 2, the tendency to disavow reality is supposed to begin with every child's discovery that girls lack a penis or, alternately, that boys possess one. Children initially gloss over the apparent contradiction between their observation of the "missing penis" (in the case of the girl, the presence of a penis in boys) and the expectation—based on his preconception—of seeing one. The boy disavows the stark absence of the girl's penis and "hallucinates" one instead. Yet, what is the reality in question? Is it the mere perception of the missing penis, which the child, horrified, disavows; or the child's conception of what is lacking, fueled by his anticipatory imagination? Laplanche and Pontalis suggest:

> If the disavowal of castration is the prototype—and perhaps even the origin—of the other kinds of disavowal of reality, we are forced to ask what Freud understands by the "reality" of castration or by the perception of this reality. If it is the woman's "lack of a penis" that is disavowed, then it becomes difficult to talk in terms of perception of a reality, for an absence is not perceived as such, and it only becomes real in so far as it is related to a *conceivable* presence. If, on the other hand, it is castration itself which is repudiated, then the object of disavowal would not be a *perception* . . . but rather a *theory* designed to account for the facts. (1973, 120; emphasis added)

If psychotics can't accept reality but choose, instead, to disavow and then remodel it with delusion and hallucination, what purpose does this "renovation" specifically serve? Wouldn't they seek to obtain happiness because the reality they disavow is inherently frustrating? When psychotics resort to delusions and hallucinations to fend off—in fact, to change their idea and perception of—reality, to rearrange and remodel it, they do so, not to find alternate ways to achieve their desires but in order to protect themselves from them. But that isn't enough. They have to dismantle the interhuman world that serves as the foundation, the scaffolding, of their existence. This is why, in the final analysis, reality isn't the mere "concreteness" of a world that is perceived or ignored. It is the community of relationships where we reside and take part, where we take chances, commit errors, suffer failures, and enjoy success. Reality is our abode. It isn't "inside" or "outside"—it's where we live, suffer, and survive.

Freud's essential insight into the nature of psychosis is epitomized by the significance he attributed to delusions and what they, in turn, tell us about our experience of reality. He realized that ostensibly crazy beliefs—just like other forms of phantasy—conceal a meaning that, when properly understood, makes our suffering intelligible, once we recognize how delusions—no matter how bizarre—convey a purpose. They tell us something about the people who experience them. The trend in psychoanalysis, however, increasingly conceives of psychosis as a "process"—impersonal to be sure. This process is governed less by drives and intentions—with meaning—than it is by "mechanisms" and "defense." Whereas Freud was the first to employ denial as an essential feature of psychosis, he emphasized the inherent intelligence at the heart of delusion. Because of this intelligence we are able to know these people in their psychosis. They are not that different from ourselves, because they are a reflection of ourselves. They are us, and we, them.

Delusions, like phantasies in general, are a door to the unconscious. They are crucial elements of a dialogue that psychotics are having with themselves. Delusions, like all linguistic expressions, are actually acts of revelation. They contain a truth that, if discovered, can explain the nature of the reality that has become so unbearable to the person who avoids it. On the other hand, psychotics aren't the only ones who suffer delusions! Freud's most famous obsessional patient, the Rat Man, suffered them, too (see Part Five). Perhaps it is reasonable to say that there is a bit of the psychotic in all of us, that the gap said to separate "us" from "them" isn't as wide as it seems.

5

Real Love and Transference-Love

One of Freud's most valuable insights was the discovery that falling in love frequently occasions a peculiarly pathological reaction. The phenomenon of falling in love with one's analyst, though initially perceived as a hindrance to the progress of therapy, soon became an essential and anticipated aspect of the treatment. Freud mused over the mystery of love in a variety of contexts and the question of its nature has become a cornerstone of analytic theory in general. My present concern, however, is more limited. I would like to examine Freud's efforts to differentiate between "transference-love" on the one hand and real, "genuine" love on the other. Nowhere does Freud explore this distinction more poignantly—and ambiguously—than in "Observations on Transference-Love" (1958d). I will explore the practical import of this paper later when I review its contribution to psychoanalytic technique (see chapter 19), but for now I would simply like to examine those aspects of the paper that pertain to Freud's conception of reality.

Freud's objective in this paper was to advise analysts how to handle expressions of erotic yearnings manifested by their patients. While arguing that erotic demands should never, under any circumstances, be returned, Freud sympathizes with the unique difficulty analysts face if they hope to avoid alienating their patients in the process. Freud believed analysts "must recognize that the patient's falling in love is induced by the analytic situation and is not to be attributed to the charms of his [her] own person" (160–61). Naturally, a person falling in love with her doctor (Freud typically uses a female patient as the prototypical example) may become the object of a scandal in the eyes of her relatives and friends. Yet, Freud insists that one's patients should never be admonished against these feelings; nor should they be enticed to concoct them:

It has come to my knowledge that some doctors who practise analysis frequently prepare their patients for the emergence of the erotic transference or even urge them to "go ahead and fall in love with the doctor so that the treatment may make progress." I can hardly imagine a more senseless proceeding. In doing so, an analyst robs the phenomenon of the element of spontaneity which is so convincing and lays up obstacles for himself in the future which are hard to overcome. (161–62)

Freud characterizes this phenomenon as one in which the patient "suddenly loses all understanding of the treatment and all interest in it, and will not speak or hear about anything but her love, which she demands to have returned" (162). Under this "spell of love," the patient typically loses or denies her symptoms and "declares that she is well" (162). On encountering this behavior, some analysts may be tempted to assume that they've achieved a miraculous cure and that her being in love is tangible proof of the treatment's success. On the contrary Freud suggests that, faced with this development, "one keeps in mind the suspicion that anything that interferes with the continuation of the treatment may be an expression of resistance" (162). The reason for this degree of caution is due to Freud's efforts to distinguish between expressions of affection, on the one hand, and signs of resistance, on the other. He explains that an affectionate transference (i.e., a positive transference) is a welcome development because it motivates the patient to cooperate with the analysis. But passionate expressions of erotic attraction are something else again. At the time this paper was written, Freud had not distinguished between erotic and positive transferences, though virtually all that he subsequently had to say on this subject is contained in this discussion on transference. For one thing the emergence of an erotic (transference) reaction has a distinctively troublesome air about it because it jeopardizes the progress of the work that has been accomplished. Previous signs of comprehension and cooperation disappear:

Now all this is swept away. She has become quite without insight and seems to be swallowed up in her love. Moreover, this change quite regularly occurs precisely at a point of time when one is having to try to bring her to admit or remember some particularly distressing and heavily repressed piece of her life-history. (162)

Freud's painstaking distinction between "love" and resistance now comes to the fore. "If one looks into the situation more closely one recognizes the influence of motives which further complicate things—of which some are connected with being in love and others are particular expressions of resistance" (163). However, the emergence of erotism itself isn't synonymous with resistance, per se. Expressions of erotism in analysis merely strive to achieve the same purpose they might on any other occasion: to transform the object of such feelings into a willing partner. The part resistance plays, however, is far more subtle, even devious. Freud warns that any effort on the analyst's part to satisfy these longings will probably only arouse his patient's aggression. In fact, "the patient's condition is such that, until her repressions are removed, she is *incapable of getting real satisfaction*" (165; emphasis added). In other words, the patient's erotic feelings, once manifest, tend to engender a resistance to the analysis that, in turn, acts as an agent provocateur by seizing on this love and exaggerating its passion. The consequence is a deepening of the repression against the patient's capacity for genuine love.

The emerging resistance acts against whatever feelings of love that are aroused, and takes their place while masquerading as genuine love in order to resist the psychical changes that were beginning to occur. This is why, if the analyst commits the error of responding to the patient's entreaties, "in the further course of the love-relationship she would bring out all the inhibitions and pathological reactions of her erotic life, without there being any possibility of correcting them" (166). But if the initial expression of love for the analyst—the "affectionate" transference—is a welcome, and crucial, development for the work of analysis, why shouldn't these feelings be encouraged rather than "analyzed"? In fact, Freud warns the analyst against inadvertently hurting the patient's feelings by behaving in a rejecting manner: "To urge the patient to suppress, renounce or sublimate her instincts the moment she has admitted her erotic transference would be not an analytic way of dealing with them, but a senseless one. . . . The patient will feel only humiliation, and she will not fail to take her revenge for it" (164).

Some patients become so overwhelmed by their emotions and the frustrations they engender that they opt to quit if the analyst doesn't comply. Freud describes them as "children of nature who refuse to accept the psychical in place of the material, who, in the poet's words, are accessible only to the 'logic of soup, with dumplings for arguments.' With such people one has the choice between returning their love or else bringing down upon oneself the full enmity of a woman scorned" (166–67). The only possible response, according to Freud, is to resign oneself to accept their limitations, and wish them good luck.

Obviously, a love that is so demanding and intolerant of frustration must be distinguished from one that is "less violent," which can accept the analyst's neutrality and is capable of assuming an analytic attitude. The "analytic attitude"—in fact, a form of love—entails compliance with the analyst's efforts at "uncovering the patient's infantile object-choice and the phantasies woven round it" (167). Freud conceived of the analytic attitude as one that was consistent with the kind of love he characterized as genuine. "Genuine love, we say, would make her docile and intensify her readiness to solve the problems of her case, simply because the man she was in love with expected it of her. In such a case she would gladly choose the road to completion of her treatment, in order to acquire value in the doctor's eyes and to prepare herself for real life" (167). Indeed, is genuine love even possible within the scope of psychoanalysis? Is it possible, in other words, for a patient to experience genuine feelings of love for her analyst in the course of therapy from the vantage of her analytic attitude—or is this genuineness only possible after her analysis is over, once she is "cured"? Freud believed that evidence of genuine love actually precedes resistances that only subsequently undermine it. In other words, our capacity for love is manifested in our adherence to the analytic attitude, demonstrating a capacity for cooperation that is already inherent in each patient's personality. That is why one's capacity for genuine love needs to be harnessed to a willingness to collaborate with one's analyst by acknowledging—and striving to overcome—resistances that arise.

Not everyone, however, is capable of genuine love. Sometimes the analyst encounters a patient who is dominated by a form of resistance that only pretends to love, already poisoned by the forces of repression. According to Freud, "she is showing a stubborn and rebellious spirit, she has thrown up all interest in her treatment, and clearly feels no respect for the doctor's well-founded convictions. She is thus bringing out a resistance under the guise of being in love with him" (167). Having drawn this elaborate distinction between transference-love (compromised by resistances), on the one hand, and genuine love (which tolerates the analysis of those resistances), on the other, Freud questions whether so-called transference-love isn't actually real when compared to ordinary, everyday love. "Can we truly say that the state of being in love which becomes manifest in analytic treatment is not a real one?" (168). What, precisely, does Freud mean by the term *real* in this context? Does it refer to a love whose achievement is the culmination of a successful analysis? Or is he describing, as he seems to have been implying, a love that is sincerely felt, the kind of love that any "analyzable" person is capable of at the beginning of analysis?

For those who always assumed transference-love, by definition, isn't "real" because, after all, it's the consequence of unabated infantile longings, Freud's question must come as a shock—even bewildering. Furthermore, what place could real love enjoy in psychoanalytic treatment? Isn't the basis of transference rooted in phantasy? In response to this entirely unexpected, and frequently overlooked, question, Freud says something that in hindsight is truly amazing: "The part played by resistance in transference-love is unquestionable and very considerable. Nevertheless the resistance did not, after all *create* this love; it finds it ready to hand, makes use of it and aggravates its manifestations" (168; emphasis added). To make sure we understand what Freud has in mind, he goes on: "Nor is the genuineness of the phenomenon disproved by the resistance. . . . It is true that it repeats infantile reactions. But this is the essential character of every state of being in love. *There is no such state which does not reproduce infantile prototypes*" (168; emphasis added).

If there isn't any kind of love that doesn't derive from "infantile prototypes"—genuine, real, or transferential—then what distinguishes the real from the transferential? Throughout this paper, Freud contrasts the two in respect to their aims. Genuine love presumably aims at a "real" object, whereas transference-love aims at "the patient's infantile object-choice and the phantasies woven around it" (167). What's more, Freud adds, "It is precisely from this infantile determination that it receives its compulsive character, verging as it does on the pathological" (168). In other words, the relationship between love and infantilism doesn't define the pathological, but merely "verges" on it. What, then, distinguishes "transference-love"? "Transference-love has perhaps a degree less of freedom than the love which appears in ordinary life and is called normal; it displays its dependence on the infantile pattern more clearly and is less adaptable and capable of modification" (168). Recall that it is love's aim that characterizes the difference between the infantile and the normal, rather than the specific emotions that we customarily attribute to our experience of love. But if love is in its essence rooted in the infantile, how does it become "normal"? Does it find an object that approximates the infantile wish? Or does it abandon the infantile wish altogether? Even Freud seems at wit's end when he exclaims, "By what other signs can the genuineness of a love be recognized? By its efficacy, its serviceability in achieving the aim of love? In this respect transference-love seems to be second to none; one has the impression that one could obtain anything from it" (168).

Even the attributes of resourcefulness and determination prove irrelevant when attempting to determine the nature of normal love. If the degree of passion fails to persuade us of its genuine nature, then by what criteria might we hope to distinguish the genuine from the pathological?

> Let us sum up, therefore. We have no right to dispute that the state of being in love which makes its appearance in the course of analytic treatment has the character of a "genuine" love. If it seems so lacking in normality, this is sufficiently explained by the fact that being in love in ordinary life, outside analysis, is also more similar to abnormal than to normal mental phenomena. Nevertheless, transference-love is characterized by certain features which ensure it a special position. In the first place, it is provoked by the analytic situation; secondly, it is greatly intensified by the resistance, which dominates the situation; and thirdly, it is lacking to a high degree in a regard for reality, is less sensible, less concerned about consequences and more blind in its valuation of the loved person than we are prepared to admit in the case of normal love. We should not forget, however, that *these departures from the norm constitute precisely what is essential about being in love.* (168–69; emphasis added)

Let's look at these three criteria more closely. To suggest that transference-love is provoked by the analytic situation is true enough, but hardly exclusive. Any situation in which one person, placed in a position of authority, brings to bear all his attentiveness and sympathetic concern about the other person's trials and woes of living—including sexual and romantic grievances—will inevitably provoke a "transference reaction," an affectionate appreciation. Traditionally, aunts and uncles assumed this function in families. Furthermore, perhaps most importantly, resistance to analysis—or, generally speaking, resistance to revealing oneself to the person whom one idealizes—frequently evokes the kind of hostile reactions Freud attributes to the effects of repression. Yet, if resistance to analysis—a resistance that makes use of the transference-love reaction—obtains a regression to infantile love, a love that lends the transference its compulsive character, then how can this regressive-pathological element be reconciled with the statement that love in general—the genuine included—is no different? Finally, what does Freud mean by "lacking in regard for reality" when he adds that this very quality constitutes love in its essence? Earlier Freud said that being in love (with one's analyst) is initially genuine, but subsequently arouses resistance. On the other hand, a presumably "healthy" patient—one who is truly devoted to her analyst—would willingly succumb to the treatment and "prepare herself for real life," the very thing that her analyst wants from her. How does one manage to achieve this degree of compliance? Freud tries to resolve these ambiguities with the conclusion that "she [the patient] has to learn from him [the analyst] to overcome the pleasure principle, to give up satisfaction which lies at hand but is socially not acceptable, in favor of a distant one, which is perhaps altogether uncertain" (170). Thus her capacity for love should lead the patient to conclude she needs to make a sacrifice, momentarily forego her pleasure and obey the "reality principle" for which she will be rewarded—later.

But why should delaying satisfaction make the patient's love any more real than the genuineness already felt towards the analyst? Is realistic love identical to the genuine, aim-inhibited kind that epitomizes the analytic attitude, or are they different kinds of love entirely? Why can't the analyst return the patient's love if, after all, it's genuine? Is the patient's love real, but the object of her love "unrealistic"; or is the patient's love only "imagined" in the first place? What happens at completion of analysis when, healthy and cured, the patient's conflicts no longer jeopardize the genuineness of her feelings and the achievement of her aims? Why can't she be rewarded with the prize for which she so earnestly struggled? Because, "After all the difficulties have been successfully overcome, she will often confess to having had an anticipatory phantasy at the time when she entered the treatment, to the effect that if she behaved well she would be rewarded at the end by the doctor's affection" (169). Often enough, patients fail to resolve their "transference" at termination. And often enough, analysts fall in love with their patients. Occasionally, some even marry them subsequent to treatment. Of course, this is never accepted by their peers. Why not? Freud explains that

> for the doctor, ethical motives unite with the technical ones to restrain him from giving the patient his love. The aim he has to keep in view is that this woman, whose capacity for love is impaired by infantile fixations, should gain free command over a function which is of such inestimable importance to her; that she should not, however, dissipate it in the treatment, but keep

it ready for the time when, after her treatment, the demands of real life make themselves felt. (169)

This is only one of the many contexts in which Freud equates technical issues with ethical ones. Psychoanalysis comes into being where the two intersect. This is why the analyst

> must not stage the scene of a dog-race in which the prize was to be a garland of sausages but which some humorist spoilt by throwing a single sausage on to the track. The result was, of course, that the dogs threw themselves upon it and forgot all about the race and about the garland that was luring them to victory in the far distance. I do not mean to say that it is always easy for the doctor to keep within the limits *prescribed by ethics and technique*. Those who are still youngish and not yet bound by strong ties may in particular find it a hard task (169; emphasis added)

It isn't always so easy to say whose ethics Freud is emphasizing: those of the patient or the doctor? Surely both carry equal weight. In fact, the question of ethics plays a major function in Freud's estimation of what reality is comprised of. Let's return to his comments about the opposition between the pleasure principle and ethical behavior: "She has to learn from him [the analyst] to overcome the pleasure principle, to give up a satisfaction which lies to hand but is socially not acceptable, in favor of a more distant one, which is perhaps altogether uncertain, but which is both psychologically and socially unimpeachable" (170).

In other words, if patients ever hope to overcome their infantile yearnings and obtain real satisfaction subsequent to the termination of analysis, they have to renounce whatever remains of their love for the analyst and do the right thing: conform to "socially acceptable" conduct. In this particular context, Freud equates real ("realistic") love with what is socially and ethically "unimpeachable." The analysis is a microcosm of society; it helps us come to terms with—by accepting—society's rules. Freud believed it was critical to distinguish between genuine feelings of love (dominated by the pleasure principle) on the one hand, and attaining real love (the "garland of sausages") by submitting to what is practicable, on the other. It is perhaps ironic that Freud was so concerned with ethics and propriety when he devoted most of his life to rebelling against the beliefs of the society to which he belonged. In practice, Freud bent the rules whenever he was compelled to by individual judgment and tact. But we would be mistaken if we equated Freud's concern for behaving realistically (and ethically) with capitulating to the arbitrary customs of one's neighbors.

Being true to one's feelings—and to one's principles—requires sacrifice. It doesn't always obtain gratification. What is true isn't necessarily reducible to what is real. It may be true that I love somebody, but unrealistic to expect my love can be returned in the way that I want it to be. What is "socially acceptable" merely determines what is attainable. The purpose of analysis is to realize what is possible. It's easy to love one's analyst and certainly convenient, but although this love, so immediate and ready to hand, may be accessible, is it realistic? If the so-called infantile origins of all love, essentially narcissistic, can be conquered, sooner or later it is necessary to succumb to disappointment. The wish to be loved by one's analyst must inevitably go unrewarded, not because the feelings that prompt these longings aren't genuine, but because their satisfaction is simply a denial of reality, of the limitations their situation engenders. Yet, how is the patient's emancipation—so elusive and painful—finally achieved? If Freud's comments suggest anything, it's that we have to work for our freedom; and this work is of a special kind. Even if the love felt for one's analyst is genuine, it isn't enough. To be viable, love requires more than genuineness—it entails suffering. Real love needs to recognize and accept life's laws and limitations. This is what it means to be ethical. It isn't a question of doing what is "good," but of doing what is right: whatever fits the occasion.

Yet, when Freud says that genuine love—if his patient were capable of it—would lead her to become docile and submissive, that she would strive to perform the analytic work in order to please him, is this entirely convincing? If she were docile, would she cease to experience erotic longings, or simply accept them? Is normality determined by the conscious control over one's impulses, or the freedom from these impulses themselves? If hysteria, in particular, is epitomized by a demand for love that can be insatiable, is the demand itself pathological or simply one's refusal to recognize it? What is it about erotic strivings, after all, that can be said to be "neurotic" when we know that the repression of those strivings is the cause of neurosis?

In his 1914 paper "On Narcissism" Freud proposed that all children set before themselves an ideal of themselves that, in turn, becomes the object of their erotic yearnings. "This ideal ego is now the target of the self-love which was enjoyed in childhood by the actual ego" (1957c, 94).

Because every child is reluctant to give up earlier sources of satisfaction, Freud argued that "when, as he [she] grows up, he is disturbed by the admonitions of others and by the awakening of his own critical judgement, so that he can no longer retain that perfection, he seeks to recover it in the new form of an ego ideal. What he projects before him as his ideal is the substitute for the lost narcissism of his childhood in which he was his own ideal" (94). Yet, a positive, or aggrandized, ego ideal cannot compensate for the absence of real sources of gratification—in the form of genuine love—from others. Freud concluded that "idealization is a process that concerns the object; by it that object, without any alteration in its nature, is aggrandized and exalted in the subject's mind" (94). In other words, other people compensate for the individual's own sense of personal frustration and dissatisfaction. The qualities one wishes for oneself—qualities that might, in turn, be exalted by others—are projected onto someone else.

It isn't difficult to appreciate how children, who rely on the comfort of idealizing phantasies to cope with the pain of their inherently frustrating emancipation, would resort to the same tendency when they grow older: to idealize other people as a way of procuring love, *in phantasy*. All analysts are an object for such idealization by their patients. In fact, the more we repress our desires, the more likely we will idealize others as a compensation. "Being loved" becomes a substitute for one's impoverished capacity to love. This is why the tendency to idealize others is an essential component of "falling in love." Idealizing is a magical transformation of one's world. It has the power to circumvent repressions by elevating the sexual object into a benefactor. "Since, with the object type (or attachment type), being in love occurs in virtue of the fulfillment of infantile conditions for loving, we may say that whatever fulfills that condition is idealized" (101). In other words, "What possesses the excellence which the ego lacks for making it an ideal, is loved" (101).

Neurotics, who feel unloved and, in turn, are afraid to love, are in an impossible situation. They blame others for their impoverishment, yet long for them to relieve it. The analyst, the object of their "transferences," becomes the ideal for this confused devotion. They hope the analyst can save them from their agony of isolation, to be their companion. The cure they envision is one that isn't, however, the culmination of ceaseless effort, but rather a salvation at the instigation of a higher power. "This is a cure by love, which he [the neurotic] generally prefers to cure by analysis. Indeed, he cannot believe in any other mechanism of cure; he usually brings expectations of this sort with him to the treatment and directs them towards the person of the physician" (101). Inevitably, the patient's own resistances to loving, a consequence of earlier repressions, renders his plan impossible. "Falling in love," occasioning both erotic and idealized components, contains an unconscious plea for the other person—the analyst—to shower the patient with a love he is actually incapable of accepting. Freud conceived of idealization not only as a manifestation of erotism, but as a substitute for erotism too. In his book on group psychology, published seven years later (1921), Freud returned to the problem of determining the nature of love and whether or not it could possibly possess a realistic component. In this study he was specifically concerned with distinguishing between erotic love and its aim-inhibited derivative, affection. Now idealization is conceived as a "de-eroticizing" of one's sexual inclinations, due to the repression that follows the Oedipus complex. If individuals subsequently fail to overcome their earlier adherence to the incest taboo in adolescence, their experience of erotism and their capacity for aim-inhibited (de-eroticized) affection may remain split off from each other and reappear in the form of a neurosis: the inability to feel both affection and sexual attraction for the same person.

Freud finally concluded that the more repressed one's erotic longings, the more likely the tendency to idealize others. "If the sensual impulsions are more or less effectively repressed or set aside, the illusion is produced that the object has come to be sensually loved on account of its spiritual merits, whereas on the contrary these merits may really only have been lent to it by its sensual charm. The tendency which falsifies judgement in this respect is that of *idealization*" (1955b, 112). But how can we reconcile the apparent contradiction that repressed sexuality supposedly leads to an increase in noneroticized idealization, on the one hand, and the contrary idea that repression should result in increased eroticized idealization, on the other? Some patients in analysis experience a powerful erotic attraction for their analysts, whereas others manifest nonsexualized, "spiritualized" feelings of adoration. Often, many patients experience both, alternately or simultaneously. The tendency to split off the two—erotic attraction and, as Freud would say, aim-inhibited affection—is a common neurotic symptom. But Freud was intrigued by those patients who idealized their analysts without any apparent interest in or experience of manifest erotic feelings. Many patients complain that their lovers are only interested in sex. They denigrate the sexual act and narrowly define love in terms of a spiritual or mystical, nonphysical relationship. This is, perhaps, idealization par excellence: to love someone and to long for this love to be returned in the form of an intangible, mysterious "power," unreachable, yet compelling. The repressions can be so severe that love is consequently experienced as the absence of—and freedom from—erotic demands. These two forms of idealization are not mutually exclusive. One, however, can be emphasized over the other and become a favored "compromise formation."

Freud was still struggling to define the nature of love, its realistic and imaginary tendencies, in his paper on group psychology when he said: "Even in its caprices the usage of language remains true to some kind of reality. Thus it gives the name of 'love' to a great many kinds of emotional relationship which we too group together theoretically as love; but then again it feels a doubt as whether this love is real, true, actual love, and so hints at a whole scale of possibilities within the range of the phenomena of love" (1955b, 111). At bottom, the neurotic's inability to love, inhibited by unconscious fears, leads to two alternative solutions: the tendency to idealize the other person so as to be loved, passively; or alternately, to simply repress one's libidinal interest in others, capitulating to the anxieties that are inevitably aroused. Both of these responses become manifest in what Freud called "transference-love."

Freud never arrived at an unambiguous definition of real love; perhaps because even real love, according to Freud, verged on the pathological. The distinction—if there is one—emerges somewhere along the difficult transition from the so-called pleasure to reality principles. No doubt Freud was a master at recognizing the deceptions in everyday protestations of love, of the neurotic's inability to love. What is love, if its "realness" isn't a determining factor? Freud's attempt to distinguish between genuine love (a love sincere in its affect and heartfelt) and real love (one that is capable of sacrifice and that is practical) says something about his views on the nature of truth and reality. The unconscious harbors truths. These truths are contained in fantastic and unrealistic wishes. Freud realized that these truths, by their nature, are concealed. The task of psychoanalysis is to disclose them. But for what purpose and to what end? What's the point of revealing secrets if they have no practical import, if they don't eventually gratify? Freud believed that neurotics, by harboring disturbing truths, become alienated from reality. We can see from the way he conceived of real love that Freud viewed reality, essentially, as our encounter with others. The so-called harsh and exasperating aspects of reality are due to the way that relationships arouse erotic yearnings whose object, amidst all the inherent frustrations, is another human being.

Real love, like life itself, is interpersonal. It can't be reduced to a feeling, however powerful and insistent that emotion may be. Transference-love, so frequently decried as merely a feeling, is more than that because, as Freud says, in terms of its efficacy it is unrivaled by any other. Whatever else we may think of it, it is a kind of love after all. Otherwise, why call it love in the first place, hyphenated or not? In his efforts to dismantle love's complexes by distinguishing the "real" from the suspect, Freud finally resigned himself to the conclusion that transference-love is only a little less real than it seems. And this conclusion tells us something about real love too, because its so-called normality even calls our notions about "normal" and "sick" into question. It isn't so easy to tell them apart. The same can be said for reality. "Psychical" reality, "transference-love," "neurotic" anxiety: When we try to measure them against the real thing, they befuddle as much as enlighten. Perhaps what is real isn't so categorical. Like existence itself, we determine its efficacy by degrees. It's more or less what it seems.

II

THE TRUE AND THE REAL
IN HEIDEGGER

The road from psychoanalysis to existential thought—or, more specifically, the road from Freud to Heidegger—has never been easy, nor one
well traveled. It has always been occasioned by hesitance, misunderstanding, suspicion. Why do these doubts persist when Freud's own
search for truth and his efforts to understand the human condition is
obviously existential in nature? Freud condemned philosophers, but he
read them seriously. Nietzsche and Spinoza were important influences, as
were Kant, the Greeks, and Brentano. Freud was well educated, yet
his mind was more speculative than scientific. In his condemnation of
philosophers—few of whom paid Freud the courtesy of taking him seriously—he was probably referring to academics rather than philosophers
in the true sense. In his essay, "The Question of a *Weltanschauung*,"
Freud suggested that philosophy "has no direct influence on the great
mass of mankind; it is of interest to only a small number even of the top
layer of intellectuals and is scarcely intelligible to anyone else" (1964c,
161). This dismissal of the academic who Freud believed was lost in an
ivory tower, cut off from the everyday passions of "normal folk," isn't
unlike the attitude most people today share toward the so-called academic
egghead who is divorced from the practicalities of real living. In that
sense, Freud could be seen as a man of the people rather than, strictly
speaking, "anti-philosophical."

Ironically, it is just this kind of criticism of academic philosophy that is
shared by modern existentialists and phenomenologists such as Martin
Heidegger, Jean-Paul Sartre, Maurice Merleau-Ponty, Gabriel Marcel,
Paul Tillich, Miguel de Unamuno, and a host of others. Although Ed-

mund Husserl is credited as the father of phenomenology—the philosophical foundation for modern existentialism—Heidegger is credited
with the "existential turn" away from the tedious abstractions of Husserl's
thought. He based his philosophy of existence on a more passionate,
everyday, and concerned interpretation of Husserl, borrowing heavily
from the nineteenth-century philosophers, Friedrich Nietzsche and Soren
Kierkegaard. Whereas Husserl—who, like Freud, was Jewish—became a
devout Christian, Heidegger, an agnostic, was deeply concerned with
theological questions, such as the nature of Being, revelation, and truth.
Although Heidegger wasn't a religious man, his philosophy was adapted
by theologians and atheists alike due to the extraordinary power of his
thinking and its applicability to everyday, and contemporary, ethical concerns. Yet, there was no kinship expressed by Freud toward the existentialists and apparently no relationship between them. Attempts have been
made to link Freud's early education to Franz Brentano, Husserl's mentor, but even the most casual reading of Brentano's work would show a
clear antipathy toward the very notion of anything akin to an "unconscious" (Spiegelberg 1972, 128). On the other hand, Freud was apparently influenced by Brentano's lectures on Aristotle and attended several
of them. Brentano's Christian background seems to have touched Freud
and for a time he was so taken with this strikingly handsome and charismatic man that he once confided to a friend, "Under Brentano's influence
I have decided to take my Ph.D. in philosophy and zoology" (Vitz 1988,
52). But mysteriously, Freud neglected to acknowledge this debt in any of
his published writings. Even if Freud might have looked on Heidegger's
philosophy more favorably than he did Husserl's, a philosophy much
closer to the Greeks, they were hardly contemporaries. Freud was an old
man in 1927 when Heidegger published his first major work, *Being and
Time (Sein und Zeit)*.

Still, Freud's quest throughout his life, by his own admission, was a
search for truth, a philosophical quest. Freud's professional life was concerned with establishing the universal acceptance of psychoanalysis—the
"science of the unconscious"—which aimed to disclose the nature of
reality. This is an unusual thing for a scientist to be concerned about. Few
psychoanalysts today talk about the nature of reality. It is simply accepted
as a given. We all know what it is. As far as the question of truth is
concerned, there aren't even many philosophers who are preoccupied
with it; most deny that it's knowable! But Freud's life was devoted to

unravelling the nature of truth and what it means for something to be real. Perhaps the most distinctive concern that set Heidegger apart from his contemporaries, and this is even more relevant today, was his criticism of modern philosophers whom he accused of having forgot to ask the following question: "What is the nature of truth, and what is the nature of a being who can ask this question?" Perhaps Freud and Heidegger— unlike so many of their contemporaries in psychiatry and philosophy— were asking the same question: "Who are we, what are we doing here, what do we want?"

Although Freud never openly asked about the nature of truth, he instructed his analytic patients "to be truthful" in order to obtain the most beneficial outcome of their analysis, knowing it was impossible for them to be entirely successful. His reflections on the nature of reality (see Part One) are philosophical queries, not scientific "investigations." His use of the word *real* is frequently meant to convey a sense of what is inherently true rather than what is objectively factual. He wasn't looking for accuracy but rather for what a person sincerely and genuinely believed to be so. Freud's use of concepts such as phantasy and repression were invaluable for determining what was true about the things that were said, felt, experienced, and actually occuring in the analytic situation. What, then, is the nature of this truth, and the reality it imposes on us?

Freud's conception of reality fostered irreversible consequences for the development of his views about psychic structure, emotions, and the nature of psychopathology. If your conception of reality, for example, were rooted in your experience of anguish, as was Freud's, you might, in turn, conceive of phantasy as an alternate reality that you could retreat to—Freud called it a "reservation"—in order to escape from the pain of existence. These phantasies would, you might infer, be experienced as reassuring and pleasurable. Psychic structure, if it were faithful to this premise, would be conceived accordingly. If my experience of reality is frightening, then my conception of reality should be frightful. In the face of it, I might contrive to split myself into separate entities or "selves" in order to avoid my experience of un-pleasure. My ego (I), in order to cope with reality, may have to employ a subterfuge (call them defenses) to protect my secret (call them unconscious) wishes, as added security from the possible intrusions of an environment (reality) that is frequently opposed to those wishes. Freud's conception of reality depicts it as inherently uncooperative. Whatever my wishes may be, reality is my master.

Yet, my phantasies allow me to be master, in a fashion. Although they temporarily appease, reality can't, however, be held in abeyance forever. Freud's conception of primary and secondary thought processes is based on this view of reality. It conveys a quality of harshness and difficulty, but it isn't inherently pessimistic, as some have supposed. In fact, a closer reading would suggest the contrary. When Freud characterized "real" love as the kind that submits to the reality principle while upholding a capacity for genuine pleasure, the seemingly irreconcilable barrier between pleasure and reality, between primary and secondary thought processes, between id and world, dissolved.

Freud's tendency, however, of equating reality with what is externally valid compromised his philosophical quest for truth, diluted further by the limitations imposed by empirical verification. By articulating his search for truth within the confines of observable data, Freud's hopes for establishing the foundations for an epistemology of the unconscious—which is intrinsically unobservable—became increasingly remote. This is why there is no "philosophy of truth" in Freud's body of work—even if psychoanalysis is concerned with no other question. The unconscious, by definition, can't possibly be observed. It can only be thought. If psychoanalysis is going to be used to explore experience, this exploration needs to answer the most fundamental questions about human knowledge—its truths and its reality. If Freud's vocabulary obscures this question, how can we justify the inherently philosophical interrogation his clinical work introduced? If a psychoanalytical conception of truth was never finally articulated by its founder—who nonetheless devoted his life to this task—where might we find one?

Why not turn to philosophy itself? And what better philosopher to ask than the de facto founder of existential philosophy, Martin Heidegger? Why Heidegger? After all, we know the contempt that so many analysts feel toward existential philosophy generally and against Heidegger, the acknowledged Nazi collaborator, specifically.[1] When we talk about a road less traveled—the one between psychoanalysis and existentialism, between Freud and Heidegger—we know the obstacles must be real,

---

1. Space doesn't permit me to go into Heidegger's relationship with National Socialism, prior to and during World War II. A heated controversy has recently ensued over the extent of Heidegger's involvement with the Nazis and why (Farias 1989; Rockmore and Margolis 1992; Wolin 1991). For a balanced view of this controversy, which examines the motives surrounding Heidegger's complicated identification with German culture, see Zimmerman (1981, 169–97).

even passionate. But there is more to the rift between psychoanalysts and Heidegger than "the Nazi question." Even if Heidegger is sometimes accused of anti-semitism—whether justly or not—or if his betrayal of his former teacher, Husserl—a Jew—was politically motivated or personal enmity, there is more to these accusations than personalities or politics. Heidegger's thought is assumed to be fundamentally opposed to any psychology that is founded on the notion of an "unconscious." This perception, I believe, is wrong. Existential thought has always entertained the dimension of the latent and concealed, that place from which consciousness belatedly appears under the guise of "symptomatic" expression. The problem we all face, philosophers and psychoanalysts alike, is determining the nature of this latency and a method by which it may be understood. Once this misunderstanding about existential philosophy has been corrected, we can travel that road from Freud to Heidegger and see what is there.

What of those who preceded us? Some who went from psychoanalysis to Heidegger never came back (Laing 1961; May 1958; Boss 1963). Others took what they could and returned, faithful to their analytic identity (Loewald 1980; Leavy 1988; Rycroft 1966). Loewald, who studied with Heidegger personally, candidly acknowledged his debt to his former teacher (1980, viii–ix) and Leavy, in a recent article (1989), explored Heidegger's influence on Loewald's thinking. Leavy (1980, 1988) has also discussed his own debt to Heidegger's thought. That influence is as apparent in Leavy's compelling style as it is in his clinical theories. On the other hand, R. D. Laing and Rollo May, both of whom trained as psychoanalysts, turned away from and abandoned their principal identities as psychoanalysts (though not entirely) in order to pursue more freely an Heideggerian and existentialist path—a path, nonetheless, significantly indebted to Freud. The British analyst Charles Rycroft—who was, coincidentally, Laing's training analyst—was also influenced by existentialism, yet chose to stay in the mainstream of psychoanalysis. Still, Rycroft eventually resigned from the British Psychoanalytic Society, feeling that his attempts to broaden analytic dogma never made an impression (Rycroft 1985, 198–206).

Obviously, there were other analysts interested in and indebted to existential philosophy—Ludwig Binswanger (1963), Alfred Adler (Van Dusen 1959), Paul Federn (1952), Angelo Hesnard (1960), Jacques Lacan (1977), Erich Fromm (Burston 1991)—and many psychiatrists who were interested in both—Paul Schilder (1935), Viktor Frankl (1968), Erwin Straus (1966), Henri Ey (1978), David Cooper (Laing and Cooper 1964), Ludwig Lefebre (1957). All of them owe a debt to Heidegger in important ways, and all of them discovered that the respective thought of Heidegger and Freud was mutually beneficial. None, however, to my knowledge, has explored their respective views on truth and reality in the context of analytic technique. Perhaps Heidegger's conception of truth might open the way to a reappraisal of this question and help us, in turn, learn something about the psychoanalyst's experience of reality, its truth, and the nature of his endeavor.

6

Heidegger's Conception of Truth

Heidegger's concept of truth is alluded to throughout his writings, but the ones that occasion his most extensive arguments are his classic, *Being and Time* (1962, 225–73), and a shorter essay, "On the Essence of Truth" (1977a, 113–42). The question of truth isn't merely a preliminary to Heidegger's philosophy; this question is his philosophy in its entirety. His approach to this question startled and even dismayed many members of the European academic community. With the publication of *Being and Time* (*Sein und Zeit*) in 1927, Heidegger abandoned the conventional approach to this question that had been preoccupied with scientific applications. Also unsettling for many was the literary manner in which Heidegger chose to write his magnum opus. It was almost impossible to decipher. Heidegger believed that contemporary European society had lost its way and had strayed from its essential nature. He blamed this to some extent on the direction science had taken, a direction obsessed with technology and its potential for "protecting" mankind from the fears inherent in everyday living. To suggest that Freud was captivated by this "scientific spirit" may be unfair, but we can assume he didn't share Heidegger's skepticism about the course science was taking. Of course, the problem with modern culture—a problem many would argue is even more evident today—wasn't created by contemporary society. Heidegger argued that its seeds were sown in ancient Greece. Heidegger did believe, though, that the problem had gotten out of hand with the technological revolution and that we're now in danger of completely forgetting what our nature really is. Our attitude about truth, Heidegger insisted, is at the heart of man's nature, which we've apparently repressed.

What is this nature? What do we think truth is? The conventional attitude about truth is that it's something that is so. If I were to say, "I am truly enjoying this moment," I would mean that I am actually enjoying myself, that I'm accurately describing my feelings. In other words, it's my statement that is true, because my statement conforms to how I feel. But we also talk about truth as some thing as well as a statement about that thing. For example, it's possible to distinguish between true gold and false gold. True gold, actual gold, is genuine. It really is gold. It's real gold. Does that mean that false gold isn't real? After all, it really is something. It's something or other, though it may not be gold. I don't hallucinate false gold. It—whatever "it" is—actually exists. So wouldn't it be true to say that although it's false, it's still real? This is why something can be actual yet false. Whatever it is that's true about real gold can't be demonstrated by its actuality. So what is it that we mean when we say something is genuine or true? Genuine gold is gold that is in accord with, that corresponds with, what we understand as gold. False gold is something, but it isn't the thing that we know *as* gold. We're still talking about a statement that concerns gold, not gold itself. The statement, "this is gold," is true or false. So, the statement is either in accord with this thing, or it isn't. Thus, you can't reduce the genuineness of something to the thing that it is; you can't omit the statement or proposition that something is what it is. In a psychoanalytic session, patients are declaring that something is true every time they say something. But how do we know that what they say is really so? Isn't this principally what the psychoanalyst is trying to determine? According to Heidegger,

> The true, whether it be a matter or a proposition, is what accords. . . .
> Being true and truth here signify accord, and that in a double sense: on the
> one hand, the consonance of a matter with what is supposed in advance
> regarding it and, on the other hand, the accordance of what is meant in the
> statement with the matter. . . . This can be taken to mean: truth is the
> correspondence of the matter to knowledge. (1977a, 119–20)

The problem with this approach to the problem of truth, though it's true as far as it goes, is that propositional truth relies on material truth, thus whether or not the proposition, "This thing is gold," is true, is decided, in the end, on the thing that is gold. The truth of a declaration depends on whether it's correct, which depends on the thing the statement is about. According to this definition, a truthful statement is nothing more than a factual statement about the thing the statement depicts.

Heidegger isn't suggesting that this theory about truth is necessarily wrong. It just doesn't get to the heart of the matter. Where did that theory come from? We would have to start with Aristotle, whose correspondence theory was gradually adopted by Jewish and Arabian philosophers, then by Christian medieval thinkers, then the scholastics, and now us. It was during the medieval period, however, when Heidegger thought this theory had its biggest impact. According to Christian theologians, whether or not a statement was so depended on whether that statement was faithful to a corresponding idea in God's mind. This is the mind of the God who created human beings, the world, and everything in it. If a statement conformed to God's intentions, then that statement was true. Humankind's capacity to gain knowledge and wisdom was presumably bestowed on human beings by God Himself. "If all beings are 'created,' " says Heidegger, "the possibility of the truth of human knowledge is grounded in the fact that matter and proposition measure up to the idea in the same way and therefore are fitted to each other on the basis of the unity of the divine plan of creation" (1977a, 120).

In other words, truth, according to Christian philosophers, implies conformity to God's plan and His intentions. People could determine what was true by making sure their beliefs corresponded to the "order of creation." But hasn't this way of thinking become archaic? Can we now be accused of relying on a "preordained" plan that is supposed to justify our beliefs? According to Heidegger, the answer is yes. "But this order," he warns,

> detached from the notion of creation, can also be represented in a general and indefinite way as a world-order. The theologically conceived order of creation is replaced by the capacity of all objects to be planned by means of a worldly reason which supplies the law for itself and thus also claims that its procedure is immediately intelligible (what is considered "logical"). That the essence of propositional truth consists in the correctness of statements needs no further special proof. Even where an effort is made—with a conspicuous lack of success—to explain how correctness is to occur, it is already presupposed as being the essence of truth. (121)

One of the most obvious objections to propositional truth is its conditions for validity. Its credibility has to rest on something else that is incontrovertibly obvious to everyone, whether that something is the word of God or the latest scientific finding. Truth is supposed to be obvious, even irrefutable. We don't have to search for it, we can learn it in schools or from whomever else we can turn to when we're too lazy to sort it out for ourselves. According to conventional education, truth isn't something we need to ponder, it's just an answer to a question that some expert is supposed to have worked out for us. Besides, how do we ever know if anything is correct? How can we be certain that a statement actually depicts the thing it describes? The notion that ideas represent things has been around a long time. Freud adopted the representational theory of language to explain his ideas about psychic structure, the unconscious, the nature of phantasy, even his concept of reality. We use words to depict the things that go on in our minds, yet words can't correspond to these things with accuracy or precision. According to Heidegger, "Correspondence here cannot signify a thing-like approximation between dissimilar kinds of things. The essence of the correspondence is determined rather by the kind of *relation* that obtains between the statement and the thing" (123).

In other words, words, strictly speaking, don't actually correspond with the things they describe. They merely point to them. They guide us to them. Take his statement about gold coins, for example. "The statement regarding the coin relates itself to this thing in that it presents *[vor-stellt]* it and says of the presented how, according to the particular perspective that guides it, it is disposed" (123). The German *vorstellen* means to present something or introduce it. But it can also be understood to *re*present something, and the connotation becomes drastically altered. Heidegger plays on the nuance of *vorstellen* to "present" things to us, though we're not used to thinking this way. The difference is striking. It makes a lot of difference whether I'm introducing, or presenting, someone to you or whether I'm representing that person in his or her place, by standing in for them. Do words actually "stand in" for the things they reference, or do they introduce us to things, instead? With this distinction Heidegger's conception of truth now comes into being.

One of the implications of distinguishing between words representing (i.e., corresponding to) things and words presenting (i.e., introducing us to) them instead is that if words simply direct our attention to phenomena, we don't need to be concerned about how accurate or correct those words are in order to establish the truthfulness of the statements they comprise. That doesn't mean the words we use don't matter. It means that the relationship between words and the phenomena they describe has changed. My relationship with words has changed too. Do I use words and manipulate them to convey what I'm thinking, or do words introduce me to things I'm just discovering that I believe? When patients talk to their analysts, are they merely characterizing the things that happen to them in life, or are they introducing us to the life they're living, and the underlying existence it implies? The fact that we interpret their utterances confirms that we're looking at something more radical than what is being talked "about." We're looking at the Being of the person who is speaking to us. When we urge people to speak freely, we're proposing that they suspend their preoccupation with explanations and simply talk to us, spontaneously and unequivocally. We're not looking for information. We're trying to get at something that isn't so easy to put into words.

And even when words do serve to represent my thoughts about things in nature, how do these ideas ever occur to me in the first place? Do I instruct my mind to elicit the right word or idea that "correctly" represents it? Or do the words just come to me, unsolicited, freely, more or less of their own accord? It's only when I have a mental lapse and can't remember someone's name, for example, that I deliberately look for the word that's missing. But even this example proves Heidegger's point, because it shows how helpless I really am when trying to make a word appear on command. Words have a life of their own, just as the thoughts I collect together have a will of their own.

Words don't just present things to me. They speak to me. I listen to the words I say, I don't just conjure them up. Words, when I think them, occur to me. In fact, listening to words comprises thought. They show themselves in the same way that truth makes its appearance, spontaneously and often unexpectedly. If words don't just depict things but exist on their own, what is their relationship to things? Words show me things that stand by themselves, in their own right. That is why I can use any number of words and convey different meanings to point to the same thing. When I'm describing people for example, they don't change every time I use a different adjective or noun. But my perspective of them achieves greater scope because of the words I use to describe them. And this larger perspective enriches my feelings about them and may take my relationship with them into unexpected regions. Through it all, they stand by themselves, inhabiting their own space, "the openness of which is not first created by the presenting but rather is only entered into and taken over as a domain of relatedness" (Heidegger 1977a, 123–24). On the other hand, when I say something about somebody I'm not merely describing someone who is who that person is and nothing more. I'm also revealing my relationship with the person and how I see the person. Through my relationship with others I, too, come into being. Whenever I say something, whether I speak accurately or ridiculously, I disclose something about myself. In other words, truth, when it shows itself, is bound to be personal and biased.

Even while Heidegger traces the correspondence theory all the way back to Aristotle, the theory he feels closest to is much older. In fact, it's based on the oldest name for truth in Greek philosophy: *aletheia*. The key to this word lies in *lethe,* which conveys a number of closely related ideas: concealment, hiddenness, veiledness, coveredness. The *a-* has the function of reversing the connotation of hiding something. In addition to the more cumbersome English equivalents—un-concealment or un-hiddenness, for example—we have recourse to a number of ordinary everyday words with which we're all familiar: discover, disclose, reveal, unveil. These words convey the idea of *alēthēia*—of truth—as lifting a veil from something that's hidden or obscured, of uncovering what's been disguised beyond recognition. Truth is disclosed when I discover something I couldn't see but was there all the time. In other words truth comes into being by being revealed to someone. It doesn't exist as a "fact," in and of itself. This conception of truth isn't as quaint as it seems. After all, it was adopted by science to designate the "discovery" of its latest findings. On the other hand, the word *revelation* has traditionally been associated with mystical or religious insight, but these distinctions are conventional rather than etymological. Because language discloses truth instead of merely describing it, truth is based on the manner in which it is revealed instead of someone's "depiction" of it, however complicated that depiction may be.

Of course, when I discover something I can tell others about it and "pass it on." This is hearsay, but it contains a certain truth because it may be, in a certain sense, correct. But do the people who receive truth in this way and pass it along to others know this truth themselves? Not necessarily. Yet, that doesn't stop this truth from getting talked about and even written about and, eventually, it may become recognized as "objective" truth. Why? Because so many people adopt it. People study these truths in universities where they're supposed to learn how to discover these truths themselves. But how often is this really the case? These truths become abstract and divorced from everyday life and the context that gives rise to them in the first place. The process of gathering and even memorizing truths becomes equally abstract. We forget that these truths were once discovered by someone, that real truth—truth that you know for yourself—has to be discovered; it can't just be "learned" in a vacuum. Contemporary education has lapsed into a process of acquiring, collecting, and disseminating information about truths that are simply learned by rote. These truths are impersonal in the extreme. It shouldn't be surprising that this kind of learning—the norm of modern university— has little relationship to the way truth is actually handled by us, personally and collectively. These truths are just handed down, divorced from their context and devoid of any personal recognition. The truths we're expected to learn must in turn conform to those that have been "established" beforehand. If we expect to find the kind of truth that arises from our own experience in the world we actually inhabit, we're more likely to discover that truth by talking to a psychoanalyst than by listening to a college professor.

This is no accident. Truth isn't academic. It isn't the property or the province of "higher learning." Truth is what being human is all about. Truth isn't something I covet simply for the sake of knowledge. Knowing the truth is what it means to be a person, a being who's always showing and hiding who that person is.

7

Heidegger's Conception of Un-truth

If truth becomes known by revealing what is hidden, then untruth must be the concealment of truth, a reversal of *alētheia*. Because we use words to reveal and conceal things about ourselves, everything I say converges this way or that. My speech is always directed toward either disclosing truths or concealing them. There is no neutral position. Freud believed that every thought, emotion, and behavior employed a purpose even if that purpose was unconscious. His theory of the unconscious allowed him to account for those truths that are most hidden. In his "Recommendations to Physicians Practising Psycho-analysis," he advised his readers to remain open and alert with their patients if they hope to understand the unconscious (i.e., hidden) material (i.e., truth). "The doctor must put himself in a position to make use of everything he is told for the purposes of interpretation and recognizing the *concealed unconscious material* without substituting a censorship of his own" (1958g, 115; emphasis added).

Freud's conception of repression is remarkably similar to Heidegger's understanding of concealment. The decisive aspect of Heidegger's conception of truth is that it rests, not on the notion of a truth that simply "is" what it is, but rather a truth *revealed* for what it is. Truth, by its nature, has depth. It has to be discovered. If it weren't already hidden in the first place, we wouldn't have to go to such pains to determine what it is. Conventional notions about truth depict it as something that is what it is already. Our ability to establish a relationship with truth is supposed to depend on our comprehension of it. This reduces it to a strictly intellectual conception of knowledge. Heidegger, on the other hand, claims that truth is alive. It is inherently personal. How could Heidegger's conception of truth have any relevance to psychoanalysis, when psychoanalysis relies on an epistemological premise that traditionally depicts the unconscious as impersonal?

Stanley Leavy referred to Freud's notion of "counter will" to shed light on this question.

> The truth of the matter is that the progress of our life enforces a steady discrimination between what we choose to notice, inside and outside ourselves, and what we choose to ignore. Note that I have said "choose," although it is easy to protest that there is no choice in the matter: for instance, I didn't deliberately go about ignoring the affront implicit in some words of mine, I simply said them "in all innocence," thereby compounding the concealment. Psychoanalysis, by insisting on close attention to the details of what I said, might reveal that I intended the malice and, further, that I intended to protect myself from noticing it. In short, when I refer to the "I" who acts, I am often referring to another than the one who carries out my actions with conscious purpose. We come back to Freud's "counterwill", and it is in this sense that we speak of choosing." (1988, 45–6)

When we look at Freud's (abandoned) use of this concept, we come face to face with the problem of agency, or subjectivity, in psychoanalysis and the mysterious nature of a subject who doesn't know what he knows. If we were to ask Freud, "Who performs the concealment inherent in the concept of repression?," he might answer, "Defensive forces perform this task"; or, he might say, "That aspect of the ego which is assigned the task of protecting the organism from anxiety." In other words, "No one." The person who is being psychoanalyzed has succumbed to the "workings" of his or her mind, or apparatus, or unconscious. But it wasn't he or she specifically who concealed the material, which is why he or she is little help in discovering—and eventually freeing—the repressed material.

The basic difference between the Freudian and Heideggerian responses to this dilemma revolves around the question, who is it that performs this bit of concealment and what is it that is being concealed? This distinction echoes Sartre's accusation that the psychoanalytic theory of repression poses the notion of "a lie without a liar" (Sartre 1953, 203–24). There is some truth to his assertion. The word *lie* is a provocative term, though Sartre takes care to distinguish self-deception from the willful—and conscious—deception of others. If the id isn't a subject but merely a metaphor for what remains obstinately hidden from awareness, then to say that the ego is deceiving itself by its failure to get to the truth of what's hidden would be absurd. However, if the id were indeed a subject (even the subjective core of our being) and the ego was simply a mask or facade (an intermediary) erected to play a role, then the id doesn't merely possess the truth but even uses the ego to deny that truth, by soliciting its ego to enact an alternative truth in the service of concealing it. This is what Sartre calls the "sliding away" of truth; or a "lie." Living this lie, "bad faith," according to Sartre, is our normal condition, interrupted by occasional glimpses of the truth whenever it catches us unaware through insight and parapraxes. This somewhat pessimistic tone is in contrast with Heidegger's, which advocates a more optimistic appraisal of our condition and the deception it occasions. Whereas it may be painful to admit certain truths, we wouldn't avoid them in the first place if we didn't care what they were. Contrary to Sartre's fundamental lie, which we can never hope to transcend, Heidegger believed that the experience of guilt ultimately saves us from ourselves because it reminds us of what we are: a manner of being whose existence is condemned to discovering who we are, whether we like it or not.

Yet, if truth is, by its nature, hidden, why should we feel guilty for concealing something that is already concealed? Heidegger's answer isn't easy to grasp, because his notion of un-truth—of concealment—isn't, strictly speaking, the opposite of truth, in the way that wrong is the opposite of right. Revealing and concealing are intertwined because what is being revealed isn't some "thing" that, once exposed, is no longer hidden. What's being revealed is one's Being, which by its nature is always hidden, so our truth, whatever it is, never loses its inherently mysterious quality. Freud more or less intuited this when he pointed out that symptoms are overdetermined because our interpretations of latent content into manifest meanings are potentially inexhaustible.

Unlike scientific truth (see chapter 8) which is based on the "correctness" of data, Heidegger's is based on the intrinsic mysteriousness of existence itself. Getting to know something is an endless process of acquaintance and familiarity that unfolds a bottomless reservoir of discovery, repression, and recovery. It's impossible to get away from the intrinsic concealedness of things. Nothing is ever entirely revealed because everything unfolds in time. The things that are concealed from us, including the repressed, are alive, so their mystery is constantly changing and adapting to the situation, including the consequence of analyzing them. This is why psychoanalysis is interminable, because no one can ever be totally known. The date of termination is never based on the exhaustion of analysis; it is terminated when the "time" has come to end it (see Part Six).

The mystery of who we are can't be reduced to a riddle that is solvable. It's not like the "mysteries"—really puzzles—described by Conan Doyle or Agatha Christie. Actually, Freud often compared psychoanalysis to detective work and talked about "solving" one's neurosis in a similar vein. But none of his case histories ever supported this analogy, which, handy as it was, is misleading. Humans aren't mysterious because they're neurotic, as though the well-analyzed individual ultimately becomes transparent. If anything, our mysteriousness is deepened by analysis, and with it the intrinsic concealedness of who we are. The better we get to know someone, the more of a mystery that person becomes. This is why diagnosis is misleading. In fact, it is contrary to the spirit of analytic inquiry. Psychoanalysis relies on the notion of diagnosis and treatment in an analogous sense only. It is principally concered with determining what is true. Freud's term *excavation* is equally apt for that reason. But this mysterious aspect of our concealedness isn't simply inherent in who each of us is; our hiddenness is also determined by the situations—and the people in them—we encounter. That's why one analyst will see a patient one way and another will see that person differently. The manner in which we're interrogated adds a dimension to our mysterious nature and even determines the direction that the latent within us employs.

Concealment doesn't merely obscure truth. It contains it. Truth, untruth, revelation, and concealment each implicate the others. The key to obtaining the truth about one's suffering doesn't lie in diagnostic accuracy. Every analyst knows that. It lies in patients' willingness to plumb the depths of their nature. Freud called this capacity the "analytic attitude," a willingness to be led down a path over which we haven't any control. However, if truth, according to Heidegger, is inherently concealed, how might we distinguish between ordinary forms of concealment and neurotic manifestations of resistance and repression? Surely they aren't the same. In fact, Sartre's notion of "bad faith" was meant to address this problem. Sartre, following Heidegger, believed that we repress—conceal—whatever is objectionable. This is how Freud characterized the nature of repression, that it helps us avoid painful disappointments. Heidegger called this "erring." According to him, "Man's flight from the mystery toward what is readily available, onward from one current thing to the next, passing the mystery by—this is *erring*" (1977a, 135). This form of "carelessness" depicts typical neurotics, afraid of their own desire, too anxious to get to the depth of their existence. Resistance to the analytic process epitomizes this aspect of erring, of fighting against the discovery of the things we want to stay concealed.

Another sense of erring comes from the Latin *errare*, "to wander from the path," to be lost without knowing it. To err in this sense doesn't refer to common mistakes. It suggests a deeper dimension of our personalities that is prone to getting stuck. We err because we've already made a stubborn commitment to a specific manner of being, falling further and further astray without even knowing how far off track we've become. In other words, "error is not just an isolated mistake but rather the realm (the domain) of the history of those entanglements in which all kinds of erring get interwoven" (Heidegger 1977a, 136).

The most obvious complement to this dimension of errancy—of wandering—in psychoanalysis is the act of free association whereby individuals are invited to let their mind wander and to "fall" into the typical kinds of defensiveness, parapraxes, and phantasies that characterize their particular way of being lost. Freud's conception of cure was based on the capacity for allowing one's mind to wander, that is, "free associating." In so doing, the mind eventually rights itself, of its own accord. Blake's admonition—"the road of excess leads to the palace of wisdom"—is an apt characterization of what Heidegger and Freud were advocating, each in his own conceptual framework. Free associating, by revealing our errings, allows us to grasp the truth that is concealed in our hiddenness, by revealing the unconscious secrets contained in our everyday speech.

All of this would be rather academic and even specialized if it wasn't for Heidegger's central message: to *be* human is to seek truths. We don't search for answers just because something's gone awry. All cultures, whether they're primitive or advanced, want to know things and learn. Yet, in the modern era, science has taken hold of education and made it impossibly conceptual, divorcing us from our nature (see chapter 9). Freud's hypothesis of a "scopophilic urge," which drives children to spy on their parents during intercourse, was a precurser to Heidegger's observation that every human being simply needs to know. Freud recognized that we especially want to know what's forbidden, what is oftentimes none of our business. Having found it, we are partially blinded by the weight of its power.

8

Truth and Science

Humans, by their nature, are always revealing themselves and showing themselves off. We wonder who it is that we are and what we're after. We're obsessed with the truth, especially the truth about ourselves. Who are we? What kind of truth can answer this question? Whatever it is, we know it can't be measured, weighed, or calculated. How does this type of truth—personal, to be sure—differ from the truth of science? Science, which claims to know so much, models its truth on the precision of mathematics. Its exactness, however, doesn't necessarily coincide with what is true. Measurements of space and time are always inaccurate to some degree. But when a person says that the distance from here to there is "an hour's walk," or "a fifteen minute drive," we appreciate that the truth-value of these personal communications contains a truth that is handier and more useful than the so-called exactness that a scientific response can convey. That's because personal communications inhabit a real world. People who use this way of talking know it's an hour's walk. They don't have to be exact in order to benefit from the knowledge of their experience. Real truth, existential truth, always contains this handy quality. It is faithful to the everyday world we live in.

Another claim of science is that its truths, because they strive to be exact, are more strict than other truths. But what does this criterion for truth say about history or anthropology, studies very concerned with accuracy and strictness of information gathering? None of these specifically human sciences would ever presume to be "exact." One of the fallacies of modern psychology is the suggestion that it's possible to study human behavior—which is to say, human beings—by scientifically "objective" standards. In claiming to be objective, these truths are supposed to be free of the contamination of the investigator's personal bias. This claim is so absurd that it's astonishing that it is still being made. It's gotten to where the truth-value of any area of human knowledge— including philosophy, religion, psychoanalysis—is rejected out of hand unless it conforms to the so-called precision and strictness of scientific procedure. But what exactly do we mean by a procedure that claims to be "scientific"?

Heidegger believed that our approach to science changed dramatically in the sixteenth and seventeenth centuries when modern science turned violently away from the scholastic and medieval philosophical tradition, a tradition indebted to Aristotle's conception of nature. It wasn't until Newton challenged Aristotle's theory of motion that scientists began to adopt a specifically mathematical approach to science. In a lecture course on metaphysics that Heidegger gave in 1935–36, subsequently published under the title, *What Is a Thing?* (1967, 65–111), he argued that modern science is indebted to mathematics, not because the "mathematical" is essentially concerned with numbers and computation, but because the original meaning of the mathematical—*ta mathēmata* in Greek—embodied a theory of learning that was essentially conceptual and abstract. Unlike many contemporary critics of psychology (and even psychoanalysis), who claim that these disciplines are too indebted to empiricism, Heidegger argued that the essence of modern sciences is even more indebted to the curse of "conceptualization," a way of validating knowledge that divorces it from practical experience. Unwilling to acknowledge a critical distinction between the empirical and social sciences, Heidegger maintained that all the post-sixteenth-century sciences are equally cut off from the everydayness of human experience. In contrast, in Aristotle's time one's experiences were the primary source of the sciences.

Roughly speaking, the Greeks broke the sciences down into five basic groups. Aristotle slightly altered them and added more, but the essential character and rationale of these distinctions remained more or less the same. *Physica* concerned things that already existed in nature. *Poioumena* concerned things that were produced by the human hand, the so-called productive sciences, which included crafts and the study of medicine. *Chrēmata* specifically concerned the use of things that were at our disposal, whether these things were found in nature (such as rocks for sling-shots) or manmade (the proper way to administer an injection, for example), all of which embodied what we now call "technical" skills.

Pragmata was by far the most extensive science because it encompassed human pursuits, including ethics, politics, and poetry: the so-called practical sciences. Finally, *mathēmata* concerned "the things insofar as we take cognizance of them as what we already know them to be in advance" (Heidegger 1967, 73). In other words, the mathematical referred to the concept of learning, what was learnable and teachable. But the type of learning it concerned can't be reduced to obtaining information or a facility for memorization. It was concerned with learning how to conceptualize something we already know. *Mathēmata* embodied what we now call "academics," learning things about that which we already have some experience, whether those things are plants, animals, the body, the mind, and so on.

This way of distinguishing amongst the sciences was abandoned a long time ago. Aristotle revised them and transformed the sciences into the structure with which we're now familiar: biology, politics, physics, botany, economics. The way the Greeks originally categorized disciplines suggests how dependent each was on the others. The sciences were effectively "interdisciplinary," yet individually distinguishable. Learning to conceptualize, which included the study of numbers but not exclusively, required a special use of the mind that adds another dimension to the study of all the disciplines. However, it wasn't the principal discipline. The thing that most characterized Aristotle's approach to science was its intrinsically intuitive quality. His approach to nature, for example, was based on the assumption that knowledge was revelation. In other words, one's knowledge about nature relied on the mind's grasp of personal experience. There wasn't anything especially mathematical about his theories, even those concerning metaphysics. They were more speculative than abstract.

All that changed with Newton's *First Law of Motion*. In effect, Newton rejected Aristotle's experiential approach to science, which had dominated Western thought for about eighteen centuries. With Newton, man's ability to conceptualize about the nature of bodies took precedence over simply observing them. Basing his abstractions on the axiom that "all bodies, left to themselves, move in a straight line," Newton repudiated Aristotle's belief that heavenly bodies moved in a circle. Newton also argued that all bodies are the same, so each isn't determined by its own nature as Aristotle proposed. In fact, one of the remarkable effects of Newton's theory was how it altered our conception of nature itself.

Instead of establishing the intrinsic qualities of things in order to determine what they were, those things were conceived in terms of how each was constantly changing its position in respect to the others. This was as true for objects in space as it was for the atoms that comprise our very being. In other words, the nature of an object could be discerned by studying its relationship to other objects instead of, as Aristotle held, exploring what the object itself could tell us. Astronomy was only one of the sciences transformed by this approach. Virtually all of the other sciences eventually followed suit (Heidegger 1967, 76–88).

The important thing to keep in mind is how "mathematical"—in the original sense of abstractness—Newton's theory was. This inaugurated a shift in our thinking that subsequently epitomized scientific "validity." But what is that validity based on? Newton's "bodies" in motion don't actually exist in reality; they're merely theorized conceptually, and computed accordingly. Whereas science had previously been rooted in concrete experience, the modern emphasis on the scientist's ability to conceptualize about existing bodies achieved greater validity, based solely on the relative elegance of one's theory—and its "predictability." Experience gave way to "experimentation," yet experiments weren't expected to prove one's theory but to simply support it. A perfect example was Galileo's experiment at Pisa. He hypothesized that falling bodies of different weight and mass would descend at the same velocity, disputing Aristotle's assertion that heavier bodies would descend faster. Actually, the two balls that Galileo used didn't arrive at the same time, but close enough to support his theory. That's because, as in life, there's nothing exact about science. But ever since Newton's axiom was "proved" to be valid, scientists have been claiming a capacity for exactness that has never actually been demonstrated. The so-called precision of science only exists in theory, worked out by computation and conceptualization.

After all this time, Newton's *First Law of Motion* is now being challenged. Newer theories based on Einstein's work suggest that the universe is curved after all, so the axiom that bodies travel in a straight line is in doubt. Could Aristotle have been "correct," all along? But the point to keep in mind isn't who is or isn't correct, but whether our knowledge about things can really be reduced to such a notion. Aristotle never strived for correctness. It wasn't an essential aspect of truth, as he saw it. Yet, science bases a lot of its credibility on the myth that knowledge about things can be reduced to the accumulation of accurate information: "data." This approach to knowledge isn't limited to the so-called natural or hard sciences. It includes all sciences because each advocates a predominantly conceptual framework. They are generally skeptical of human experience and universally dismiss the "bias of subjectivism." The more abstract and removed, the more valid knowledge becomes. According to these criteria, psychology is among the most abstract sciences of all. Does that make it the most valid? Although it has increasingly relied on human behavior as its object of investigation, Freud's psychological theories about the mind and its workings—epitomized by the structural theory—is no less abstract than Newton's *First Law of Motion*. Just as Newton didn't require actual, existing bodies in order to theorize about their nature, nor did Freud—following the spirit of modern science—require actual "agencies" in the mind in order to speculate about their powers. The importance was in the elegance of his theories and whether they happened to satisfy the analysts who accepted them, which is to say, who believed them.

Modern psychology, since separating from philosophy in the nineteenth century, has become increasingly identified with a scientific methodology modeled on what Aristotle called the "theoretical sciences," rooted in mathematics. Psychologists believe that by studying human behavior they can determine laws about how and why we behave the way we do. Then they devise ways to apply this knowledge in order to alter our behavior in a clinical setting. This basic tenet of psychology applies equally to those who believe they can determine the nature of the mind so they can make it "work," or think, differently.

The terms psychologists embrace as "valid" determinants of knowledge are radically impersonal. Statistical studies—the literal application of mathematical abstraction to a theory based on numbers—are increasingly quoted in order to support a hypothesis about the nature of psychopathology, for example, or the effects of psychotherapy. What is this evidence based on? Random questionnaires, the accumulation of the personal opinion of thousands of therapists or their patients. What is remarkable about these studies is how simplistic and unreliable they are. Yet, they call these opinions "hard evidence." How can you believe what these people say? Typical psychologists are more liable to embrace the data produced by these random, anonymous samples than they would the opinion of an analyst with thirty or more years of experience. Why? Because psychology is based on the same principles as the other sciences, which, in turn, are founded on abstract computation and supporting data. But these computations are even more abstract—and hence, "mathematical"—than the physical sciences. If psychologists want to be scientific, they have to have a theory at hand that guides what they expect to observe in their patients. This is how theory dominates contemporary science. We take this so much for granted that it sounds astonishing to question it, let alone to suggest that science may even be contrary to what truth is about.

When Freud devised his mechanistic metaphors to characterize the nature of the unconscious he was talking in a language already familiar to his medical audience. They were predisposed to see the conscious or unconscious mind as an extension of the body and to think of psychopathology in terms consistent with medical pathology. Freud embraced psychology as the foundation for psychoanalysis because it already conformed to the basic conceptual laws of science that governed neurology and psychiatry. Freud was schooled in this model and never abandoned it. As far as his medical colleagues were concerned, "unconscious" mental causes of psychopathology could be understood as analogous to "undetected" microscopic bodies that occasioned disease. This is because psychology, like medicine, adopted scientific criteria as the basis of knowledge. Science, which in Latin literally means "knowledge," has always been touted as that discipline by which knowledge can be demonstrated, in the same way that Galileo demonstrated his theory at Pisa. Although this requirement became less crucial after the influence of Francis Bacon, proponents of "scientific knowledge"—a tautology—have continued to seek physical, or empirical, evidence to support their claim that it offers the most rigorous way of obtaining truths about the world. Even now, science has been loathe to abandon its naturalistic tendencies. The more abstract its theories, the more it yearns to obtain complementary physical evidence—evidence that can be interpreted any way you like.

In Aristotle's day, sciences were concerned with the nature of living. Philosophy emphasized human relationships and the pursuit of the "good life." Ethics and politics were among the important sciences. Today sciences are more preoccupied with the narrower questions of life itself and how to prolong it, or create it. Improving one's life isn't conceived in terms of ethics but in terms of easing life's burdens through technical interventions. This is why newer theories are intrinsically valued over old ones, because the sciences have fostered the assumption that "discoveries" will reveal something startling and new rather than something we've forgotten, hidden, overlooked—something, perhaps, neglected.

Ethics and politics are no longer thought of as sciences because we can't make them exact. There's no way to test their results. Since their method is so ambiguous and blatantly human, we now think of them as arts—or worse, as philosophical! We can see why psychoanalysis, to obtain credibility, aligned itself with science. The bias of science toward certitude is inconsistent with philosophical aims, and with those of psychoanalysis. Where did the search for certitude begin? Newton's impact on science and philosophy was so profound that when Descartes, in turn, sought to found his philosophy on the principle of certitude, it easily gained influence. Everyone already assumed that certitude was possible. And when he suggested that the only thing people could be certain of was to doubt their own existence, the elegance of his hypothesis was irresistible. He convinced his colleagues that our capacity to conceptualize is more reliable than anything we could possibly experience. Since science, following Newton, learned to equate knowledge with our conception of it, Descartes's rejection of sensual experience easily found favor. Ironically, he circumvented the limits of certitude by proposing that the only possible certainty is the certitude of one's limits to knowledge. This logical irony apparently confirmed the possibility of certitude once and for all. It even seemed foolproof. I can only be certain of my thoughts, even if my thoughts doubt my own existence!

Nobody doubted the sincerity of Descartes's motives for seeking certitude. No one thought that such a quest was even quite mad. Whereas many today might smile at the thought of Descartes's test for certitude— the mind's capacity to doubt itself—how many have abandoned certitude itself? Science continues to search for certainty, precision, and accuracy in its quest for the foundations of knowledge. This bias has served as the paradigm for the sciences since the sixteenth century. Ironically, Freud rejected Descartes's conception of the mind though he was profoundly influenced by it. Descartes's reliance on rationality (the *ego*) as the foundation for knowledge was replaced by the theory of the "unconscious," a more subtle (and certainly less certain) source of knowing than simple reason. On the other hand, Freud's structural theory was based on a model of subjectivity that is indebted to Descartes's radical skepticism. The Cartesian ego is a subject without a foundation because it isn't based on one's existence. Because it is rooted in our capacity for doubt, it is a subject without subjectivity, without being. For this reason I doubt that Descartes was as responsible for having introduced subjectivism into modern psychology as some have claimed. He introduced an abstraction of subjectivity that is inherently de-centered. It even characterizes Freud's structural theory, a model of subjectivity that hasn't one, but three "subjects." None of them is a true subject, and put together they don't constitute a subject, either. His model, like Descartes's, is an abstraction of subjectivity that serves to encourage an increasingly aloof technique.

Science is based on "facts," the raw data of observation, which, when combined, may or may not compel us to accept the hypotheses that prompt its inquiry. Philosophy, on the other hand, isn't really concerned with facts. Philosophy is concerned with the validity of what we believe to be the case. These beliefs are based on intuitions, not data. Intuition—an idea that spontaneously occurs—isn't an observation, though it may come to us while we're observing something. Philosophy invites us to be thoughtful and think things through. While thinking, we form judgments and make decisions about our thoughts, feelings, and inclinations. Philosophers are concerned with being true to the direction their thoughts happen to take them. They aren't concerned with being "correct." They think and, like any thoughtful person, theorize. But their theories don't lead to necessary conclusions. Philosophers—in the Greek sense—hold conclusions in abeyance. They don't form their thought or mold it by building one thought upon another to comprise a series of conclusions, each supported by the previous ones, the way that scientists do with their facts, data, and hypotheses. Nothing binds the thoughts or beliefs of philosophers together, no tangible evidence or conceptual elegance or statistical study. The only thing they have going for them is their fidelity to their point of view, based on what makes sense to them, personally. This is why psychoanalysts are philosophers, not scientists. Psychoanalysts are thoughtful people, concerned with helping others take the time they need to think things over. They hope that, in time, their patients will understand and accept the things that have troubled them all their lives. Their dilemmas are essentially existential in nature; Freud never suggested they were just "mental."

Psychoanalysis doesn't achieve its purpose by proving that something is so. It simply moves us to think through the things we're usually too anxious to even think about. Its truths can't be scientifically validated because they can only be realized, through personal experience. Science may offer mastery of our physical world, but it will never shine the light on one's sanity.

9

Truth and Technology

Freud and Heidegger, as different as two men could be, were ironically aligned in the same purpose: the pursuit of truth as a singular aim. For Heidegger, this aim was his philosophy; for Freud it was his life. If the purpose of psychoanalysis is to obtain truth, its technique must be such that it accomplishes this goal. Freud's "technical papers" were devoted to no other task. But from where does the very notion of technique derive? What does it mean? Does it imply one thing to one person, and something else to another? Heidegger devoted an entire paper to this question, *The Question Concerning Technology* (1977b). His conclusions about its nature were remarkably consistent with Freud's. Perhaps this question, more than any other, links Heidegger's thought to Freud's in ways that are especially beneficial for the work of analysis.

Derived from the Greek word *techne,* the *Oxford English Dictionary* defines technology literally as "a systematic treatment." It's used to denote an art or craft, a discourse about art, a scientific study of the arts, or the terminology used in describing the production of a specific art, the so-called technical term. Each art has its own nomenclature. Technical terms refer to a performance that is artistic in nature. Not one of these definitions, however, tell us anything about the essence, or nature, of what technology is. Technology isn't specifically concerned with science, yet the term has become increasingly associated with modern science in ways that have compromised its original meaning. How has this happened? This is the question Heidegger was asking when he devoted an essay to this problem.

> According to ancient doctrine, the essence of a thing is considered to be *what* a thing is. We ask the question concerning technology when we ask

what it is. Everyone knows the two statements that answer our question. One says: technology is a means to an end. The other says: technology is a human activity. The two definitions of technology belong together. For to posit ends and procure and utilize the means to them is a human activity. The manufacture and utilization of equipment, tools, and machines, the manufactured and used things themselves, and the needs and ends that they serve, all belong to what technology is. The whole complex of these contrivances is technology. Technology itself is a contrivance—in Latin, an *instrumentum*. (1977b, 4–5)

One might characterize this depiction of technology as a rough and ready notion of what technology basically means. This is how the term is typically used. The technical refers to an instrument of some kind, a contrivance. This is how Freud referred to psychoanalysis, as a tool, an instrument whose use served a particular aim. But Heidegger isn't content to leave it there. We haven't even begun to appreciate what the technical—a term we use every day—actually means. Giving something a definition doesn't necessarily determine what something is. If we want to know what technology means, we need to go beyond definitions. We need to determine its essence. To do that, Heidegger believed we must ask:

What is the instrumental itself? Within what do such things as means and end belong? A means is that whereby something is effected and thus attained. *Whatever has an effect as its consequence is called a cause.* But not only that by means of which something else is effected is a cause. The end in keeping with which the kind of means to be used is determined is also considered a cause. Wherever ends are pursued and means are employed, wherever instrumentality reigns, there reigns causality. (6; emphasis added)

In order to understand the nature of technology we have to understand the nature of cause—means and ends. You have an end in mind concerning something you want to achieve and you try to determine the means by which you can achieve it. The combination of the two fall under the domain of technology. But it isn't the one or the other—ends or means—that "cause" something to happen. Both means and ends are, by definition, causes. The end causes me to seek means, and the means cause the task to be completed. The one depends on the other. Yet, the nature of cause is more complicated than we usually assume. Historically, there are four kinds of causes, not two. Heidegger explores them in detail.

The four are *causa materialis, causa formalis, causa finalis,* and *causa efficiens.* Each plays a vital role in what we mean by technology. *Causa materialis* is the matter from which something is made—silk, wood, metal. *Causa formalis* is the shape or form that something assumes. *Causa finalis* refers to the purpose that something serves, what it will be used for. And finally, *causa efficiens* refers to the work that is employed in making something. This fourth kind of cause, *causa efficiens,* concerns labor. It is the one most commonly associated with the specific "work" that technique implies. It is also the most ambiguous. Another aspect of cause concerns its relationship to debt. According to Heidegger, "What we call cause and the Romans call *causa* is called *aition* by the Greeks, that to which something is indebted" (7). In other words, a cause elicits a debt from the thing that is beholden to it. Causes aren't blind; they tie things together: "The four causes are the ways, all belonging at once to each other, of being responsible for something else" (7). Whatever, or whoever, causes something to come about assumes responsibility for it. This measure of responsibility applies equally to all four causes.

Let's find an example that shows what Heidegger is getting at. How about the technology employed in building a house? Let's say that a man is planning to get married and wants to build a house for him and his wife to live in, and to raise a family. If he chooses a wooden house, then the wood is one element or "cause" of the house's existence. The wood is the matter, the material, from which the house is made. In that sense, the house is indebted to the wood for its existence. But the house is also indebted to the form the house will assume, the plans and blueprints that determine its design. It won't be a wooden chair or a wooden boat, but a wooden house when it's finished. Both the wood and the design are co-responsible for the house's creation, its coming into being. But there's a third factor that is also responsible for the house's existence. What purpose will it have? The man who is building this house plans to use it for a home where he can live with his wife and their family. Naturally, a building may serve other purposes as well. But whatever the *finalis* may be, a purpose is always in mind. Things aren't built just for the sake of it. And what about the fourth cause that is needed to make something? This fourth aspect, *causa efficiens,* entails the work that is employed in building the house. But this aspect can't be reduced to the labor alone. In order for work to occur there has to be a worker, someone who actually builds the house and sees that it's finished. The builder is the person who gathers together the three other causes of the process of building something. The builder may be the person who is going to live in the house, or the contractor who plans to sell it, or the person who makes it by hand. It could be anyone. Whoever it is, it's not necessarily the carpenter or the construction worker who performs the actual labor. It's the person who conceives of the house and is principally concerned with its completion. The essence of *causa efficiens* belongs to the individual who is employed to finish the house, who nurtures it along. This person's function isn't defined by the notion of "toil," as crucial as that function is. This is the person who ponders the development of the building as it evolves. The individual is party to each of the elements as they join together, guided to their eventual completion. This person sees that it gets done. The "builder" isn't just somebody who's doing a job, who's merely punching a clock and following orders. The builder is the principal instrument in a creative process, the one who makes it happen.

Debt, cause, and responsibility are three aspects that are vital to the meaning of technology, of what it means to make something. What ties them together? What links them to the specifically human dimension that the technical entails? In order for technology to be human we know that it has to reveal something, because being human always entails the act of disclosure. In other words, when something is made, something is revealed for what it is.

> The four ways of being responsible bring something into appearance. They let it come forth into presencing. They set it free to that place and so start it on its way, namely, into its complete arrival. The principal characteristic of being responsible is this starting something on its way into arrival. It is in the sense of such a starting something on its way into arrival that being responsible is an occasioning or an inducing to go forward. (9)

There are no blind causes, no purposeless aims. A cause doesn't just have an effect, as though it could trigger a chain reaction whose outcome is unfathomable. Causes conspire to bring about their effects, which, in turn, are causes too. Together, they comprise an intelligent aim. It's not because of the effect alone that a cause has significance. A cause brings together the collaborative elements that combine in a single purpose. In other words, a cause is specifically human. Yet, the very concept of "cause" has become so fraught with materialist connotations—due to the encroachment of modern science—that Heidegger suggests we use an alternative term in order to grasp its original meaning. The Greek word for causality, *aitia,* may be translated as *occasion* or *occasioning,* a word that immediately conveys the collaborative connotations of causality that we've lost. To cause or occasion something to happen, to bring it into being by revealing what it is, entails a concomitation of elements that are bound together in a united purpose. What is that purpose? Bringing what is in concealment into unconcealment.

In other words, the essential purpose of technology is "revelation." The technical is a form of revelation, not just a means to an end. Technology is a way of revealing things for what they are; for what, in fact, they become. Most people think of technology as simply constructing something by joining the component parts together. But we would be truer to its actual meaning if we thought of technology—"technique"—as an instrument that reveals something in its unfolding. When we think about a work of art, for example, we wouldn't say that its purpose is to make a painting. The purpose of the artistic endeavor is to reveal something through its painting. This is a distinction we commonly make between a work that is artistic and one that isn't; one whose purpose, for example, is to "make money."

Yet, is technology only concerned with things? Can't technique be applied to works of the mind, as well? Technology is a way of revealing. The Greek word *technē,* usually understood in the narrow sense of a "manual skill," has a wider meaning that goes much farther than the skill of a craftsman. It also encompasses the arts of the mind and the so-called fine arts. In other words, theorizing itself is an art of the mind. It encompasses the pondering of philosophical questions, as we're doing this very moment. Freud's conception of "free association" is another technical use of the mind, whose sole aim is to "reveal the concealed." This is because *technē* is essentially poetic. As with all poetry, it is concerned with bringing something out and into the open. All arts are technical in this respect. But are all uses of the mind exclusively technical? There's an even older meaning to the word *technē* that was common before Plato, when it was linked to *episteme. Episteme* is the root of epistemology, a word that was only adopted as recently as the sixteenth century to denote "philosophy of knowledge." According to Heidegger, "Both words are names for knowing in the widest sense. They mean to be entirely at home in something, to understand and be expert in it" (13). They share in common a type of knowing that reveals something by opening it up. However, *technē* and *episteme,* equally concerned with revelation, aren't exactly the same. What makes them different? *Technē,* according to Aristotle, depicts a process of revelation that can't be completed of its own accord, whereas *episteme,* which is concerned with thought for its own sake, is capable of revealing itself. *Technē,* which conforms to the "four modes of occasioning," is a type of revelation that can't reveal itself by itself. It needs help. A contrivance needs to be employed, whether one is building a house, painting a work of art, or performing a psychoanalysis.

In fact, this distinction shows just how subtle an instrument psychoanalysis really is. Free association is both a *technē* and an *episteme.* It is a use of one's mind that must be allowed to act of its own accord, but a contrivance is utilized in order to facilitate it. Otherwise, associations wouldn't occur, freely, on their own. Analytic patients don't have the full use of their mind because they're tied up in knots. They need help. Psychoanalysis is a contrivance, a *technē,* that is brought to bear for a purpose, to deepen one's capacity for *episteme. Technē* evolves into *episteme* as one's thinking begins to flow more freely and autonomously.

But what if the contrived nature of technology—whether it's applied to psychoanalysis or something else—gets out of hand and loses contact with its true purpose? Is it possible that the tools designed to serve our needs—in thoughtless hands serving thoughtless motives—might be used for some other purpose? Is there a danger that *technē* could be used to conceal more than it reveals, to build something useless or even monstrous? Nowadays, we have a real problem with technology. The problem is what has become of modern technology. If technology is supposed to be creative, an instrument of revelation and truth, a human enterprise, how is it that technology has developed such a negative connotation? When we think of technology today, we think about "machines" instead of tools. We think of something detached and impersonal. We see this even in the way that psychoanalysis has developed. Nowadays, most people think of psychoanalysis as a specifically un-personal form of treatment. They hardly think of it as a relationship between two people united in common cause: to determine what is going on. The development of analytic technique during the course of this century has repeated in this brief span of time the gradual corruption of technology over the last two thousand years. This is epitomized by the changes that have occurred during the last three centuries, including the industrial revolution and the turn toward the mathematical, inaugurated by Newton and Descartes. What's happened to technology? What's the matter with it?

For one thing, it's gotten so big. Today, modern technology is less of an aid in our relationship with nature than a challenge to nature itself. It steals nature's riches and gives nothing back. The most obvious example is the incredible size of industrial enterprises like coal mining, oil exploration, farming combines, dams, nuclear plants, big business, the global economy, even tourism. All these examples of contemporary technology share one thing in common: their immensity. Modern technology hungers for the large scale. The insidious motives for its size ultimately rely on economic gain. What happens when we compare the scale of modern technology with simple farmers, for example, who work their plot of land with the help of their family? They take out of the soil but they also give something back. The land is alive and prospers. It conforms to a chain of life that is reciprocal. Naturally, farmers use technical skills that help them to farm. In turn, these skills obey the "four means of occasioning," which are so vital to the way technology is supposed to work. These farmers would be lost without those skills, just like the tailor, or baker, or lawyer, or doctor would be. But compare the ecology, a concept with which we're all increasingly aware, of the people whose labor is rooted in the skills they personally embody with the immensity and depersonalization that is involved in raping forests that are irreplaceable and establishing corporations whose scale, power, and advantage drive the small farmer, professional, or businessman out of business. You have to wonder what's going on. Where is it headed? How has it changed *us,* without our even knowing that it has?

Heidegger calls this recent development a monstrosity that grabbed hold of our existence and altered it in ways we don't realize. It's even altered psychoanalysis in the way that it's used by the marketplace, employed by its practitioners, perverted by the "mental health" industry, and controlled by its institutes and societies. How does Heidegger characterize the nature of this monstrosity?

> In order that we may even remotely consider the monstrousness that reigns here, let us ponder for a moment the contrast that speaks out of the two titles: "The Rhine" as dammed up into the *power* works, and "The Rhine" as uttered out of the *art* work, in Hölderlin's hymn by that name. But, it will be replied, the Rhine is still a river in the landscape, is it not? Perhaps.

But how? In no other way than as an object on call for inspection by a tour group ordered there by the vacation industry. (16; emphasis in original)

The vacation *industry*. A contradiction in terms, isn't it? Tourism offers an apt example of how insidiously modern technology has affected—and infected—our everyday lives. Yet, there's more than the mere scale of tourism that exemplifies the spirit of technological progress in our age. There's also the problem of economics. Without it, modern technology and the tourist industry, the mental health industry, and all the other "industries" couldn't survive. The thing that makes tourism specifically modern isn't simply its scale. It includes the financial return that fuels the machinery of that industry at its source. Modern technology mass produces the intrinsic pleasures of travel. But it also divorces our experience of travel from the sense of adventure that originally inspired it. Tourism has no purpose except to make money. It isn't concerned with seeing the world. It's goal is to capitalize on the public's urge to travel, at a "bargain" that few can resist, or truly afford. Inexorably, we all become implicated in its appetite for "fuel": more money. Cities like San Francisco, a place of such beauty and charm that many would like to see it, become dependent on tourism for their prosperity. This is because tourism seizes on what was there to begin with, then prompts growth in order to service the demands of its consumers. Hotels, shops, restaurants, and entertainment are created to accommodate the increasing number of travellers. Airports, airplanes, tour buses, and taxis need to be bought and operated to serve all this need. San Francisco, such a beautiful city to live in, soon becomes something else. It is less a habitat than a convention center, more a spectacle than a home. San Franciscans hate it. But what happens when tourism falters and the numbers of travellers subside? San Franciscans worry. They hope the tourists come back.

That is how modern technology works, and how it comes to control what was once its master: us. The magnitude of modern technology and its violation of our existence are truly monstrous. If that's all there was to worry about, perhaps we could contain it. But even that isn't the most insidious or damaging aspect of modern technology. If it were, we could possibly stop it. What is truly ominous about technology concerns the way it's become master of its former masters, the way that it orders us about. This works in two ways. Modern technology, due to the immensity of its scale, imposes an order on the life of the community it serves. This is how San Franciscans, on the one hand, benefit from tourism and, on the other, can't live without it. It establishes "order" over our lives, promulgated by incentive and reward. Modern technology tries to order nature, for the benefit of all. But in that ordering we become its pawns, not its captains. We welcome the orderly routine and economic return of its successes, but we pay for this apparent security—a false sense of security—with a price. In fact, that price has no limit. Modern technology has introduced miraculous cures in the "health" industry, which increase the span of our lives longer than ever before. We envision more radical cures in the future. But can we really afford them? As our lives are prolonged, we become less capable of paying for it. We demand it anyway, just because it's possible to have it.

But there's another way that modern technology hurts us. If you ask the employees who work in these industries why they do their jobs—why the forester cuts down trees, why the nuclear engineer endangers his community, why any of them perform the odious functions that many of these jobs entail—they give the same reply: "It's my job. I was only following orders. One has to earn a living." We need to support its machinations for our economic survival. It's not so simple to stop it, even if we want to. We can't just walk away. The term *order* has a double connotation. Through technology we impose a sense of order on the social blueprint of our community. Then we become subservient to it. We can't live without it. We follow wherever it leads us. This is when oppression replaces revelation as the essence of technology. Expediency displaces truth. It's true that modern technology continues to reveal, but what it reveals has changed. The nature of this revelation is no longer poetic or faithful to Man's highest aspirations. It reveals instead the jeopardy our lives are in. It reveals how dangerous technology has become in the age of thoughtlessness we inhabit. Now we service technology instead of technology serving us.

How did that happen? How did this transformation in technology occur? Technology belongs to art. But it is increasingly dominated by science. By appropriating technology, science transformed it and subverted its nature. What science has added to technology is its notion of precision, based on Descartes's quest for certitude (see chapter 8). Oblivious of the intrinsic mystery that the revelation of our existence entails, science appeals to the pervasive concern for security, predictability and control over our day-to-day lives. Science seeks to protect us from ambiguity, from the things in nature that frighten—poverty, infirmity, even death. It has taken what was creative, flexible, and imperfect and tried to make it bigger, better, safe. Though technology was once the tools of our integrity, we have become the "tools" of its infamy. It's determined to make us immortal, even if it kills us.

10

Truth and Psychoanalysis

How has the transformation that technology enjoys in our culture affected psychology and, more specifically, psychoanalysis? Freud embraced science and couched psychoanalysis in scientific terms. He even insisted that psychoanalysis—a quest for truth—conform to the empirical rules of validation that science employs. He compared the observability of psychoanalysis to astronomy, which bases its findings on the observation of the heavens. But there was nothing scientific about Freud's conception of the unconscious, or his theories about psychopathology. Freud once boasted that psychoanalysis had demolished, once and for all, Descartes's claim of certitude because he discovered the existence of an unconscious that wasn't consciously knowable. The man who subverted the basic premises of the father of modern science could hardly be a spokesman for what the sciences now epitomize.

The same holds for Freud's conception of technique. It was always an artistic conception—in Heidegger's sense—rather than a scientific one. In Freud's day, technical rules weren't as rigid as they are now. They were offered in the form of advice and suggestion. Freud shared those rules with analysts who wanted to know what they meant to him. They merely described the way that psychoanalysis worked for Freud, personally. Many of his recommendations simply suited his personality. Other analysts were encouraged to follow his advice, but to stay faithful to what suited their personalities. His rules were sketchy, subtle, and ambiguous. They were conveyed in the spirit of an artist talking about his craft to fellow artists. There was little of modern science in the manner with which Freud discussed the practicalities of psychoanalysis.

Today this has all changed. We study technical manuals of encyclopedic length that don't merely advise or suggest—in effect, they order us about. They are modern to the core. We're not invited to be thoughtful about the techniques we might use. We're not asked to experiment. We're told there's a "correct" technique and there are deviations from that procedure. Naturally, the deviations are wrong. They're even "unanalytic." Freud's technique, especially, is increasingly dismissed as wrongheaded—even deviant! Freud is dead. Others have taken the mantle and carry the torch. But do they come to praise or to bury him? Sometimes they do both, simultaneously. A rock in one hand, a wreath in the other. Today, the weight of professional societies is used for the purpose of telling analysts what to do. They order us about in the spirit we have learned to expect from the institutions of modern technology. Psychoanalytic institutions today—grant me this generalization—are terribly concerned with being modern. They don't want to be left behind. One analyst told me how he was on the "cutting edge" of psychoanalytic thought and practice. He knew all the *latest* ideas. Freud knew this would happen. He saw the Americanization and modernization of psychoanalysis in the winds of its future. It couldn't wait till his death. Now, Freud is old-fashioned. Most of his ideas were over two thousand years old. What could be more old-fashioned than that?

Without realizing it, psychoanalytic institutions have fallen prey to the very thing that psychoanalysis was originally conceived to destroy: the rigidification of the mind, the thoughtlessness of behavior. The way they "order" us about is a perfect example of modern technology run amuck, bringing order to our lives while imprisoning our creativity—and our liberties. Increasingly, in their zeal to be right, analysts talk more and more about ethics, but a peculiar form of ethics, in fact. It's an ethics predetermined for us. It talks about rules and civil codes. It doesn't encourage responsibility. Instead, it advocates conformity and compliance. Even confidentiality, strictly speaking, in certain cases, it's against the law. You might get arrested. So we comply. We do so not out of respect, or gratitude, or indebtedness, but out of fear. It can be dangerous to speak a truth; and it can be dangerous to protect a truth that's been uttered.

More and more, analytic technique is dictated by authoritarianism. This, in turn, is inspired by legalistic distinctions between right and wrong behavior: This is "psychoanalysis." That is "psychotherapy." By splitting hairs into the finest gradations psychoanalysis has followed the trend in modern technology of cutting itself off from its source. Instead of gathering together the four modes of occasioning that comprise the original meaning of technology, it severs each from the others. It conceives its technique in terms of behavior alone, while its vision and its perspective are left to something called "theory." The way it distinguishes, for example, between theory and technique reduces technical considerations to applications of theory. On the other hand, one's technique should be consistent, whatever the theory might be. People even talk about "the theory of technique." This is how the conceptualization of modern science, and modern technology, has affected theory. It's cut off from its body. It exists by itself, in thin air. Originally, technology included the theory from which subsequent concepts were extracted. Freud himself confirmed this, because his psychoanalytic theories followed his technical behavior, not the other way around.

What could we learn about analytic technique if we were to apply the four original causes of technology to it? First, the matter with which we're dealing would comprise the patient's suffering and the concern it arouses. Secondly, the shape of the matter would comprise the means by which expression to that suffering is realized—meeting together in confidence, listening to what each has to say, alert to the responses elicited. Third, the purpose of this endeavor is to determine what that suffering is; to let it come into being by making itself heard. Finally, the actual work the analyst and patient are engaged in is comprised of talking and listening—free associations, interpretations, and other conversational interventions that help to reveal the depths of one's suffering and what it means.

This fourfold constellation of cause and effect includes theory—literally, one's way of seeing things. If it didn't, technique would be blind, like a hammer falling in space. When technique is reduced to only the last of the four causes of technology—*causa efficiens*—it, in effect, flies blind. In its blindness, it holds onto itself even more tightly and becomes rigid. It's like reducing the technique of building a house to the method employed by driving in nails: When something goes wrong, drive the nails in even harder. Psychoanalysis isn't comprised of technique on the one side and theory on the other. It is technical in its essence. It isn't anything else.

What, then, is the essential purpose of technology? It is composed of many elements, as we've seen. That's why it can't be reduced to a "means to an end." It presupposes an end in its means. This is what modern technology neglects. When technique is divorced from its purpose and cuts itself off from its roots, it becomes a depersonalized technology, serving disembodied means. The path modern technology has taken, because of its size and its power, overwhelms the personal dimension. Technology is no longer simply a "tool." It isn't an extension of ourselves. It's a machine that usurps us. We're its "workers" and "consumers." We serve its ends instead of our own. Worse, we become machines ourselves as we compete—and identify—with its power and success.

This trend is nowhere more prevalent than in contemporary psychiatry and psychology, the "mental health" industry, even psychoanalysis. It even includes the terminology we use to convey our most private concerns. We talk about suffering as though it's apart from our selves: distant, microscopic, chemical, even "mental." We reduce who we are to particles and components, displacements, defenses, drives, part-objects, and the like. Always the appropriate "technical term," but to what end? What are we saying? Are we revealing anything, or just satisfying a yen for abstraction? Freud introduced this way of talking into his vocabulary, but a careful reading of his terms shows that he applied them metaphorically. Why do we take them so literally? We probably have science to blame. In its triumph, it reduces our existence to its literal components, the "stuff" that we're made of. It builds edifices and monuments to Man's cleverness, but it stifles thought and dismisses its inherent wisdom. Some psychiatrists even suggest that humans don't merely resemble machines, but are machines. In the words of Warren McCulloch,

> Everything we learn of organisms leads us to conclude not merely that they are analogous to machines but that they are machines. Man-made machines are not brains, but brains are a very ill-understood variety of computing machines. Cybernetics has helped to pull down the wall between the great world of physics and the ghetto of the mind. (1965, 163)

McCulloch believes that despair, alienation, depression, joy, enlightenment, suffering, even love are manifestations of chemical processes that germinate in our brains. According to McCulloch, we are our brains. In fact, "we" are machines, because the brain, he says, is a "computer." On the other hand, we don't become more *human* by simply replacing McCulloch's brain theory with a more psychological one. "I" am no more a mental mechanism than a cerebral cortex. Yet, that is what many psychologists and psychoanalysts happen to believe. This is where science, in the service of technology, leads us. It takes us out of ourselves and into the abyss, where exactness reigns supreme. This is how technology infected the most intimate recesses of our existence, and killed it. We don't merely use machines and, so, depend on them more and become helpless. Technology has also infected our minds and what we have left of our sanity. The way that we talk to each other shows it. We reduce our suffering to a "problem" and then we demand "solutions." This reveals a technological way of thinking, in which we incorporate technical concepts into our very being. It epitomizes the contemporary man and woman of our age.

There was a time when poetry and the arts epitomized technology. Science subsequently coopted the technical and corrupted it. That doesn't mean science is bad, but modern science stifles the artistic license that lies at the heart of technology. The purpose of technology is to reveal what would otherwise remain concealed. Technology helps us free what is trapped in concealment. That is why technology, in its essence, is about revelation, discovery, truth. Psychoanalysis is essentially technological— in the true sense of that word. It strives to reveal what is hidden, to make it more or less what it is. How it proposes to do that is what psychoanalysis is.

III

THE TRUTH ABOUT DORA

Never has a case history provoked as much attention, examination, criticism and praise, controversy, disgust, or appreciation as Freud's treatment of Ida Bauer, known to us pseudonomyously as simply "Dora." Why does this case continue to arouse so much passion and debate when Freud himself freely acknowledged that the treatment was a failure? One might suspect a lengthier analysis, more ambiguous in its outcome or misguided in its execution to elicit the measure of debate that has surrounded this all-too-brief psychoanalysis. Yet, Dora was one of only five major cases that Freud published, and of the five (the others were Little Hans, the Rat Man, Schreber, and the Wolf Man) she was the only woman. Obviously, Dora's analysis assumes a remarkable significance if we wish to understand how Freud viewed women, and, more importantly, treated them.

Freud thought of Dora as a woman and treated her like one though she was only eighteen years old when he analyzed her. One of the most frequent criticisms of her analysis is Freud's alleged failure to appreciate how young she was, both in his manner and his interpretations of her symptoms. This accusation, and others like it—that he lacked sympathy for women generally and was prone to male prejudice—is frequently used as evidence of a flaw in Freud's character and of his limitations as a psychoanalyst.

Even so, psychoanalysts couldn't imagine their education complete without a thorough study and appreciation of Freud's understanding of Dora's neurosis and his treatment of it, even if the technique he used is frequently rejected as inadequate, myopic, even "unanalytic." Dora's analysis continues to be taught in virtually every analytic institute in the world. It is the first and often only case study that college courses on Freud use as an example of how psychoanalysis is practiced—even if the heart of this teaching is increasingly occupied with emphasizing the errors of the case; "errors" that go considerably beyond what Freud himself acknowledged.

You can't help but wonder if criticizing Freud is as important for the contemporary psychoanalyst as praising him used to be. This seems especially apt when the subject being discussed is Freud's technique. Whether we praise or condemn him, coming to terms with Freud is the only way we have of establishing our credibility as psychoanalysts, because being a psychoanalyst implies a necessary, if wary, relationship with Freud's published views. It isn't that easy to maintain an allegiance to a figure as powerful as Freud's while carving out some independence of thought and behavior that doesn't lose contact with him altogether. Are the criticisms we raise genuine disagreements, or do we sometimes seek things to criticize in principle, as evidence of our professed emancipation? And if our disagreements are genuine, does it make them credible just because they're raised half a century after his death? Perhaps Freud's importance in every psychoanalyst's life invites us to seek flaws in his work, whether they are real or imagined.

There are many details, and so many places to look. There are so many things that Freud is supposed to have overlooked, misunderstood, or misinterpreted about Dora, women, and even hysteria; so much that we claim he didn't grasp about technique, good manners, humanity. Had he lived longer, surely we could have taught *him* a thing or two ourselves. The debate about Dora concerns much more than the success or failure of one analytic case. It involves a debate about psychoanalysis itself, the direction that it's taking and whether that direction is identified with Freud or something else.

In my inquiry into Dora's analysis, my purpose is less to belittle Freud than to admire him, less to criticize than to learn. This tack may appear, I admit, unusual. My purpose is primarily concerned with Freud's technique; in other words, with how he conducted himself. Naturally, one can't look at Freud's technique in isolation. The thoughts that occur in an analyst's mind are just as important as how the analyst behaves; how an analyst thinks should coincide with what that analyst does. Freud was preoccupied with the way he talked to his patients. His aim was to get to those truths his patients concealed—from themselves as well as from others. The way Freud elicited these truths allowed him to discover some incredible things about the kind of suffering his patients only alluded to and sometimes denied. Freud's theories didn't "guide" his practice. Rather, his interrogative manner gave rise to what he learned about human suffering.

When we explore Freud's treatment of Dora, embodied in his relationship with her, we should emphasize what it was he was after, what it was that he set out to do, and what it was that he did. What was Freud's conception of the analytic cure? To what extent has that conception been adopted or modified? And finally, how faithful was Freud's conduct to his purpose and his views about analytic technique?

It's been suggested that Freud revised his views about technique as a consequence of his treatment of Dora. Freud's realization that he neglected to appreciate the full force of Dora's transference with him subsequently informed his discussion on transference in the "technical papers." In fact, two of the six papers that comprise his technical writings are devoted specifically to this problem. Yet, there is little evidence to support the notion that Freud altered or modified his technique as a consequence of his analysis of Dora. The basic principles of his technique were apparently fixed at the time he treated her.

It is possible—and I think, even likely—that the so-called errors Freud committed with Dora weren't as consequential as they have subsequently become in the minds of those who came later. They were the sort of mistakes any analyst might make, at one time or other, with any patient, especially a difficult one. Had Freud to do it all over, I doubt he would have treated Dora differently. He may have added this or that interpretation in hindsight. But these kinds of considerations don't comprise a revision in technique. Freud was satisfied with his technique when he treated Dora and believed that it basically served his purpose. On the other hand, he was never certain to what extent this or that person could benefit from psychoanalysis, no matter how skilful the analyst is.

I believe that Freud's analysis of Dora was true to the "classical" technique as he envisioned it. He tried to help Dora discover the truth about her symptoms, her longings, her grievances, and the unequivocal meaning of her place in the orbit of her family and their world. I hope to show how faithfully his conception of psychoanalysis was demonstrated by his memorable encounter with this remarkable young woman.

11

The Paradox of Neurosis

Freud's preface to the published account of his treatment of Dora reads less like an introduction than a warning; more like a battlecry than an invitation. Peter Gay, in his biography of Freud, calls its tone "combative" (1988, 247). Freud waited five years to publish the case and it was only then that the preface was finally composed. He had a long time to think about it. It's fair to assume his remarks were carefully considered. They comprise as forceful a statement as the text that follows.

There is no mistaking that Freud assumed this book would be rejected by its audience. He anticipates criticism, ridicule, condemnation, even "ill-will." He wastes little time in striking back at the expected onslaught that he imagined would follow. Gay suspects that Freud's mood and apparent emotion were the result of unresolved feelings about Dora and the abrupt termination of her analysis. While Gay falls short of suggesting that Freud was in love with her, he does allude to his "involvement" with Dora and how it was probably "more unsettling than Freud suspected" (247). No doubt Freud still felt a degree of passion about the case if not Dora herself. And no doubt Freud was in anguish when he wrote the preface, and frustrated with the same public that more or less ignored his *Interpretation of Dreams,* published the same year Dora was analyzed. Five years later, Freud was still struggling to achieve the recognition and acceptance for his ideas that he eagerly anticipated.

Dora was to have been his "test case." The original title, *Dreams and Hysteria,* was eventually abandoned sometime after the treatment ended so precipitously and prematurely, hence the revised title, *Fragment of an Analysis of a Case of Hysteria.* Freud had hoped to demonstrate how dream interpretation could cure a hysterical neurosis. What he got instead was a lesson in how unpredictable an analysis can be! If nothing else, the preface serves to alert us that a psychoanalysis is not an easy thing to complete, and how important the completion of it is if one hopes to meet with success.

Freud opens his "Prefatory Remarks" with a warning: don't expect too much from the case you are about to read. The nature of the criticism Freud anticipates is extraordinary. It wasn't his lack of success that especially concerned him. After all, no one else was succeeding in treating hysteria, so Freud could hardly be faulted for encountering the same difficulties himself. He says he was criticized for a poverty of case materials to substantiate his theories, then predicts that "now I shall be accused of giving information about my patients which ought not to be given" (1953a, 7). Freud felt he was damned if he failed to publish details about his work (in order to substantiate his rationale for it), but would be damned as well for publishing those very details once the public (in fact, Freud's medical colleagues) discovered its nature. This is probably the first time a physician was ever compelled to conclude that his method of treatment would create a scandal once it was disclosed. What was it about psychoanalysis that was said to be scandalous? Does that scandal continue to haunt psychoanalysis, or do we reserve our disapproval for Freud alone?

Freud confesses his apprehensiveness from the start. Because hysterical symptoms are the expression of the individual's most secretive desires, the only hope for relief from these symptoms and the condition that underlies them must derive from "the revelation of those intimacies and the betrayal of those secrets" (8). But how many patients would enter into analytic treatment in the first place if they understood from the beginning that its success depended on revealing their best-kept secrets to a person they didn't even know? Of those who are, however, willing, how many would remain committed if they suspected their secrets would some day be published? Freud, nevertheless, felt it was his duty to tell the story to the scientific community in the interests of reaching those people who might benefit from psychoanalysis. Obviously, the publication of one's failures, and the reasons for them, would be just as invaluable as championing the successes. But wouldn't patients stand to be even more embarrassed by the public disclosure of these failures than their analyst? After all, it would be the analyst's decision, not theirs, to have these details published.

Freud was understandably sensitive to the matter of disclosing secrets learned in confidence—learned to a considerable extent without the knowledge of the patients who, after all, show more than they realize. He employed every caution to prevent Dora's identity (Ida Bauer) from being learned. But what if Ida Bauer herself comes across Freud's account of "Dora's" treatment and recognizes this woman as herself? Mightn't she be shocked—even dismayed—at all the things she now discovers about herself that she hadn't learned when she was being treated? Incredibly, Freud says that even if she were to read his report, "she will learn nothing from it that she does not already know" (9). This is a remarkable thing to say, when you take into account all of the many details that he discloses about Dora's character; her sexual proclivities; her attitude toward men, women, and her family; her bitterness; and all the other things we learn about her. It's astonishing that Freud would conceal none of these details from her and, presumably, his other patients. How many analysts today would make such a claim? His audacious candor may partly explain why Freud was so concerned about the future of his great enterprise. And what about the enmity of those patients who failed to hold the course, or the medical colleagues who were, at best, suspicious of his motives or, perhaps, envious of his achievement? Freud excised a number of things from his account of the treatment in order to protect Dora's identity. But he refused to omit some graphic details he believed had to be disclosed. Freud was unusually candid with all his patients, even with the young Dora.

Beneath the semiapologetic tone of Freud's less than successful experience with Dora, and the combative—even hostile—remarks against his colleagues, two important themes were introduced in his preface to this case. The first concerns a question of ethics and the obligation of protecting one's patients from harm. Ironically, the potential danger that Freud had in mind wasn't the analysts themselves but those colleagues he feared would use his revelations to attack his former—and through them, potential—patients. The second cause for concern is even more ironic. Psychoanalysis aims at uncovering secrets. These secrets are of an extraordinary nature, because they refer to the innermost longings and beliefs of the person being analyzed. Neurotics suffer from these secrets because they deny them to themselves and guard them from discovery by others. The only way out of this impasse is to willingly—though not necessarily "wittingly"—disclose these secrets to another human being. In so doing, the peculiar form of alienation that characterizes neurosis—in this case, a hysterical neurosis—is transformed.

But this makes psychoanalysis—the experience of it and one's compliance with it—a scary proposition. It involves a risk with no guarantee of reward. The paranoiac would approach this arrangement with considerable reluctance, if at all. There has to be some capacity for trust on the part of the potential patient or the requisite confidences will never be shared; if shared, they will only lead to even deeper mistrust. This was one of the crucial lessons learned from Dora's analysis. The willingness to share one's secrets is essential to the success of treatment. Freud also learned how difficult it is to overcome the paradox of neurosis. If one holds onto secrets out of fear, increasing the anxiety until it is intolerable, how will one ever find the courage to disclose these secrets—while still afraid of them—in order to diminish the fear one was harboring in the first place? How, in turn, can one describe such a process to the public without frightening them away before they've even begun? These were some of the questions that perplexed Freud when he finally decided to publish the most controversial of all his analyses.

12

A Case of Secrecy

When Dora's father took her to Freud's office for treatment, an association had already started between Freud and the young girl two years earlier, when she was sixteen. At that time she had been suffering from a cough that was tied to other conversion symptoms that would follow. Freud tried to enlist her into analysis even then, but was rebuffed, apparently because the symptoms spontaneously disappeared on their own. But that wasn't the first contact Freud had with Dora's family. Four years earlier still, when Dora was twelve, her father had visited Freud with a problem of his own, a bout of syphilis. He was referred by a friend who figures prominently in the events that would later drive Dora into treatment: the notorious "Mr. K." Freud's successful treatment of the father instilled in him an abiding faith in this discreet physician and subsequently prompted him to take his own daughter to see him.

Because of these earlier contacts, Freud had already formed a positive impression of Dora's father. He gave the appearance of possessing a fine character of moral integrity, and seemed in all a most capable individual. In short, Freud was taken with him, perhaps because he was so candid and trying his best to cope with a miserable marriage. This positive regard was obviously mutual as Freud was the first to be consulted when new difficulties arose. As Freud would discover, his initial impression of this man couldn't have been further from the truth.

One day Dora's parents discovered a half-written letter, which said, in effect, that she was miserable with life and could no longer go on. They were concerned, but couldn't accept she meant to kill herself. They didn't say anything. But Dora's father became alarmed when she fainted after an argument with him. He decided to take her to see Freud. She protested, but eventually consented. Prior to their visit, Dora's father provided Freud with a brief history of what was, in his opinion, the matter with his daughter. Years earlier he and his wife had befriended another couple—the K's—at a resort they frequently visited to relieve his poor health. The acquaintance between the two families grew progressively friendlier over the years. Mrs. K even nursed Dora's father when he was recovering from tuberculosis. Though his condition quickly improved, Dora's family stayed there the better part of ten years, apparently to ensure against relapse. During this time the two families became very close. Mr. K grew fond of Dora and she in turn became fond of him, Mrs. K, and their two young children whom Dora looked after. In fact, when Dora and her father had visited Freud two years earlier, they had been on their way to join Mr. and Mrs. K, who were vacationing in the Alps. Dora was to be dropped off to spend some weeks there while her father returned home. But as he was about to leave her, without explanation she suddenly insisted on leaving with him. It was not until later that her father learned why she became upset. She accused Mr. K of making a pass at her while they were walking by the lake. This was why she refused to stay alone with Mr. K and his family. But when her father confronted Mr. K with his daughter's accusations, he flatly denied the occurrence. He even suggested that Dora had imagined it. He added that Dora was frequently occupied with sexual thoughts and that he had caught her reading erotic novels at their house by the lake.

Her father told Freud that he believed Mr. K's account of the incident was the more reliable one. "I have no doubt," he said, "that the incident is responsible for Dora's depression and irritability and suicidal ideas" (Freud 1953a, 26). Even while her father was convinced that the "incident" that Dora recounted never actually occurred, she insisted that he break off his relationship with Mr. K and Mr. K's wife—a woman, her father exclaimed, Dora used to "positively worship." But this her father wasn't about to do. For one thing, he had decided to accept Mr. K's side of the argument and suspected that Dora had invented the scene by the lake. Playing the analyst now, he interpreted her "recollection" as nothing more than phantasies that had found their way into her mind. Anyhow, his relationship with Mrs. K was too important to sacrifice simply for the sake of humoring his high-strung daughter. Freud could see where this was leading. Next Dora's father confessed a deep-felt pity for Mrs. K on account that her husband was such a wretch. He acknowledged that he and Mrs. K had grown quite close, but insisted they were merely "friendly." Then he claimed that he, of course, got nothing from his wife; his pitiful relationship with Mrs. K was all that he had to enjoy. And now his daughter was insisting, because of her condition, that he give it up. Wouldn't Freud try and bring her to reason?

Freud wasn't fooled for a minute. He concluded the account Dora's father gave him wasn't especially credible and decided to reserve judgment until he heard from Dora herself. From a technical standpoint, this was a remarkable attitude for a psychiatrist to adopt, but one that was axiomatic of Freud's conception of psychoanalysis. If Dora was to be his patient, it was her account that mattered, not her father's. Dora's version of events was crucial for determining the significance of her symptoms and whether or not they were treatable.

The chronology of events that followed isn't so easy to determine. Facts, recollections, bits and pieces of material from one session and then another bombard us on every page. Freud dazzles us with one surprising discovery after another, reflecting the way that knowledge actually emerges in a psychoanalytic treatment. The story of Dora—if not her actual analysis—is a tour de force. It won Freud Germany's highest literary prize, the Goethe Award. Freud even hoped he might win the Nobel Prize for the invention of a new idiom: the "case history." It's a pity he didn't. The reading of Dora's analysis grows more remarkable with each passing generation of analytic publications. Only Freud could have got away with it. He didn't even try to provide a blow-by-blow account of her analysis. For a book that was supposed to demonstrate his clinical theory, there's little discussion of technique in it. What he offers instead is one of the most astonishing stories ever written by a psychoanalyst. We are staggered by the impact his words have on us, recreating the same type of experience we derive from our own analytic patients.

Analysts today typically treat us to the most boring, chronologically astute, clinically "correct," and dispassionately faithful accounts of their work with patients anyone could ever hope to endure. Who could get away with an account like Dora's today? "Process notes" were irrelevant to Freud's way of thinking. He doesn't try to confuse us with them. Nor does he wish to make things too clear, by stripping the case of its inherent ambiguity. This is because the truth of a patient's neurosis can't be spelled out, one step at a time. It has to unfold, gradually, imperceptibly, with its share of surprises. Dora's story is nothing if not shocking—as, in some instances, is Freud's own behavior. The events that comprise Dora's analysis are stunning, yet deceptively simple. Freud believes Dora's account of what happened by the lake with Mr. K. He never doubts her for a moment. This is an eighteen-year-old girl, a bundle of neurotic symptoms whom Freud hardly knows and who is less than eager to confide in him. Yet she has more credibility with Freud than the father he has known for six years, the same father who created an altogether positive impression on Freud—that is, until now.

Dora is convinced her father has been having an affair with Mrs. K for some time, though she only put it together herself recently. She suspects her mother knows about it but doesn't care, and Mr. K knows and does care, but has worked out a deal with her father to look the other way while he attempts to seduce Dora. This "arrangement" must have been unfolding for a long time, as Freud learned that the incident by the lake wasn't the first time Mr. K made a pass at her. Two years before that incident, when Dora was only fourteen, Mr. K arranged to be alone with her at his office, unbeknownst to Dora. With no warning, he suddenly grabbed Dora and kissed her passionately on the lips. She pushed him to the side and ran away in tears. They acted, however, as though nothing had happened and didn't breathe a word of the incident. Freud was the first to hear of it.

Something that Dora said about this incident—the first time Mr. K had made his intentions known to her—caught Freud's attention. She had felt disgusted when he kissed her. Freud thought this was an odd reaction for a young girl to have. Not that he thought she should have welcomed his advances. But Freud had met Mr. K himself (he had, after all, originally brought Dora's father to see him). He was strikingly handsome, and Freud's impression of Dora was of "a girl of intelligent and engaging looks" (23). In other words, Freud wasn't surprised that Mr. K found her attractive, even at fourteen. By her own testimony Dora was especially fond of Mr. K too. She was nevertheless stunned when he forced himself on her. Her reaction of disgust intrigued Freud. Wouldn't a normal girl feel some measure of sexual excitement, along with the fear, shock, and confusion? Freud's interpretation of Dora's reaction is as controversial now as it was when the case was published. He suggested that her behavior was symptomatic of a condition that must have predated the scene by the lake. In fact, Dora's reaction to Mr. K was surely connected to the symptoms that had prompted her father to bring her to Freud in the first place, predisposing her to react in the way that she did.

Dora had one sibling, a brother who was a year and a half older. She was extremely close to her father and her devotion to him was only enhanced by the assorted illnesses he developed as she was growing up. Her father's health became a family preoccupation, though the seriousness of his condition is unclear. Her mother was by all accounts a trying woman, obsessed with cleanliness and order. Dora wasn't close to her. And her mother, by all accounts, wasn't especially fond of Dora. Dora suffered her first hysterical symptoms at age eight, when she developed a nervous cough and lost her voice. Even her family doctor put this down to a psychological condition and it gradually disappeared. The same symptoms resurfaced when she was twelve, but were complicated by migraine headaches. The headaches gradually went away, though Dora was never entirely free of her intermittent coughing. When she was sixteen, her father took her to see Freud for the first time, but the symptoms unexpectedly went into remission. And again, when Dora returned a second time for depression and blackouts, she suffered from the same coughing attacks. But now she was somehow different. She was seriously depressed and her attitude toward her father wasn't the same. She no longer adored him and was increasingly critical. The last two years of her life had changed everything.

Freud was confident that Dora's symptoms could be traced to the one she had suffered when she was eight. That was around the time her family met the K's and when Mrs. K began nursing her father. But it wasn't until much later, when Dora realized something was going on between them, that her devotion to her father started to wane. This change in her feelings, however, was predated even earlier by Mr. K's passionate kiss in his office. Yet, that incident occurred six years after her family and the K's began their friendship—six years after Dora's first conversion symptoms. She had already started to feel ambivalent about her father, perhaps denying the jealousy she must have felt for Mrs. K, when Mr. K kissed her. This may explain why she wasn't "free" to feel even slightly aroused by Mr. K's maneuver in the office. Could her initial disgust have been the product of her developing suspicions about her father's relationship with Mrs. K?

Freud suspected that the duplicitous intrigues that were unfolding in

Dora's family didn't actually cause but rather exacerbated conflicts that had already erupted inside her. She was torn by her extreme attachment to her father and the violent jealousy she felt for Mrs. K, a woman whom Dora herself had once loved. In fact, Freud's inquiry into the sources of Dora's neurosis never strays very far from the intrigue that characterizes her family's relationship with the K's. Dora knew what was happening. She took note of every nuance of the sordid goings-on between her father and his not-too-subtle affair with Mr. K's wife. As she shared her suspicions with Freud, he began to realize the degree to which jealousy was at the bottom of her symptoms. He saw how much she hated this woman. To make matters worse, Freud discovered that Mrs. K's affair with Dora's father—which they still denied—was persisting during the course of Dora's analysis with Freud! Apparently nothing—not even Dora's illness—could cool their determined liaison. According to Freud, this was when "Dora's criticisms of her father were the most frequent: he was insincere, he had a strain of falseness in his character, he only thought of his own enjoyment, and he had a gift for seeing things in the light which suited him best. I could not in general dispute Dora's characterization of her father" (34).

This insight into her father's character was a turning point in her analysis. Freud more or less agreed with Dora's characterization of the events she described. She was furious over the bargain that had been negotiated between her father and Mr. K. Her father had betrayed her in the most unscrupulous and cowardly way, pretending he was ignorant of Mr. K's intentions and leaving Dora to fend for herself, unprotected.

Then Freud made a startling discovery. He realized that Dora had really been in love with Mr. K all along. When he proposed this to her, she claimed she couldn't "recall having ever felt that way" (37). But then she admitted that a cousin had once said to her, "Why you're simply wild about that man!" (37). Faced with these recollections, Dora confessed that she might have been in love with Mr. K at one time, but the scene by the lake had erased those feelings for good. She acknowledged, however, that Freud was admittedly on the right track. He was getting closer to the truth.

What were the specific elements that prompted Dora's neurosis? What did she gain from her symptoms? The aim, in Freud's estimation, was apparent: "to detach her father from Mrs. K" (42). Moreover, Freud was confident "she would recover at once if only her father were to tell her that he had sacrificed Mrs. K for the sake of her health" (42). Dora was overwhelmed by the enormity of her jealousy for Mrs. K. She couldn't bring herself to accept the reality of the situation, that her father had spurned her for another woman. Yet, Dora had been tacitly aware of her father's affair with Mrs. K for some time. She even went out of her way to protect their tryst from discovery. She tried desperately to cope with the unsettling nature of their affair while maintaining control over her attraction to Mr. K. Something had to give. She "attacked" Mrs. K with her symptoms, which were intended to spoil the affair and win back her father. This was, at bottom, the source of her resistance against the treatment. Its success would only deprive her of her anticipated victory over her father's mistress. This was the paradox of Dora's and, by extension, every neurosis. Why would someone abandon the only weapon in her arsenal—her neurotic symptom—only to capitulate to a reality she is fundamentally opposed to?

This was the problem that Freud had to resolve as he was developing his novel technique. Freud's treatment of Dora was based on the principle that the revelation of her unconscious motives would free her from the conflicts her repressions had created. But the secrets that her repressions had secured weren't that easy to get at. The truths her neurosis concealed weren't obtained "in" the account of her history but rather *through* it—whether that account was "accurate" or fallacious. Freud's skill at observation and interpretation was critical in bringing these truths to light. Dora resisted his efforts throughout her brief analysis. Not once did she invite Freud to share his observations about the nature of her illness. After a while Freud found her behavior—endless diatribes and contemptuous accusations—trying. Dora didn't really care what Freud thought one way or the other. Yet, in spite of her "incessant repetition of the same thoughts about her father's relations with Frau K" (54), she couldn't completely deny the circular nature of her complaints. She admitted there was something the matter with her take on reality. At one point she wondered why she couldn't forgive her father, as her brother had urged her to. In fact, she told her brother they should be glad that at last their father had found someone in Mrs. K whom he could love and, in turn, be loved by. But no matter how hard she tried, she couldn't bring herself to accept his love for this woman.

Freud told Dora that she couldn't forgive her father because she loved him too much. But the kind of love she felt wasn't altruistic. It wasn't, for example, *carritas*. It was pure passion. Dora loved her father like a school-girl with a mad crush. "Her affection for her father was a much stronger one than she knew or than she would have cared to admit: in fact, she was in love with him" (56). This insight into the cause of Dora's antipathy finally exposed the source of her neurosis. She loved her father so passionately she couldn't give him up. This proved to be Freud's most radical discovery about the nature of hysteria. It explained why sexual desire or affection, once suppressed, becomes displaced onto symptoms. The intensity of one's passion is too compelling to abandon.

This also explained why Dora couldn't acknowledge her love for Mr. K. She was attracted to Mr. K and loved him "like a father," but couldn't give herself to either of them. Her jealousy for Mrs. K was so profound that it wouldn't permit (a) her father to love anyone else, or (b) her (Dora) to love anyone either. But just when Freud was beginning to grasp what was happening, yet another revelation came to light about Dora's relationship with Mrs. K. Once upon a time Dora had demanded that her governess be fired when it she discovered that the woman was in love with her (Dora's) father. She felt betrayed. She had thought that the governess was a friend but realized she was only being used to get close to her father. Later, a similar incident occurred between Dora and Mrs. K. Dora told Freud that she and Mrs. K had been confidantes. They were so close that "there was nothing they had not talked about" (61), including Mrs. K's marital frustrations. When this story was recounted, Freud observed an unmistakable excitement in Dora's feelings for Mrs. K. She had always given the impression that the reason she was angry with her father's mistress was because of their affair. Suddenly, Freud realized it was Mrs. K who had filled her husband's head with all those rumors about Dora's absorption in "sexual topics," the same rumors that were used against her when her father confronted Mr. K about the incident by the lake. In fact, it was Mrs. K who had filled Dora's head with those topics in the first place, and had given Dora the books she was subsequently caught reading. Only Mrs. K could have known, and passed on, all the things Mr. K learned about, and hoped to share with his would-be mistress. These details hadn't even occurred to Dora until Freud pointed them out to her. Mrs. K had betrayed Dora and turned against her when she was needed the most, when Dora was accused of "imagining" Mr. K's intentions. She used Dora and pretended to befriend her to get close to Dora's father, just as the governess had done before her.

With these new discoveries, Freud could see why Dora was unable to forgive her father. He understood how hurt she must have felt by Mrs. K. She was probably just as upset about her father's relationship with Mrs. K as she was about her former confidante's relationship with him. Not two secret lovers, but three, had conspired to betray her: Dora's father, Mr. K, and Mrs. K, probably the most painful betrayal of all.

13

Dreams of Vengeance and Farewell

The rest of Dora's analysis revolves around Freud's interpretation of two dreams that were pivotal to the outcome of her treatment. His account of the dreams seems less intended to demonstrate how dream interpretation plays a part in the potential cure of a neurosis than to simply show how they may be useful in supporting discoveries already made or anticipated. Freud said in the preface that he had decided to abandon his original title, *Dreams and Hysteria,* because the analysis turned out to be only a "fragment." It is remarkable, nevertheless, that he chose to discuss only two of Dora's dreams in a book that was originally intended to offer a clinical demonstration of the theories he outlined earlier in *The Interpretation of Dreams.* Freud analyzed Dora the same year *The Interpretation of Dreams* was published, and then wrote the case material in a few weeks. If his intention was to follow the dream book with another that would show its practical application, why not discuss all of her dreams, or at least a representative sample in order to show their relevance to the treatment itself?

Maybe the title wasn't the only thing that had changed since Freud originally conceived it. He wondered if the public's reaction to *The Interpretation of Dreams* mightn't have been more favorable than it turned out to be. Perhaps the Case of Dora would be more successful. Surely these thoughts began to weigh heavier as the publication of her analysis grew closer. He wasn't even sure he would publish it at all. In the space of the intervening years between publication of the two books Freud reflected on what he had learned about dreams and their relation to psychoanalysis. He apparently concluded that dream analysis is only one of the many tools of analytic treatment. It doesn't comprise analysis in its entirety, though at one time it had seemed to. By choosing only two of Dora's dreams to discuss, Freud put dream interpretation in perspective. In Dora's case, he used her dreams to show that his insights into her neurosis were supported by the dreams themselves.

The first dream, in Dora's own words:

> A house is on fire. My father was standing beside my bed and woke me up. I dressed quickly. Mother wanted to stop and save her jewel-case; but Father said: "I refuse to let myself and my two children be burnt for the sake of your jewel-case." We hurried downstairs, and as soon as I was outside I woke up. (1953a, 64)

Though this was a recurrent dream, this was the first time it had occurred since Dora had begun her analysis. Freud concluded that the dream symbolized her relationship with Mr. K. (He explained that dreams are comprised of wishes that have been repressed, and intentions that serve as protection against those wishes.[1]) The father in the dream was actually Mr. K. The jewel-case was ostensibly a symbol for Dora's genitals. The fire alluded to her passion and the imminent danger suggested that Dora felt tempted to yield to Mr. K's propositions, at least when the dream had originally occurred (immediately after the incident by the lake). The dream revealed that Dora was deeply troubled by Mr. K's behavior, but only because she had felt tempted in the first place to submit. Escaping from the fire symbolized her intention to get away from Mr. K's irrepressible advances.

But, the dream revealed more than Dora's anxiety over being pursued by Mr. K. What about the underlying wish that prompted her dream in the first place? Dora had wanted to give Mr. K her "jewel-case." The dream seemed to confirm what Freud had been saying all along, that Dora had rejected Mr. K, not because she hated him, but because she was in conflict with her feelings. She also loved him. The dream intimated the degree to which Freud had penetrated her unconscious. Since Dora's feelings for Mr. K were enmeshed in her conflicts with her father, the

---

1. Freud's distinction between "wishes" and "intentions" seems idiosyncratic at first, but in fact is a critical component of his conception of the unconscious. According to Freud, a wish isn't the same as an intention. One's intention—desire—reveals a purposeful aim—whether or not one is consciously aware of it. A wish, on the other hand, is a remnant of the past, a memory of a *forgotten* desire that persists. That is why a wish isn't personal, whereas an intention is. Freud implies that neurotics are invested in "protecting" (defending) themselves from wishes that are repressed, giving rise to an antipathy between wishes and intentions, which together comprise neurotic conflict.

more she was drawn to Mr. K the more she hated her father. This is why the recurrence of the dream at this time convinced Freud it alluded to her transference feelings about him. Freud told her that:

> The re-appearance of the dream in the last few days forces me to the conclusion that you consider that the same situation has arisen once again, and that you have decided to give up the treatment—to which, after all, it is only your father who makes you come. (70ff.)

Freud predicted that Dora's transference reactions would probably prompt her to act out the same conflicts that she felt for her father and Mr. K. Because Dora was in love with her father, she couldn't acknowledge her attraction to Mr. K. She invested her efforts instead at keeping her father from Mrs. K, and punishing him for betraying her. This was what Freud suspected she had in mind for him as well. His interpretation of Dora's first dream, however, brought him no closer to unraveling this knot. It was followed by a second dream that was even more revealing than the first. Material is now disclosed at a breathtaking pace. It starts with Freud's unexpected announcement that the solution to her second dream was achieved at a dismaying cost: Dora's decision to break off the analysis. The gist of the dream is as follows: Dora had left home and one day received a letter from her mother saying that her father had died. She is offhandedly permitted to come to his funeral. Dora rushes home but meets many difficulties along the way. When she finally arrives, she discovers her family has already left for the cemetery without her.

Both of these dreams foretell Dora's abrupt termination. The first one hinted that Dora may be contemplating to leave. But the second dream culminated in Dora's actual decision to terminate; the acting out, as it were, of what had been intimated earlier. Dreams not only contain clues to a past concealed; they sometimes presage things to come. The most important thing about the second dream, however, was a pattern of revenge that lay beneath Dora's symptoms. Freud elicited five components to this pattern. Four of them were derived from the dream itself; the fifth from her decision to terminate. One of the questions that puzzled even Dora was why she had run to her parents when she complained about "the incident by the lake." Dora couldn't understand why she had hesitated to tell her parents in the first place. Then, having delayed, why tell them at all? Freud explained that ordinarily a woman—even a young woman such as Dora—would have preferred to take her complaints directly to the man himself. She must have told her parents in order to make life difficult for him, as a way of getting even. This had been her first act of revenge.

The dream suggested that Dora had left home without warning or permission. Her mother was so angry with her she hadn't even told Dora her father was ill—the illness that killed him. His "illness" was in fact the broken heart Dora's running away had inflicted. The third motive for revenge nearly escaped Freud's notice. When Dora arrived at her parents' home only to find that everyone had left for the cemetery, "she went calmly to her room, and began reading a big book that lay on her writing table" (100). This dream element symbolized books that Dora had read without her parents' approval. With her father dead and the other members of her family away, Dora was free to read "forbidden" books at her leisure. Because her father was dead she could "read"—actually love—as she wished. Her fourth motive for revenge was when Dora impulsively slapped Mr. K by the lake, as he tried to seduce her. This motive came to light at the beginning of their final session. The previous session had ended when Freud suggested that Dora had been in love with Mr. K and was in love with him still. Freud noted, however, that this time Dora's rejection of his interpretation was weaker than before. His hopes for a breakthrough were high. At the start of their next session Dora announced it would be their last. When she told Freud she had made the decision two weeks earlier, it reminded him of how a maid gives a "two-week notice" when terminating her employment. Freud's remark elicited the following association. A former governess of Mr. K's children had taken Dora into her confidence and disclosed that she'd had a brief affair with Mr. K, her employer. He had implored her to become his mistress, using the very same words he subsequently shared with Dora that fateful day by the lake: "I get nothing from my wife." The governess gave in to him, but then he dropped her. She left her employment when she realized it was finished between them, *two weeks* later. Now Freud realized why Dora had spurned Mr. K so violently when he repeated those words to her by the lake. Dora was in love with Mr. K, but when he uttered the very words he had used to seduce the governess she was furious. Was he treating her like a maid? Were his intentions that facile, as they were with the governess? Dora reacted the way that any woman might if she was being duped by the man she loved. She felt hurt and confused, unsure of Mr. K's intentions. Her slap made it clear he had better mean business if he hoped to win her over.

Like the governess before her, Dora waited to see what he would do next. Would Mr. K come begging to explain? Would he divorce his wife in order to marry her? Dora had acquiesced to her father's liaison with Mr. K's wife, so his road to freedom was secure, if he wanted it. But Mr. K stood still. He said nothing. She waited *two weeks*. Then she acted. She reported the incident to her family, thereby avenging herself against Mr. K for wounding her honor. Freud was sympathetic. The full impact of Mr. K's proposition by the lake had finally struck her. Dora listened intently. They shared a moment of sadness. Beneath the haughty exterior, Dora was still a little girl. She loved her daddy, who wounded her. Nothing would bring him back. Mr. K was exposed as a scoundrel. But this knowledge hardened Dora's heart even more. Who knows what turn these events might have taken had Mr. K's intentions been sincere? Their hands had been played, yet Dora was nobody's fool. She thanked Freud, wished him a happy New Year, then left. It was over. Freud said that "her breaking off so unexpectedly, just when my hopes of a successful termination of the treatment were at their highest, and her thus bringing those hopes to nothing—this was an unmistakable act of vengeance on her part" (109). Her abrupt termination, though unexpected, was consistent to the end. Her last act of revenge was exacted against Freud himself.

14

Freud's Last Word

Freud's handling of Dora's termination aroused no less controversy than his interpretation of her dreams. What might he have done to save the analysis? What was Freud's actual goal in her treatment: to further science or help Dora get over her illness? These questions are hinted at in the postscript, which had to have been written at least fifteen months after their final session, though the date of its composition is unknown. Its final edition might even have been drafted just prior to publication, about four years after the analysis was terminated. Even at that late date there's no denying that Dora's departure was still a source of considerable anguish for Freud.

Some have cast Freud as self-serving in his treatment of Dora, suggesting that he merely used her to support his theories. Freud subsequently wrestled with what alternate actions he might have taken when Dora announced on that fateful session it would be their last. He questioned the wisdom of "acting a part," of imploring her to continue the treatment. Had he adopted that ploy, he felt he would have played too great a part in what had to be her decision, not his. Any encouragement on his part might have led her to misunderstand his motives. Freud decided that "there must be some limits set to the extent to which psychological influence may be used, and I respect as one of these limits the patient's own will and understanding" (1953a, 109). He concluded that whatever Dora's reasons for leaving, however neurotic they may have been, they were still hers. Even if her decision was ill-advised, it was her choice to make and she should feel free to make it.

Dora's decision to quit her analysis undoubtedly dismayed Freud, which is implied in his statement, "No one who, like me, conjures up the most vile of those half-tamed demons that inhabit the human breast, and seeks to wrestle with them, can expect to come through the struggle unscathed" (109). Great though his pain was, Freud believed her decision to leave was her responsibility and hers alone. In turn, she would have to live with it—as would he. When, in hindsight, he wondered what he might have done differently, Freud acknowledged that he hadn't realized the extent to which Dora's transference had prompted her termination, which was nevertheless hinted at in her first dream. Had he thought of it in time, he might have helped her to see how she was transferring her erotic feelings for Mr. K onto him. On the other hand, given her unwavering suppression of those feelings, it's unlikely such an interpretation would have swayed her. Besides, any such interpretation, even had he thought of it when Dora announced her termination, would have proved futile for the reasons he already explained. Any effort he might have made to dissuade her from leaving would have had the same effect, the presumption he was imploring her to stay.

The termination of a psychoanalysis ultimately depends on a decision, a choice that analysands alone must come to terms with. Even when analysts impose the termination, patients choose how to contend with it, and how to resolve it in their mind. Freud's closing comments to Dora's treatment epitomize all analytic patients' struggle to distinguish between what is really happening and what they imagine—what they prefer— should happen. Even if they are able to determine the unconscious motives that incline them away from reality and toward phantasy, they still have to choose—in an existential sense—what to make of their situation. There isn't anything analysts can do that will sway their patient's decision one way or the other. That is why Freud believed that "it is never possible to calculate towards which side the decision will incline in such a conflict of motives: whether towards the removal of the repression or towards its reinforcement" (110). Paradoxically, neurotics, mistrusting their unconscious drives, almost always prefer the fantastic solution over the real one:

> Incapacity for meeting a real erotic demand is one of the most essential features of a neurosis. Neurotics are dominated by the opposition between reality and phantasy. If what they long for the most intensely in their phantasies is presented to them in reality, they none the less flee from it; and they abandon themselves to their phantasies the most readily where they need no longer fear to see them realized. (110)

That doesn't necessarily mean it's hopeless. Many manage to free themselves from their neuroses. Some eventually opt for the rewards of reality over phantasy, submission over obstinance, love over repression. No one can predict the course particular patients will take, but that course, whatever it is, will be theirs to assume, whether they accept that fact or not. All analysis can do is to bring those inclinations to light.

Freud believed he understood the motives behind Dora's termination. Still, he wished he could make it more intelligible to his readers. He apologized for not having written the "technical manual" his audience might have hoped he would give them. Such a work "would have to be illustrated by numerous examples chosen from a very great variety of cases and which would not hope to take the results obtained in each particular case into account" (112). Such a work would be a marvel to see, but Freud never wrote it. Though other cases would follow, Freud never wrote anything like a manual that explained *how* analysis should be conducted. Dora's analysis is as exhaustive an exposition of analytic technique as he ever composed. This is because the efficacy of psychoanalysis can't be demonstrated, as in science, by the outcome of this or that case. Its value can only be determined by first principles. That is what "rules" are. They are not meant to instruct but to guide. Analysis is rooted in truth, thus its "first principles" are concerned with the means by which truth has its say. Due to the nature of resistance, the emergence of this or that truth could just as easily result in a premature termination as a permanent remission of symptoms.

Freud's postscript to Dora's analysis was probably written in stages, commencing some time after her termination. The surprising addition of her unexpected return visit fifteen months after she broke off her analysis throws the treatment into momentary temporal confusion, a déjà-vu experience. We are struck by the realization that even when the treatment seems to have ended, we may discover there's more to come, something that throws us onto an unforeseen, even transformative, path. The epilogue is, without a doubt, Freud at his best. Its tone is deliberately didactic. Yet, Freud is more intent on exploring the nature of hysteria than explaining how to treat hysterics. If his emphasis had been reversed would the analysis have been successful? Probably not. Freud's experimental and unwaveringly theoretical tone is reprised time after time in all his subsequent case histories. Instead of advocating a predetermined technique, he suggests that we listen to what each analytic case has to teach us. In fact, the process of observation, discovery, and learning is fundamental to what psychoanalytic treatment is, in its essence. In other words, analytic treatment shouldn't be conceived as an application of theory, but rather a relationship through which knowledge about a person's unconscious is discerned.

What of Dora's sexual symptomotology and its relevance to the case? After all, it was Freud's view that "sexuality is the key to the problem of the psychoneuroses and of the neuroses in general" (115). And, "neuroses have an organic basis" (113). And again, "No one, probably, will be inclined to deny the sexual function the character of an organic factor, and it is the sexual function that I look upon as the foundation of hysteria and of the psychoneuroses in general" (113). The link between sexual repression and neurotic symptoms was remarkably evident throughout Dora's analysis. That the two are connected had been established earlier in Freud's thinking, dating from his collaboration with Breuer (Freud and Breuer 1955). Psychoanalysts everywhere concur that this link exists. But Freud went even further. He maintained that the abatement of normal sexual functioning—a biological function because it pertains to an aspect of our physical being—causes pathological symptoms to occur. This was assumed to be especially pronounced in hysteria. This is the argument from which all the psychoanalytic schools diverge, each in some form of disagreement with Freud's radical position.

Due to his presumption of this connection, Freud took care to establish a link between the sexual function and matters of the heart. In fact, he was convinced that Dora's neurosis was the consequence of a broken heart. The apparent disappointment of her erotic infatuation with Mr. K was the catalyst for her revenge. Freud wondered why she would deny her feelings and sacrifice the burgeoning of youthful sexuality had she not had a reason for doing so? That reason was obviously her frustrated attempts at love, beginning with her mother, then the jealousy aroused by her father's affair with Mrs. K, Mr. K's clumsy attempts at seduction, and finally the betrayal of Mrs. K herself, whom Freud suspected that Dora still loved, perhaps like a mother. Ironically, no ostensible "cause" for Dora's chronic hysteria was ever established, not even in the postscript. Perhaps it is even unanalytic to think of hysteria in terms of cause and effect, in the empirical sense. Instead, Freud emphasizes the numerous circumstances that revolved around and intersected with a neurosis that was always *already* in motion. All the things that happened around her, to her, inside her, historically and existentially, psychologically, emotionally, and physically obviously exacerbated her symptoms and gave them more meaning. Not one of them, nor all of them combined, can be claimed to have caused her pathological condition to manifest.

In the same way that a neurosis is able to seize on an already existing physiological illness and transform it into a conversion symptom (in the form of somatic compliance), it is also capable of seizing on the circumstances that occasion one's existence — like the intrigues that surrounded Dora — to play out its secretive drama. The more one looks for the ultimate causes of neurosis, the more likely one will be to encounter "predispositions" that were there already, inclining that person further along a path previously chosen. This discovery even led Freud to hypothesize "constitutional" factors in his effort to determine the bedrock of neurotic complexes (see Part Six). A specific cause could never be found, no matter how much he looked for one. Another way of conceptualizing this point — more philosophically, perhaps — is to attribute the formation of neuroses to a person's existential inclinations. At the heart of every neurosis are subtle yet discernable choices. Freud himself kept coming back to this conclusion in roundabout ways. Nothing necessarily causes a person to choose this or that path, but the choices we make subsequently lead to consequences that we later forget helped to determine our current situation. Even when we choose compulsively, the choice is ours. Perhaps our choices cause us to become who we are rather than the other way around.

Whereas no one can say with any certainty that arrested sexuality caused the intractable symptoms that characterized Dora's neurosis, neither can anyone deny that her sexuality was at least an accomplice to her symptoms. Our erotic inclinations inevitably visit their claims on the morbid thoughts and emotions we attribute to a person's "psychopathology." To what extent love depends on sexuality and sexuality on love is a riddle no one has solved. The primacy of sexuality has always been a cornerstone of Freud's theory, but this unwavering bias — even if we don't accept it — needn't compromise the less speculative arguments of his case. Nor should its dogmatic presentation deflect our suspicion that this bias gets "tacked on" here and there in ways that are occasionally dubious and, sometimes, even forced. When he turns his eyes to transference, however, Freud enlists the allegiance of all. Due to the passion that drives transference phenomena, Freud allowed it is the most difficult issue one encounters in analysis. He believed this was because "transference is the one thing the presence of which has to be detected almost without assistance and with only the slightest clues to go upon" (116). It is also that aspect of treatment that occasions the most persistent expression of feelings about one's analyst. While the transference alerts us to a variety of idealizations concerning "who" it is the analyst supposedly is, the *person* of the analyst must eventually materialize from the debris of shattered illusions and deal with the consequences of the treatment, whatever those consequences are. Freud admits he hadn't recognized the intense nature of Dora's transference, which, had he seen it, might have been interpreted as a new edition of her feelings for Mr. K (as we noted earlier). But he argues that even had he made this interpretation, no one can say whether it would have altered the course of her analysis. In this part of the postscript, it is Dora who is teaching rather than Freud. It was Dora, after all, who taught Freud the most important lessons he was to learn about the pernicious nature of transference and its unpredictable course.

In his final comments to the postscript, Freud saves the best for last. In a scant two pages, he startles us with the announcement that Dora had returned to see him some fifteen months after she terminated the treatment. Something told Freud when he saw her that whatever Dora had in mind, nothing had really changed since the last time they met. She told him the following story: Nearly six months after her termination, Dora had visited the K's to express her condolences for the death of one of their two children. Yet, she seized on this unlikely opportunity to confront them. She got them to acknowledge that, indeed, Mrs. K had been carrying on with her father and, yes, the scene by the lake wasn't imagined but happened the way she said it had. Dora felt vindicated. She then told her father of her encounter with the K's, a victory of sorts against him too. She hadn't talked to any of them since. The matter she had ostensibly consulted Freud for was a bout of painful facial neuralgia that had broken out just *two weeks* earlier. She said that six months before that she had again lost her voice, but it returned about six weeks later. Freud traced each of these symptoms to incidents that had aroused her familiar pattern of sexual excitement followed by repressive anxiety, incidents that involved Mr. K and even Freud himself. The loss of her voice had followed a chance encounter with Mr. K on the street (five months after her final meeting with Mr. K and his wife). The facial pain arose following an article in the newspapers announcing Freud's appointment to a professorship, which Dora confirmed she had read.

Freud's synopsis of Dora's unexpected return gives us his driest and most inscrutable side. He doesn't interpret her performance, allowing us to draw our own conclusions. He did not offer her a resumption of treatment. We can appreciate, nevertheless, how very much he must have wanted to. He suspects that Dora's visit was not prompted by an urge for reconciliation. Her decision to confront the K's on the occasion of having lost their child was a deliberately callous—but effective—act of revenge. Though she cut them off afterwards she told Freud that she felt "no further concern" about them. She was hardly being candid about her true feelings in the matter. In fact, she still wanted to hurt them any way she could. Freud attributed the bout of neuralgia to her unconscious guilt for the vindictiveness she continued to harbor against himself and Mr. K.

The real reason for her return visit was shrouded in mystery. Freud couldn't believe that she came to see him simply for "her alleged facial neuralgia" (122). In a poignant yet moving conclusion, Freud admitted that he "did not know what kind of help she wanted from me, but I promised to forgive her for having deprived me of the satisfaction of affording her a far more radical cure for her troubles" (122). Perhaps, feeling alone, Dora wanted the attention that further analysis could offer. Perhaps she wanted to toy with Freud's unfulfilled wish for a cure, to punish him even more. Whatever her motivation, however unconscious or concealed, her lack of candor mitigated against any hope of resuming the analysis. Freud had no alternative but to say good-bye to one last chance for success.

15

Love and Reality

Innumerable criticisms have been raised about Dora's analysis, and newer ones are added to the list of the old with each successive generation of psychoanalysts. Most of them concern Freud's technique, that he failed to recognize, analyze, and appreciate the nature of Dora's transference reactions. Others question his understanding of women and accuse Freud of a paternalistic bias that was out of date even at the turn of the century. Perhaps the most disconcerting criticisms concern Freud's alleged countertransference feelings about Dora. This is probably the most unsettling accusation because Freud never acknowledged that they existed. Because this criticism persists, it virtually challenges, to a profound degree, how Freud envisioned the very nature and practice of psychoanalysis.

No less a Freud booster than Peter Gay took him to task over his treatment of Dora, accusing him of insensitivity and even hostile behavior. He believes that "Freud's inability to enter Dora's sensibilities speaks to a failure of empathy that marks his handling of the case as a whole" (Gay 1988, 249). Gay also suggested that Freud lacked sympathy for Dora, epitomized by his suggestive interpretations of Dora's relationship with Mr. K. Moreover, he accuses Freud of having been so compromised by his role as "critic of bourgeois morality" that his perspective on Dora was blurred and his interpretations biased. In effect, Freud "refused to recognize her need as an adolescent for trustworthy guidance in a cruelly self-serving adult world . . . [and] to appreciate her indignation at this coarse violation of her trust" (249). And, "Freud's interpretations leave the impression that he viewed Dora less as a patient pleading for help than as a challenge to be mastered" (250). Finally, Gay accuses Freud of dogmatism and even arrogance in the cavalier manner with which he offered his interpretations to her. "What matters is his insistent tone, his refusal to take Dora's doubts as anything but convenient denials of inconvenient truths. This was Freud's share in the ultimate failure" (251).

These criticisms are understandable. Mind you, Peter Gay is a psychoanalytic historian, not a practitioner, so his insights naturally incline toward the historical context in which Freud practiced—what was going on in society, what was happening in Freud's life and his personal development—rather than from Gay's experience in treating hysterics. That being said, his criticisms aren't new. They were anticipated by others before him. Gay doesn't know why, but in his mind Freud seemed to overlook the inherent "helplessness" of Dora's position. Though Freud had already learned the lessons of transference before analyzing Dora, for some mysterious reason he apparently failed to apply those lessons in her case. This leads Gay to conclude that Freud was overwhelmed with unacknowledged feelings of countertransference. Although one of the important lessons Freud learned from Dora was the extent of her transference (Freud acknowledged this himself), Gay believes that "the problematic influence of patients on the analyst never loomed large in his mind or in his technical papers" (253–5). Gay concludes that Freud never took countertransference all that seriously: "In recent years, some psychoanalysts have forcefully argued that they often find it profitable to enlist the unconscious feelings their analysands arouse in them to deepen their understanding. . . . But this position would have found scant sympathy with Freud" (254ff.).

There's no denying that Freud said little about the "handling" of countertransference. He was also remarkably direct in his manner when compared with contemporary standards. However, virtually all analysts can be, and usually are, accused of countertransference when their behavior doesn't conform with another analyst's views. Because Freud didn't enlist countertransference as a "technical aid" to the treatment, some analysts believe he overlooked it entirely. Yet, if Freud indeed lacked sympathy for Dora, and if this lack of sympathy was the consequence of "countertransference blindness," then why did Freud never recognize this himself years later when his feelings about her would have abated with time? Gay concludes his critique with the comment that he finds it less astonishing that Freud delayed publication of the case for four years than that he published it at all. Perhaps it is more remarkable still that some ninety years after Freud's analysis of this woman, our views about the nature of countertransference have assumed such extraordinary proportions.

In another study titled "Reality and Actuality" (1985), first published in 1962, Erik Erikson examined the importance of truth as a central theme in Freud's analysis of Dora. In it, he noted the tendency in analytic publications of equating the nature of reality to what is "actual." Erikson believes that one's views about the nature of reality are significant, particularly when exploring the neurotic's aversion to it. One's understanding of reality inevitably conforms with one's conception of truth, a subject that played a critical role in Dora's preoccupations.

Erikson generously applauds Freud's efforts to get to the underlying truth about Dora's neurosis. He believes that Freud's extraordinary interest in her was bound to have impressed Dora and even swayed her—to a point. He explains that two forms of truth confront the psychoanalyst: genetic and historical. Dora's concern was with the latter whereas Freud's was with the former. Erikson's critique is couched in terms of whether Dora should have been treated as an adolescent girl or as a woman. In fact, one of the characteristics of adolescents is a search for the "truth" behind historical events that seem to control their existence. On the other hand, the genetic form of truth that Erikson attributes to Freud concerns early childhood experience, the content of which has been repressed or hazily remembered. The specifically historical form of truth concerns recent events that the individual definitely remembers—in fact, is often obsessed with—which the victim of that truth feels must be acknowledged and even "exposed" for all to see. Freud and Dora met with a singular mission: to get to the truth. But the nature of their respective aims, argues Erikson, was totally different. Although Dora was preoccupied with defining the circumstances in her recent and immediate environment that were strangling her freedom, Freud was tracing the origins of her anguish to the remote recesses of her childhood. The adolescent, as Erikson characterizes Dora, is struggling with survival and emancipation. The analyst's technique needs to take this into account.

Erikson's recognition of the adolescent's preoccupation with truth was anticipated by Winnicott, most poignantly in "Adolescence and the Doldrums," originally published in 1961 (in Winnicott 1965, 79–87). Three years later, R. D. Laing echoed the same idea in a study of adolescent schizophrenic girls and their families, *Sanity, Madness, and the Family* (Laing and Esterson 1964). In that study, he and Esterson demonstrated the incredible impact that lies and deception—the sort that Dora was subjected to—can have on a girl who is repeatedly stymied in her efforts to get to the bottom of something that's being systemically concealed from her. Both Erikson and Laing emphasized in their respective work how the need to determine the truth is shared by adolescents and psychotics alike. Erikson's point, however, may lose some of its relevance in this particular case. Like Gay, he suggests that a more "protective" tone may have elicited from Dora a more willing response. Had Freud focused more on her "historical" concerns and less on his "genetic" ones, might she have felt more befriended than opposed? Perhaps. But the adolescent's search for and preoccupation with truth doesn't necessarily conflict with the kind of truth Freud was seeking. Much of what Freud was concerned with—indeed, most of what he and Dora talked about—centered on what Erikson calls historical truth: the recent and ongoing circumstances surrounding her relationship with the K's and her father. But Freud also wanted to establish a connection between her current preoccupations and the suppressed unconscious yearnings of her youthful sexuality. Rather than opting for one over the other, Freud was trying to integrate the two. That, after all, was how he conceived the essential aim of psychoanalysis.

A case could be made that Dora was mystified by her family and that the effects of this mystification compromised her sanity and capacity for trust. But even with the child who is mystified one comes across "predispositions" that incline that child this way or that (Thompson 1985, 88–117). Erikson thinks Dora was doomed from the start because Freud treated her like a woman and neglected to see her for the very young adult that she was. But even in children there burns a determined sexuality that anticipates their behavior. Can Erikson's "developmental lines" really be drawn that neatly? Whether an eighteen-year-old patient— and subsequently twenty-year-old—should be perceived as a "girl" or a "woman" or even both at the same time is a compelling issue, but one also runs the risk of patronizing a patient, as well, by underestimating the sophistication of his or her intelligence. Perhaps Dora was simply too immature or self-willed to be *psychoanalyzed,* period. In fact, the question of Dora's analyzability looms like a shadow over her treatment, just like it haunts every failed analysis. But Erikson's suggestion that Dora might have continued with hers had she been treated differently begs the question whether that treatment could still be regarded a "psychoanalysis." That is the question we are addressing.

Finally, on an altogether different note, in 1957 Felix Deutsch published a surprising footnote to Dora's analysis due to a chance encounter with "Dora" (Ida Bauer) twenty-four years after her termination with Freud (see Deutsch 1985, 35–43). By an extraordinary coincidence, Ida consulted Deutsch at the suggestion of a mutual acquaintance for symptoms that were apparently hypochondriacal. No sooner did the interview with the (then forty-two-year-old) woman begin, than she launched into a litany of complaints about the circumstances of her existence. She attacked all the men who were close to her—her husband, her son, her father—except her brother, whom she cherished. Before long she began to disclose details about her past that alerted Deutsch to the possibility of who Ida actually was (of course, he didn't know "Dora's" real name). But she spontaneously blurted out her identity herself when she realized she was talking to a psychoanalyst who knew Freud personally (Freud was still alive). She became flirtatious and even coy, obviously excited that she had met a man who "knew" her through Freud's now-famous account.

The symptoms she complained about were identical to those Freud had analyzed earlier. Nothing had changed. Despite her marriage and a family of her own, the nature of "Dora's" resentful invectives against all males—including her "disgust" with the conjugal aspects of married life—showed that the "old" Dora whom Freud had known was very much alive. Every one of her symptoms remained intact. She nonetheless appreciated the doctor's attention and requested another visit. When they met a second time her symptoms had improved, but again she proceeded to condemn her son and her husband—the latter whom she suspected of being unfaithful—and spent the rest of the hour complaining about them. She said farewell and Deutsch never saw her again.

Thirty years later Deutsch felt it was safe to publish his account of their meeting, after he had read about her death in New York. Subsequently, he engaged in a bit of detective work to learn what he could about the interval since their brief encounter. He learned from a confidante that her husband had died of a heart attack, "slighted and tortured by her almost paranoid behavior. Strangely enough, he had preferred to die, as my informant put it, rather than to divorce her" (Deutsch 1985, 42). Deutsch observed that Dora had managed to marry a man who was self-sacrificing enough to tolerate her behavior.

> Without question, only a man of this type could have been chosen by Dora for a husband. At the time of her analytic treatment she had stated

unequivocally: "Men are all so detestable that I would rather not marry. This is my revenge." Thus her marriage had served only to cover up her distaste of men. (42)

After her husband died, her son took her with him to New York where he enjoyed a distinguished musical career. Her father died, Dora's condition continued to deteriorate, and eventually her brother died too, and then her mother. The last years of her life she kept everyone around her in perpetual alarm and uncertainty, partly due to her deviousness and partly the symptoms themselves. According to Deutsch, "Her death from a cancer of the colon, which was diagnosed too late for a successful operation, seemed a blessing to those who were close to her. She had been, as my informant phrased it, 'one of the most repulsive hysterics' he had ever met" (43).

These criticisms, in no way exhaustive of the literature, nonetheless touch on the most frequently voiced complaints about Freud's handling of Dora's analysis: He was idiosyncratic in his methods and his behavior was unpredictable; he was too "personally" involved and disregarded the countertransference effect Dora aroused in him; he ignored his own recommendations about technique, including the handling of transference; there was an unanalytic quality to his behavior; he insisted on treating Dora like a woman while she was still a child. Gay implies that Freud avoided many of these "errors" with subsequent patients, though he continued to overlook the importance of countertransference. But Dora's analysis wasn't an aberration. It more or less conformed with the way Freud practiced psychoanalysis throughout his lifetime. With all the concern about the poverty of analytic propriety in Freud's behavior, it's important to remember how Freud, himself, conceived psychoanalysis. Freud believed that uncovering truths was the principal aim of analytic treatment. What Dora did with those truths was her responsibility. It's true he might have been more "supportive," more a mentor than detective. That being said, Freud's concern for Dora's recovery was unimpeachable. He believed that her emancipation depended on her assuming responsibility for her experience, by coming to terms with the circumstances in her life that were inherently beyond her control.

Of the criticisms that have been raised concerning Freud's treatment of Dora, his handling of transference and countertransference phenomena stands out as the one most frequently mentioned. This is a little surprising because Freud was the first to acknowledge this oversight. On the other hand, if we take a close look at Dora's analysis and measure its course from the perspective of Freud's "technical papers," written several years later (see Part Four), the one alteration in Freud's clinical technique that was obviously derived from his experience with Dora didn't concern transference. It pertains to his custom of introducing each patient to the "fundamental rule" of psychoanalysis: the pledge to be completely candid with one's analyst. Freud had not insisted on this rule when he analyzed Dora, because it was she who taught him that this rule was indispensable. Yet, had he introduced her to it, we can't assume she would have paid the slightest attention. Freud still assumed when he treated Dora that common sense would guide a patient's willingness to cooperate with her analyst. Once he realized that the simple wish to get well wasn't sufficient to overcome resistance to treatment, the "fundamental rule" became the criterion by which one's suitability for psychoanalysis would be determined.

In conclusion, I believe that Freud's primary purpose in publishing this case was to teach us something about the symptomatic expression of hysterical neurosis and, by extension, the nature and treatment of other forms of psychopathology. I detect three themes that play a pivotal role in conceptualizing psychopathology the way Freud specifically saw it. The first concerns pathological love; the second explores the relationship between secrecy and hysteria; the third is about the denial of reality.

If we selected one theme of the three that was essential to the case, it would have to be the one about love. Underneath all the hate, anguish, suspicion, lies and betrayal, subterfuge, vengeance, rancor and accusation, none of those feelings or sentiments could have occurred in the first place if not for the burning passion of Dora's love for her father. It plays a decisive role in the outcome of every analytic treatment, but Dora's especially. Were we to ask what Freud could have done to secure a different outcome, the sheer unpredictable nature of analytic treatment would make such a question academic at best. Had Dora's father been more honest, Mr. K more sincere, and had Freud seen what was coming sooner, might an alternative course prevail? Freud believed that the power of human passion is too unharnessable to predict what action, accidental or deliberate, could determine a specific outcome. Rather, it's our ability to gain insight into the way events affect us, not perfecting our capacity to manipulate those events, which epitomizes the analytic endeavor. The prevalence of so many unconscious conflicts makes it unlikely that "external" factors could possibly determine what our inclinations will be, whether we opt for one course or another. Like every neurotic, the direction in which Dora's choices inclined her were ultimately determined by her responses to those very developments she couldn't manipulate.

Freud returned to his thoughts about the nature of love some ten years later, in 1915, in his technical paper on "transference-love" (1958d). There the lessons learned from Dora's analysis are more explicitly articulated, though one suspects lessons learned from other patients too. If we characterize Freud's treatment of Dora too critically, we may overlook the things that he taught us about every hysteric we have analyzed ourselves. Dora is a "classic" hysteric because we can recognize a bit of her in all the hysterics—indeed, every human—we have come to know. The crux of her neurosis was simple: love was the cause of her suffering. She valiantly fought against yielding to this fact. The theme of unrequited love— Dora's story—became pivotal in virtually every case that Freud subsequently analyzed. While one's earliest experiences receive the dominant share of Freud's attention, the effect of these traumas become rooted in the context of everyday love as it unfolds. In virtually every pathological reaction, one discerns the effects of love opposed. Even in erotic transference one senses the absence of a love more benign, one that evokes submission in its essence. Freud's equation between love and submission is hard for many to swallow—especially in an age when dominance is highly regarded. All the more reason why Freud's views appear so radical, even if we call them old-fashioned. If the denial of love engenders a form of suffering that becomes "pathological," where does one turn for an antidote? Psychoanalysis, whatever else it may be, *aspires* to be "a cure through love."

The pain of love, with all its hardship, frustration, and sacrifice, may lead us, in our aversion toward a pathological solution, to the road of repression. This secretive dimension of the neurotic's troubled existence is the next theme most frequently noted in Dora's analysis, a consequence of the first. If it weren't for the pain of love and it's insupportable anguish, what would we have to hide? Freud said at the beginning of this case report that neurotics "suffer from secrets." No analyst since has been so insistent that *concealment* is the basis of psychopathology. And no other analyst has been so confident that the acknowledgment of the truths we conceal is the only path to liberation. There are other ways to "relieve" symptoms, to be sure. Dora herself enjoyed some relief from her limited experience of psychoanalysis. Other forms of therapy offering supportive attentiveness provide remarkable rates of "success." But their achievements can't be confused for the kind of emancipation that Freud envisioned. His formula for cure was simple: If secrecy has gotten us into our web of conflicts in the first place, candor offers the only viable way out. Secrets need their say, because the only way of determining what they are is to tell them. "If it is true that the causes of hysterical disorders are to be found in the intimacies of the patient's psycho-sexual life, and that hysterical symptoms are the expression of their most secret and repressed wishes, then the complete elucidation of a case of hysteria *is bound to involve the revelation of those intimacies and the betrayal of those secrets*" (Freud 1953a, 7–8; emphasis added).

Lies, secrets, betrayal, deception, subterfuge, conspiracies, and acts of mystification surrounded Dora from the first days of her father's affair with Mrs. K. But Dora wasn't simply a victim of deviousness. She had a talent for it herself. We all do. The difference between neurotic forms of deviousness and the covert acts of deception that characterized Dora's family is in the way the neurotic becomes *dishonest with himself*. This isn't simply an ethical problem, but neither is it, strictly speaking, a psychological one. Freud's conception of psychopathology inaugurated a new kind of ethics and a novel definition of honesty. It pertained to the relationship that each of us has with ourselves. Something as simple as pretending that a slight or disappointment isn't genuinely painful, or denying that we love someone whom we do, may culminate in a *complex* of denials strung together, each supporting the other, until we no longer know how we feel or what we believe. This is neurosis in its essence, its knot. We don't know where we stand or what we want. We persist in protecting those secrets because we gain something from them. That is why we're threatened by their molestation. Freud foresaw the scandal psychoanalytic methods would elicit once they became known. It is no less so today.

Now that we understand how the anguish of unrequited love leads us to conceal the truth about loves lost, we can appreciate the pain of "reality" itself. The realities we experience elicit an even greater measure of helplessness when we ignore them. Psychoanalysis helps us face the realities we would rather avoid by compelling us to *encounter* them. The denial and avoidance of reality, according to Freud, is the principal source of psychopathology. Specifically, neurosis concerns the conflict between phantasy and reality. In fact, one of the symptoms of every neurosis is a preference of phantasy over reality:

> Neurotics are dominated by the opposition between reality and phantasy. If what they long for the most intensely in their phantasies is presented to them in reality, they none the less flee from it; *and they abandon themselves to their phantasies the most readily where they need no longer fear to see them realized*. (110; emphasis added)

Freud never explained exactly why someone would choose the phantasy of love over an opportunity for the real thing, even when the reality is ostensibly gratifying. Perhaps he never found the reason for it. All analysts have to ponder this puzzle themselves, and live with it. The struggle between reality and fiction is such an essentially *human* preoccupation that it's hard to picture how anyone could ever be free of it. Why was Dora so loyal to her neurosis? Why was she so *devoted* to it? When Freud suggested this paradox about Dora's neurosis, he didn't characterize reality as anything specifically—or even suggestively—harsh, harrowing, or painful (see chapter 2). When he described Dora's ambivalence between her phantasies about Mr. K and the real thing, the "realness" of what she rejected was presumably pleasurable. However exciting Mr. K's attraction to her may have been, it confronted her with a reality that she couldn't possibly accommodate. She couldn't accept Mr. K's proposal because, in her phantasy, she was convinced she could still take her father from Mrs. K. Had she capitulated to Mr. K—no matter how much she wanted to—her father would have got what he wanted. That was simply unacceptable. When Dora went to Freud for treatment she had finally suppressed her love for her father. Her neurosis protected her from the fact that she was still in love with him. The reality that Dora couldn't face, the one that in fact "disgusted" her, was that her father didn't—and couldn't—love her. Her neurosis fed the phantasy that someday, somehow, he would. Of course, he never did.

Freud was emphatic about getting at the truth of experience and learning to accept the realities of a sometimes tragic existence. This is a tack that is difficult for many analysts to take. Increasingly, psychoanalysis is conceived as a form of "applied" psychology, the kind that concerns itself with solving puzzles. Freud conceived it as a form of ethic that is solely committed to *determining what is so*. Historically, this is a metaphysical preoccupation, not a psychological one. Determining what is real and false about one's experience and the situations that give rise to it is an explicitly existential aspect of Freud's approach to psychoanalysis. Some analysts find this dimension to Freud's technique objectionable, perhaps because the existential bias is personal in the extreme. Freud's "directness" with Dora is typical of how existentialists frequently behave. The truth about one's behavior can only be determined by *being* who one is. This conception of truth goes deeper than Erikson's "dual" theory, since the deepest layer of truth is always hidden. The distinction between historical and genetic dimensions of truth misses this point, because there are hidden determinants to both.

Freud believed the only hope he ever had of winning Dora's cooperation and her trust was to level with her, by calling a spade a spade. He thought if he was candid with her she would, in turn, be more likely to reciprocate. If she couldn't meet him halfway, then what? Perhaps, as he took stock of the case, he realized that becoming a more honest human being is not such an easy thing to do.

IV

THE TRUTH ABOUT
FREUD'S TECHNIQUE

Freud published approximately fifteen papers during his lifetime devoted to psychoanalytic technique, a remarkably small output when contrasted with the voluminous material devoted to theoretical subjects. Even the case histories—again, only a handful were ever published—as we saw with Dora, contain only a scant amount of material that is devoted to specifically "technical" considerations. In addition to the fifteen-odd papers, Freud turned to the topic of technique in only nine of his many other published works, including, for example, a section of the Dora case, a chapter in *The Interpretation of Dreams,* a section of *Studies in Hysteria,* a chapter in *Beyond the Pleasure Principle,* and so on.

Volume twelve of the *Standard Edition* (Freud 1953–73) contains a section titled simply, "Papers on Technique," comprising six of the fifteen papers (published between 1911 and 1915) that Freud wrote on the technical aspects of psychoanalysis. The story behind these papers is both fascinating and ambiguous. It is fascinating because it's something of a miracle that they were ever published at all, and ambiguous because they comprise at best a random, almost haphazard survey of thoughts and meditations Freud felt that he needed to share with the colleagues who were rapidly collecting around him. These six papers are clustered together, as Strachey (in Freud 1953–73 12: 85–88) suggests, not because they comprise a formal "manual" on analytic technique, but because Freud felt they contained the essence of what every would-be psychoanalyst needed to know about the aims and methods of analysis. A few words about their chronology in the context of Freud's other writings may be helpful in appreciating this point.

Subsequent to his analysis of Dora, Freud began to write occasional papers addressing the topic of technique. The first of these appeared anonymously in 1904 as a chapter in a book by Lowenfeld which was devoted to analytic topics ("Freud's Psychoanalytic Procedure," 1953b). It was a general account of psychoanalysis that sought to distance analytic technique from the methods employed in hypnosis and suggestive therapies. The following year—the same year that Freud finally consented to publish his analysis of Dora—Freud published a second paper on technique that had been given as a lecture to the College of Physicians in Vienna. It was titled "On Psychotherapy" (1953c). Jones points out in his biography of Freud (1955 2: 229) that the paper was ill-received and was the last time Freud ever presented a paper to that society. These two papers, however, as Strachey notes, comprise only the most cursory discussion of technique. Their significance was entirely superseded by the belated publication of the Dora analysis, which, as we saw, contained almost nothing that could be construed as "instructions" to Freud's readers.

According to Jones (1955 2: 230), Freud began to mention the possibility of writing a "General Account of Psychoanalytic Technique" in 1908. He reportedly wrote about thirty-five pages of this account, but encountered difficulties in finding a publisher, which he reported to Jung. But he apparently became discouraged and by the following year was distracted by the publication of the "Rat Man" analysis. According to Jones, he tried to resume work on this "manual" later in 1909 but again dropped the idea. In 1910 he was still struggling with some kind of version of the project, but now he had abandoned the original idea of writing one comprehensive paper and began talking instead of publishing "half a dozen essays on special aspects of it" (Jones 2: 231). The original thirty-five pages were subsequently lost, apparently forever.

Before he got around to this larger project, however, Freud published two papers in 1910 that specifically dealt with technique. The first ("The Future Prospects of Psychoanalytic Therapy," 1959a) again dealt with general aspects of technique that served to emphasize how it differed from other therapies. Freud was apparently still preaching to the unconverted while defending himself and his new method from attacks by the medical community. The second paper (" 'Wild' Psychoanalysis," 1957f) was ironically concerned with those psychiatrists who had been attracted to Freud's ideas but neglected to take the time to obtain a formal training in its application. Freud apparently felt damned from both sides: from his enemies who attacked him at every opportunity, and from opportunists who wished to benefit from his work without taking the time to earn an expertise in it. Jones remarks that, had Freud been alive in 1955, "he would have been sad had he known that by now there are hundreds of 'practitioners' in need of this obvious exhortation" (232). One has to wonder how amazed Jones would be to discover that Freud himself, in the eyes of so many contemporary analysts, would today be described as a "wild psychoanalyst"!

In 1911 Freud finally published the first of six papers that would comprise his envisioned manual of recommendations concerning the legitimate practice of psychoanalysis. The first, "The Handling of Dream-Interpretation in Psycho-analysis" (1958c), was the only paper of the six in which Freud discussed dream interpretation. This was followed a year later by "The Dynamics of Transference" (1958a). Apparently, the first two papers were intended to address the two most important aspects of psychoanalysis as Freud envisioned it: dream analysis and analysis of transference.

At this point, however, Freud drafted and published four subsequent papers that seemed to start the process all over again. All four contained the same general title—"Recommendations for Physicians Practising Psycho-analysis"—so they were obviously intended to comprise a set piece. The first of these contained instructions to beginners on how to prepare oneself for treating an analytic patient, and the second discussed how to proceed once a patient was in hand. It's amazing that these two papers—set apart from the rest in the manner in which they list "instructions" to analytic practitioners—amount to precisely thirty-five pages, the same number of pages that comprised the original lost paper. Although these two papers were published a year apart in 1912 and 1913 ("Recommendations to Physicians Practising Psycho-analysis," 58g; "On Beginning the Treatment," 58e) they obviously represent, put together, a unique booklet on Freud's specific vision concerning the rules of analytic behavior.

The two earlier papers on dreams and transference now become vaguely redundant. As if to emphasize this point, the two remaining papers on technique deal explicitly with transference issues. "Remembering, Repeating, and Working-Through" (1958h) returned to the problem of transference and the resolution of its effects, whereas the final paper in the series—Freud's favorite, "Observation on Transference-Love" (1958d)—is commonly regarded as the most important in the series.

In effect, papers three and four actually begin the series, relegating one and two to crucial points of interest, nonetheless. Paper five, on "working through," might have been saved for last because it dealt with the problem of overcoming transference and its resolution. Paper six was the heart of the series and remains one of the most remarkable papers on psychoanalysis that Freud ever published (as we saw in chapter 5).

Before I add a few words about the papers themselves, I would like to justify my reordering the sequence from the way they originally appeared. As I said before, there is reason to suspect that papers three and four were actually written earlier, perhaps in another form. They serve as the de facto introduction to the series, though it's only natural that Strachey organized them chronologically. However, the dream paper hardly seems to belong to the series at all, because it takes up the subject of dreams in a predominantly theoretical manner. I've therefore decided to begin with the dream paper, as Freud did, as a bridge between Dora's analysis and the remaining five papers on technique. I will then skip the "Dynamics of Transference" and return to it later when I consider the subject of transference. Hence, the first of the "Recommendations to Physicians" papers formally begins the technical papers as I conceive them. I follow the rest in their usual order except for the paper on "working-through," which I save for last. Whereas the order in which the papers are read isn't crucial, I have found it more convenient for my purposes to organize them in this fashion.

Now, what about the papers themselves? What did Freud mean, exactly, by the term, "papers on technique?" How is one to distinguish between the technical aspects of the analyst's conduct and the nontechnical ones? Or is all of the analyst's behavior "technical"? Furthermore, what is the relationship between an adopted technique and the analyst's *personality*? Should the analyst's personality be divorced from his or her technique, or should the two be integrated? Where does one draw the line between the personal and technical aspects of the analyst's behavior, especially if one strives to integrate the two? If all of the analyst's behavior comes under the sway of technical rules, does this mean the analyst's personality is also governed by these rules, or does it mean that technique, in its essence, is personal in the first place, so that the analyst's personality governs the technique?

Freud stated that the rules—in fact, recommendations—that he advocated for the practice of psychoanalysis were suited to his personality. Other analysts were urged to be flexible when attempting to apply his recommendations to their own. In other words, their technique should suit their personalities, just as Freud's suited his. Freud believed that each analyst's conduct required tact, sound judgment, and intelligence. Analysts couldn't be told *how* to conduct analysis, they could only be offered "fatherly advice" about what they could expect and the hazards they might wish to avoid. Freud's conception of technique was very subtle, and very personal. Like Heidegger, he realized it had to be faithful to who the practitioner happens to be. Artists can be taught how to paint, but they can't be taught how to create, that is, how to *be* artists—neither can psychoanalysts. Artists who never learn—who never discover—how to paint for themselves will only paint mechanically, predictably, and poorly. The same is true of analysts. They're on their own when it comes to becoming psychoanalysts, in their fashion and in their person.

Yet, Freud is frequently criticized for having been too personal, for not having "practiced what he preached." He said, "be neutral," but he allowed himself to be involved. There are serious implications to this accusation. If Freud wasn't master of his own behavior, if his notions about analysis were unbalanced, then why pay any attention to what he said in the first place? But who decides what comprises analytic technique, if not Freud?

When Freud was alive, he decided what comprised psychoanalysis. Adler and Jung, for example, were not recognized by Freud as practicing psychoanalysis as he conceived it. But since his death the analytic community—training institutions and their societies—decide what psychoanalysis is. This has led to problems, including disagreements with the man who invented it. Generally, analytic technique has become more circumscribed and rigid since Freud's death. This trend is rapidly increasing. "Pure" psychoanalysis is distinguished from deviations that aren't "classical" or "analytic." Yet, if classical technique doesn't derive from Freud, then from whom? If it isn't based on his rules, then whose? If all of us get to decide for ourselves what it is, then shouldn't the rules that govern it have become more flexible instead of less?

"Classical psychoanalysis," as it is currently defined, isn't what Freud himself practiced. He is frequently accused of not having been classical enough. Analysts today, if anything, seem embarrassed by Freud's analytic behavior, but when he was alive his cases were the epitome of classical technique. Gradually, a controversy has emerged concerning what is essential about psychoanalytic technique and the degree to which the analyst's personality should enter into it. Freud advocated integrating technique into the analyst's personality while now most analysts advocate separating the two. Nowhere in Freud's technical papers does he say or even imply that analysts' personalities should be excluded from their "work."

Some analysts have claimed that Freud became less personal and more "analytic" as he matured. A few draw the line after the nineties and others after his analysis of Dora. Many draw the line after the technical papers were written and still others say that everything changed after Freud formulated the structural theory. Jones notes that Freud frequently expressed affection to many of his patients and engaged in social intercourse with them, though he adds that Freud eventually refrained from the "unrestricted social intercourse" he had permitted during the nineties (1955 2: 228ff.). We are only now beginning to discover from the many recent accounts of Freud's former patients that Freud allowed himself considerable contact with his patients throughout his lifetime, up to the end of his life.

Freud advised analysts to be wary of seductive behavior, whether the seduction was in the form of unbridled erotism or appeals for sympathy. Freud's many acts of kindness, support, and sympathy are not necessarily inconsistent with these "warnings," however, because (a) Freud was an unreservedly outspoken human being who saw no harm in it, and (b) he was able to determine when tact exercised the better part of valor, and when to behave cautiously. One of the problems with this apparent dichotomy today is that it's easier to advise analysts what not to do than it is to say what they should do, and when. We have to learn for ourselves what works best, for us and for our patients.

Jones quotes from a letter that Freud wrote to Ferenczi in 1928, commenting on the "technical papers" some thirteen years after they were written. The remarks refer specifically to the problem of advising analysts what they should do when, in fact, they need to determine it for themselves:

> "Recommendations on Technique" I wrote long ago were essentially of a negative nature. I considered the most important thing was to emphasize what one should *not* do, and to point out the temptations in directions

contrary to analysis. Almost everything positive that one *should* do I have left to "tact" . . . The result was that the docile analysts did not perceive the elasticity of the rules I had laid down, and submitted to them as if they were taboos. (Jones 1955 2: 241)

Freud goes on to tell Ferenczi, who had just sent Freud his own paper on technique, that things can often go the other way and analysts who lack tact won't know what to do; they may even go to extremes. On the one hand they will be rigid, on the other they may behave arbitrarily and become reckless. In the end, there was no protection against the *lack of tact*. Perhaps they shouldn't be analysts in the first place, but who can say who they are? Freud was certain, however, that one couldn't devise a rule on how to be tactful. Ironically, Freud's rules are for the initiated, who need them the least. They are actually pearls of wisdom, to be enjoyed by those who can take consolation in them.

16

The Employment of Dream Interpretation ("The Handling of Dream-Interpretation in Psycho-analysis," 1911)

When is one called on to interpret? When you think about it, there is always something mysterious that prompts to think of interpretations in the first place. Mysteries "cause" us to interpret. This is how interpretations differ from explanations. Explanations make plain (or "flatten," in their literal meaning) the question that prompts them. The tire is flat because it has a hole in it. What could be plainer than that? There's nothing plain or straightforward about interpretations. Because they belong to the mysterious, something that—in its essence—defies explanation, interpretations are intrinsically ambiguous. There are no "flat" or "plain" interpretations. Freud's approach to dream interpretation—which, by extension, applies to all analytic interpretation—makes it plain that interpretations should never be confused with explanation. If they could, his book on dreams might have been titled, *The Explanation of Dreams*. In this case, psychoanalysis would be a true psychology, and the unconscious would have no place in it.

The first of Freud's papers on technique ("The Handling of Dream-Interpretation in Psycho-analysis," 1958c), isn't specifically concerned with the technique of dream interpretation, but rather its "handling," or its "employment." Freud explains that "the question with which I now intend to deal is not that of the technique of dream-interpretation: neither the methods by which dreams should be interpreted nor the use of such interpretations" (91). Instead, his principal—indeed, only—concern is with "the way in which the analyst should employ the art of dream-interpretation in the psycho-analytic treatment" (91). In other words, Freud takes this opportunity to distinguish between dream analysis and psychoanalysis. The two aren't exactly the same, though closely related. Freud advises against the temptation to equate the two. While dream interpretation may unlock mysteries about the dreamers being analyzed, patients will respond to their revelation according to the depth of their meanings and the strength of their resistances against them. They may simply stop dreaming and prohibit access to them; or they may over-whelm the analysis with so many dreams of abundant depth and material that the analyst can't keep up with them. "The treatment will meanwhile have fallen quite a distance behind the present and have lost touch with actuality" (92).

In other words, psychoanalysis isn't essentially or specifically defined as an analysis of dreams, however important an adjunct to the treatment it is. As valuable as dreams are in terms of the road they provide to one's unconscious, one's past, wishes, instincts, and drives, they may also be employed as resistances against the analyst's efforts to keep tabs on the day-to-day, *actual* existence of his or her patients. In other words, one's patients' reality is just as important as their dreams. If we're not careful, we may permit dreams to distract us and lose sight of the patient's conscious experience.

> It is of the gravest importance for the treatment that the analyst should always be aware of the surface of the patient's mind at any given moment, that he [the analyst] should know what complexes and resistances are active in him [the patient] at the time and what conscious reaction to them will govern his [the patient's] behavior. *It is scarcely ever right to sacrifice this therapeutic aim to an interest in dream-interpretation.* (92; emphasis added)

This is because dreams, especially in the early phases of treatment, don't always offer a complete solution. A dream may prove so central to a patient's neurosis that the resistances to its solution will only allow a fragment of its significance to emerge. But this holds true for neurotic symptoms as well. "It is the same as with the elucidation of a single symptom (the main symptom, perhaps). The whole analysis is needed to explain it" (93). In other words, some dreams, just like some symptoms, will require the entire analysis to arrive at their solution and the patient's gradual acceptance of that solution. In other words, we should keep in mind that "dream interpretations should not be pursued in analytic treatment as an art for its own sake, but that its handling should be subject to those technical rules that govern the conduct of the treatment as a whole" (94). However invaluable dream interpretation is, we mustn't allow ourselves to be distracted by the enigmatic nature of dreams or the allure of their solution. Dreams are useful, but the relationship between the analyst and patient is far more important. Sometimes, dreams serve to obscure rather than inform this important point.

Ellman (1991) suggests that Freud's advice regarding the employment of dream analysis is inconsistent with the way he conducted Dora's analysis. He says, "Freud's therapeutic stance in this case was markedly different from his present recommendations. In this 'analysis' Freud violates almost all of the tenets he puts forth in the present paper" (102). I don't agree. In fact, Dora's dreams even warned Freud that problems were brewing in their relationship! They were systematically interpreted in accordance to their relationship. On the other hand, the tenor of this paper had come a long way from *The Interpretation of Dreams* (1955c), which seemed to equate psychoanalysis with dream analysis. Somewhere in the eleven years that elapsed between Freud's magnum opus and the current paper, a shift of emphasis took place and with it a critical alteration in Freud's thinking. Now psychoanalysis concerns the analysis of the patient's unconscious and how it emerges in the relationship that develops in the course of the analysis. Dreams emerged in the context of that relationship and obtained no intrinsic status in themselves.

But isn't that the lesson Freud observed in his analysis of Dora? Both of her dreams were specifically related to the analysis and her relationship with Freud. The first warned of her termination; the second accompanied it. Somewhere in the course of her treatment he realized that dreams lacked a "curative" value, but lent themselves more to the diagnostic. One had to be careful about when to employ them and heed the dangers they foretold. Indeed, dreams may reveal too much, or more than the patient can handle. How much should analysts reveal to their patients at any given moment? How much is prudent to disclose, and when? Ironically, the more patients learn about their unconscious, the better armed they are in erecting their defenses against it: "The more the patient has learnt of the practice of dream-interpretation, the more obscure do his [her] later dreams as a rule become. All the knowledge acquired about dreams serves also to put the dream-constructing process on its guard" (1958c, 95).

In a surprising conclusion to this remarkably brief paper—it runs a scant six pages—Freud warns against instructing patients to write down their dreams upon awakening as a ploy to prevent their repression. It will only hamper their ability to associate about the dream later and, in any case, wouldn't this encourage an obsessiveness about remembering something that should be allowed to occur spontaneously? Resistance to analysis often intervenes in the guise of sincere effort. "Homework" of any kind may be detrimental, because psychoanalysis is committed to the act of spontaneity and the seemingly accidental surprises that erupt when least expected. If a concluding piece of advice could be constructed to encapsulate the essential theme of this dense essay, Freud couldn't have said it better than when he notes: "I know that it is asking a great deal, not only of the patient but also of the doctor, to expect them to give up their conscious purposive aims during the treatment, and to abandon themselves to a guidance which, in spite of everything, still seems to us 'accidental' " (94).

Before we close, there is one footnote that should be added. It concerns the technique of dream interpretation and Freud's remarkable suggestion that unusually skilled interpreters needn't use it. This refers to the laborious—Freud calls it "tedious"—process of inviting patients to list their associations to the dream components before interpreting the dream in its entirety. Many analysts today have dispensed with this complicated form of interpretation altogether and simply share with their patients spontaneous renderings of the dream's apparent meaning. Some analysts argue that this short-cut flies in the face of "correct" analytic technique. But Freud himself advises this measure, *once the analyst feels sufficiently experienced to do so*. Only "beginners in psychoanalytic practice, at any rate, are advised not to take this exceptional case as a model" (95).

This last piece of advice shows how relaxed Freud soon became in matters of technique. It's telling that this paper, the first in the series, puts so much emphasis on the analysts' discretion rather than the elusive "correctness" of their behavior. This, in turn, sets the tone for the papers that follow. Rather than instructing analysts what to do, tact and discretion in all matters is advised.

17

Freud's "Recommendations to Physicians Practising Psycho-analysis" (1912)

Freud's "Recommendations to Physicians Practising Psycho-analysis" (1958c) is the third of the six papers devoted to his technical recommendations. Practically speaking, however, it should probably be considered the first for two important reasons: (a) This and the following three papers bear the same general title and comprise a set piece that separates them from the first and second papers; (b) the style and subject matter of this paper and the following one form a series of "cautionary statements" that explicitly advise analysts how they should prepare themselves for this peculiar form of treatment.

Freud divided the paper into nine sections, each of which surveys an aspect of the analyst's mental state. Basically, Freud suggests that analysts compose themselves in a specific manner. "I must however make it clear that what I am asserting is that this technique is the only one suited to my individuality; I do not venture to deny that a physician quite differently constituted might find [her-] himself driven to adopt a different attitude to his patients and to the task before him" (111). In other words, Freud's recommendations are hardly a "riot act" by the founder of a unique method of treatment. They are thoughtful, reflective suggestions whose purpose is merely to save his colleagues from unnecessary grief and difficulty. They resemble the words of a father concerned for his children's success.

1. The first rule, or recommendation, is probably the most important. It refers to the analysts' ideal mental state, without which they wouldn't

really be analysts. It pertains to the problem of memory. How can one remember all the many facts, details, and impressions observed about so many patients without confusing one person's history with another, or simply forgetting it altogether? Shouldn't one take notes or, nowadays, tape-record sessions to insure "accuracy" and to preserve the integrity of the treatment? Today, more than ever before, this is a problem for students in training and even their supervisors. It isn't uncommon to tape-record sessions and to use their transcriptions in order to aid the task of supervising the student's work. In Freud's view, nothing could be more harmful, because it runs counter to instilling in would-be analysts the optimal mental state they need to adopt during the actual session.

Freud simply suggested that we forget trying to remember everything. Instead, he adopted a mental state of "evenly suspended attention." We should resist the temptation to remember something in particular as though that's the important thing to retain. One simply doesn't know—nor can one tell—what will turn out to be significant later on. Instead, we should adopt a "meditative" attitude. Take everything in, but then let it go. Don't be so worried about the many details and facts, as though forgetting something would prove catastrophic. Relax—but be alert! Because "as soon as anyone deliberately concentrates his [her] attention to a certain degree, he begins to select from the material before him; one point will be fixed in his mind with particular clearness and some other will be correspondingly disregarded" (112). If the analyst behaves accordingly "he [she] is in danger of never finding anything but what he already knows; and if he follows his inclinations he will certainly falsify what he may perceive" (112). Another reason to resist the urge to "note" what one assumes is important is because "it must not be forgotten that the things one hears are for the most part things whose meaning is only recognized later on" (112).

Freud's advice to surrender one's attention to the situation at hand complements, in turn, what analysts are asking of their patients: don't "prepare" for the session, or take notes, or keep an agenda, or in any way try to control what is happening. If analysts expect their patients to free associate, then they must behave in a way that mirrors the spontaneity they implore them, in turn, to adopt. The fundamental rule applies, more or less, in both directions. In other words, the analyst, "should withhold all conscious influences from his [her] capacity to attend, and give himself over completely to his 'unconscious memory'" (112). Or, to put the matter another way, *"He should simply listen, and not bother about whether he is keeping anything in mind"* (112; emphasis added).

But why is this so hard to do, when it sounds so simple? What does the term "evenly suspended attention" actually mean? Some analysts question if it's even possible to perform such a task, let alone to expect it from fledgling analysts. This recommendation is dismaying to some because Freud was proposing a different way of using one's mind than was customary, especially among scientists. What could be more alien to a scientific method of investigation than to advocate a "let the pieces fall where they may" sort of attitude? But this is just what Freud was urging. He was introducing a startling approach to the nature of memory. In time, if one is properly "attuned" to one's experience, recollection will subsequently occur of its own accord, without any willful prompting from the analyst. Instead, analysts are invited to trust their memory to serve them when they need it. But if they want to benefit from this recommendation, they have to be willing to surrender themselves, their memory and their attention to the process. This isn't easy because they're surrendering their certitude and with it the slightest pretense of being in control of the outcome.

But what if we try our best and it doesn't work? Freud suggested that "mistakes in this process of remembering occur only at times and places at which one is disturbed by some personal consideration—that is, when one has fallen seriously below the standard of an ideal analyst" (113). His response is undoubtedly disconcerting and even unwelcome for those who may conclude that this task is impossible, because it appears to eliminate them from the capacity to practice analysis as Freud conceived it. It could be argued that tape recorders might even help those analysts to adopt Freud's recommended mental state while providing them with a record of the session as well. We shall see with the next recommendation, however, why this solution isn't viable.

2. Freud discouraged against taking notes during a session for the same reason he discouraged against trying to remember something in particular. It will only detract analysts from "free-floating" attentiveness to what they are listening to in the session. This problem isn't eliminated by recording devices either. Freud didn't directly address this issue as it wasn't technologically feasible in his day. But imagine what a recording device would do to the confidentiality that is so crucial to what is said. How could patients ever feel confident that their confidences wouldn't

leak out, even unawares of the analysts themselves through loss or theft? And what effect does such a device have on analysts? If the sessions were recorded, why pay attention at all? They always know that they have a "record" to consult later. Besides, what effect does the record have on the original experience? Can it duplicate that? What about the analysts' "unconscious memory" that Freud alluded to earlier? Isn't that being dismissed and even rendered obsolete with the use of a recorder? What possible use does the recording of therapy sessions provide if not to offer opportunities to *consciously scrutinize* the sessions later? Our precious understanding would be so complete that the spontaneity Freud advocated would be lost. It would even become irrelevant.

This is why transcripts are of no value in supervision sessions either. What students need to have with them in the supervision experience is themselves, not a record of a session that they may or may not remember. Freud understood that other motives might compel analysts to seek the exception, such as working with dreams or keeping a record of the case. But even in those instances Freud suggested we commit the details to memory and write them down later. Apparently, Freud expected analysts to possess a higher than average intelligence, something that is worth remembering!

3. Another motive for taking notes could "be justified by an intention of publishing a scientific study of the case" (114). However, Freud even rejected this motive. Freud's attitude—even when it pertains to a "scientific study"—is somewhat startling. When you consider how critical "exactness" and "precision" are to scientific standards, one might expect Freud to respect the need for records and data that the scientific community demands. Instead, he argued that "it must be borne in mind that exact reports of analytic case histories are of less value than might be expected. Strictly speaking, they only possess the *ostensible* exactness of which 'modern' psychiatry affords us" (114).

This is an amazingly unscientific position for someone who was rooted in scientific decorum to assume. It shows how far afield from empirical *validation* Freud was. He dismissed the notion that psychoanalysis could ever be accepted as a "scientific psychology." Those very aspects of scientific validation that scientists deem even minimally necessary, Freud dismissed as "fatiguing." He insisted that precision of recall isn't relevant where analysis is concerned, whereas belief and confidence in what analysts are reporting is. If you don't believe the analysts' sincerity in what they are reporting, you won't believe anything they say anyway. And if they provide you with all the verbatim, rigorously "correct" reports of their work, you still won't believe them if you aren't so inclined. Freud was convinced that "this is not the way, it seems, to remedy the lack of convincing evidence to be found in psychoanalytic reports" (114). When you see how many analysts today make the amazing claim that psycho-analysis does conform to scientific standards of this sort—with virtually no acknowledgment from the scientific community—it is remarkable how prophetic Freud's remarks in 1912 turned out to be.

4. Driving home this point even further, Freud suggests that so-called scientific and technical criteria may actually be opposed. In the interest of the treatment's integrity, we shouldn't use it to prove a point or to follow predetermined paths. Dora's analysis probably convinced Freud that an analytic treatment is no place to prove the effectiveness of a given method. If anything, analysts are hostage to the course the analysis follows. We can't possibly predict where it will end. It is intrinsically experimental, unpredictable, unforeseeable. Where is the science in that? In fact, "cases which are devoted from the first to scientific purposes and are treated accordingly suffer in their outcome; while the most successful cases are those in which one proceeds, as it were, without any purpose in view, allows oneself to be taken by surprise by any new turn in them, and always meets them with an open mind, free from any predispositions" (114).

5. Freud's next recommendation concerns the risks of "therapeutic ambition," probably the most prevalent source of countertransference:

> I cannot advise my colleagues too urgently to model themselves during psycho-analytic treatment on the surgeon, *who puts aside all his [her] feelings, even his human sympathy,* and concentrates his mental forces on the single aim of performing the operation as skillfully as possible. (115; emphasis added)

This frequently quoted statement makes much more sense when it includes the one that follows. It continues: "The feeling that is most dangerous to a psycho-analyst is the therapeutic ambition to achieve by this novel and much disputed method something that will produce a convincing effect upon other people" (115). But why should wanting to *help* create such a problem? Isn't it our obligation to do all we can to effect relief from suffering? Freud isn't exactly advising against this goal, but he warns us that we may, without thinking, assume an excessive proportion of the burden that properly belongs to one's patient who, after all, is a partner in the treatment. Patients have a say in its outcome, and its success or failure is in their hands, not ours. Like surgeons who must put their feelings aside and do their best to perform their task, analysts mustn't allow their feelings for their patients to obscure the limitations of their role. That doesn't mean they aren't involved in the treatment process. They are. Nor does it imply that they shouldn't have feelings. They do. But they must put them to the side and not assume that their zeal for success can in any way compensate for what may be lacking in their patient.

In fact, there is probably no rule more controversial in Freud's technical papers than the one concerning the restraint of human sympathy. This injunction has been used by some as a justification for aloofness in analytic behavior and by others as a condemnation for Freud's alleged coldness as a clinician. The withholding of sympathy is at the fulcrum of what it means to be a psychoanalyst or, be as it may, to miss the mark entirely. What does it mean to be sympathetic on the one hand, and to withhold sympathy on the other? How might the expression of sympathy interfere with psychoanalytic aims? As Ellman points out (1991, 149–50), Freud, in another context, believed that unless analysts were able to show "sympathetic understanding" they would fail to elicit a positive transference from their patients. If patients aren't convinced that their analysts want to help in the first place, then how will they endure the limitations of their analysts' role when those limits are inevitably encountered?

One of the major symptoms of hysterical neurosis is the need to elicit sympathy from others. Certainly Dora wanted Freud to sympathize with the slings and arrows of her misfortunes, including her numerous somatic symptoms. This is because responses of sympathy are generally experienced as signs of love. This is why analysts need to be cautious when they express it and be aware of the impact that it's having. Some patients don't expect sympathy, but even self-deprecation is frequently an unconscious plea for sympathy, as Freud noted in his analysis of the "Rat Man" (see Part Five). Apparently, Freud believed that one should be aware of the degree to which one is *showing* sympathy but, above all, not to necessarily expect therapeutic results by it. Its exercise requires tact and discretion; it shouldn't be flaunted carelessly or needlessly. Even when we feel genuine pity, the expression of sympathy in and of itself can never compensate for a patient's limitations. It is only human to *feel* sympathy, nonetheless.

Analytic failures are a reality. "You can't win them all." Analysts who are driven to succeed will be poor analysts. Their personal achievements are more important to them than the needs of their patients. They believe their successes are theirs and not shared, so their failures become too painful to bear. This is untenable. Any analyst who can't accept failure and loss isn't likely to help patients who have never been able to handle theirs. Such an analyst will only inspire narcissistic ambitions in his or her patients. This form of "ambition" arises because the analyst is unable to give himself over to the analytic process, most of which is entirely beyond his control.

6. Freud's next recommendation is probably the one most readily accepted by would-be psychoanalysts. It advises prospective analysts to embark on a personal analysis of their own. Virtually all analysts today agree on this point, though a great deal of bickering has ensued concerning who should be the "analyst's analyst." What determines its successful completion? Freud wasn't concerned with these details. He did, however, give his reasons why analysts should be analyzed. Freud defined the analyst's role in the treatment as that of "a counterpart to the 'fundamental rule of psychoanalysis' which is laid down for the patient" (115). He emphasized how crucial it is that analysts be capable of assuming their part in this relationship and that they realize what their part entails. The recognition that analysts should themselves be analyzed is merely an aid in achieving this necessary capacity. The unwillingness to experience one's own analysis will only increase the potential for countertransference and limit the analysts' ability to open his or her unconscious to the other person's "like a receptive organ towards the transmitting unconscious of the patient" (115). In order to facilitate this level of openness the analyst mustn't "tolerate any resistances in himself which hold back from his consciousness what has been perceived by his unconscious; otherwise he would introduce into the analysis a new species of selection and distortion which would be far more detrimental than that resulting from concentration of conscious attention" (116). In other words, the potential harm done by the willful and deliberate control of the analysts' thoughts and attention is exacerbated even more by their *unconscious* resistances to this process. Without knowing it, they may resist certain communications

they would otherwise observe. Their own analysis might, in turn, help to purge them of some of these potential resistances later on. This has become a universal truism of analytic training, resisted only by nonanalytic practitioners.

7. How much about themselves should analysts reveal to their patients? Freud was surprisingly permissive about the temptation to share one's personal problems with patients. Some analysts hope that by doing so their patients will feel more equal and hence reduce their resistance to the fundamental rule. Yet, "experience does not speak in favor of an affective technique of this kind. Nor is it hard to see that it involves a departure from psycho-analytic principles and verges upon treatment by suggestion" (118). Revealing oneself to one's patients for the purpose of lessening resistances usually backfires because it complicates the transference. Freud even suggested that "the doctor should be opaque to his [her] patients and, like a mirror, should show them nothing but what is shown to him" (118). He said he condemned any departure from this recommendation because he feared it would transform the treatment into something other than a "true psycho-analysis" (118). Nevertheless, Freud violated this recommendation himself on numerous occasions throughout his analytic career. He had many, perhaps special, patients to whom he confided about his health and family, even about his hardships in achieving recognition. Not all of these patients were colleagues, though Freud was notoriously open with many of his analysands who aspired to become psychoanalysts. Many accounts of Freud's former patients remark on his extraordinarily personal style, his generosity, and his uncommon openness. What accounts for this apparent dichotomy?

It is perhaps helpful to keep two points in mind: (a) Freud didn't treat all his patients this way, only those who warranted special consideration; (b) when Freud advised against this behavior he included an important qualification: One should never do it for the purpose of *overcoming* the patient's resistances. This suggests that, *as a technique,* Freud believed that openness was ineffective, for the reasons he just gave. But what if the analysts behaved this way simply because they were inclined to, with those patients whom they believe are not likely to suffer adverse reactions? Peter Gay (1988) accused Freud of having his cake and eating it too, that is, of saying one thing but doing another. Jones (1955), in his biography, noted that Freud freely socialized with many of his patients, though he apparently became more circumspect in his old age. This may have been the recommendation with which Freud struggled the most, perhaps even accounting for his reluctance to publish a "technical manual" at all. Ferenczi (1980, 177–252), subsequent to these same recommendations, experimented with this rule in particular, and his experimentation initially met with Freud's approval. Later, Freud complained to Ferenczi how so many analysts were adopting *too rigid* an attitude toward his technical rules. When they lacked sufficient tact they inevitably compensated for it by becoming too literal-minded. On the other hand, when Freud eventually concluded that Ferenczi had gone too far in his experiments, it was against Freud's own behavior that he measured the lengths to which Ferenczi had gone.

Though many, if not all, analysts today reject Freud's "openness"— rule or no rule—this recommendation is often quoted by those who accuse Freud of a remoteness in manner that was never a feature of his actual behavior. He somehow loses on both accounts: for being too "classical" and too "involved" at the same time.

8. The next rule is a cousin to the one that pertains to "therapeutic ambition." This one concerns "educative ambition" and the analysts' temptation to guide their patients in this direction or that. This rule, however, is concerned less with patients' mental health than with their future vocation. It pertains to the things they will do with their *life* once therapy has relieved them of their psychical conflicts. Freud advised against this practice because no one can possibly know—not even one's analyst—what a person is truly capable of and, more importantly, what a person's inclinations will be subsequent to termination. This rule inevitably becomes more complicated when analyzing a candidate in training, because one's future vocation has been more or less predetermined by the analysis itself. Some institutes have accordingly tried to distance the students' analyst from their education. But any analyst of a student who is training to become a clinician—even if the analyst isn't associated with the training institute—will be implicated in the patient's aspirations, especially if the analyst concludes that this or that patient simply isn't a suitable candidate. Freud's recommendation alludes to an ideal that is probably impossible to apply to the analysis of analysts because it conflicts with Freud's personal analysis recommendation. But like so many of his rules, this one—no less than others—calls for a degree of latitude, tact, and discretion. After all, a rule is only a rule, nothing more, nothing less. If rules are *not* made to be broken, they apply only to the degree they

prove useful, or practicable. In the end, analysts have to decide for themselves how far they are prepared to go in the application of a particular rule. As always, the responsibility is theirs alone.

9. The last recommendation advises against enlisting the patient's intellect as an ally in the treatment. Though analytic patients should be intelligent—or at least educated—Freud questioned the view that psychoanalysis is an intellectual affair. Patients should be encouraged to abandon a conventional, logical, way of thinking and instead let their minds wander. This is why they should never be instructed to perform tasks or even solve problems. We should simply encourage patients to pay attention to the thoughts that spontaneously occur of their own accord, in their own time. This is why reading books on psychoanalysis can be fatal. Again, exceptions are invariably allowed for candidates in training, though we know this is far from ideal.

Nowadays we are rarely blessed with an analytic patient who hasn't read something about it and hasn't already formed an opinion about how it "works." We are all familiar with the amount of effort involved in weaning them off their expectations and becoming acquainted with it, instead, firsthand. The problem is no less difficult with candidates in training. Naturally, they're more interested in mastering the theory than submitting to the experience. This may explain why training institutes have become so rigid, and why psychoanalysis, as a form of treatment, has become increasingly abstract and even remote. To blame this on Freud is an amazing feat of malice given his opposition to this deplorable development.

18

On Beginning the Treatment (1913)

This is undoubtedly the most important and by far comprehensive paper that Freud devoted to technical questions. It is the heart of the current series of six and outpaces any of the other papers Freud ever wrote on technique. It contains the most specific set of instructions Freud was to make on his method of treatment. Apparently he was never certain he should have written it at all. Perhaps reflecting this hesitation, Freud suggested that rules shouldn't be taken too literally or interpreted too narrowly. In fact, they should be regarded as simply "recommendations." We shouldn't assume that he wanted "to claim any unconditional acceptance for them" (1958e, 123). His uneasiness in talking about rules of any kind is evident.

Freud compared the instruction of psychoanalysis to the game of chess, wherein the novice who seeks advice from reading books "will soon discover that only the openings and end-games admit of an exhaustive systematic presentation and that the infinite variety of moves which develop after the opening defy any such description" (123). It's ironic how few books on psychoanalysis actually discuss the beginning of treatment. Most of them concern the territory between the beginning and end, and there is no shortage of debate concerning the meaning and handling of termination. The central theme, however, of this paper is beginnings, and we shall see why this is such a vital question for the psychoanalyst to ponder.

Naturally, the first topic to consider should concern one's selection of patients. Freud refers to an earlier paper, "On Psychotherapy" (1953c), for a more exhaustive treatment of this question. But in fact, he reveals far more about this issue in the present paper. Actually, the entire paper implicitly ponders this problem. The first recommendation—a "trial analysis" to determine one's suitability for analysis—concerns an ethical issue. Why waste someone's time and money by encouraging him to suppose that analysis might help if the analyst isn't confident it can? A trial period might indicate whether a positive transference can be obtained and whether the patient's suffering was beyond the scope of psychoanalysis. Freud believed that even if people were willing to pay the cost of analysis it would nonetheless be unethical to accept them for treatment if the analyst doubted they were "analyzable."

Unlike other forms of therapy that promise immediate results, psychoanalysis requires at the outset a considerable expenditure of time and cost. This is a sacrifice that analytic patients learn to appreciate. This counsel is just as applicable today as it was in 1905 or in 1913, now that psychoanalysis is competing with literally hundreds of therapies, many of which offer quick "cures." Psychoanalysts simply can't lower themselves to this standard. They have to adopt a moral ground if they ever hope to become particularly credible, their most important tool. By whatever method analysts determine someone's suitability—whether through trial periods or diagnostic interviews or intuition wedded to experience—the point is the same. They have to believe that they can help this person through the analytic work they are making available.

Given such high standards for the analyst, what about the patient? In his paper "On Psychotherapy," Freud listed four criteria for determining a person's analyzability. In fact, the first is concerned with the question of character. Freud believed "one should look beyond the patient's illness and form an estimate of his [her] whole personality; those patients who do not possess a reasonable degree of education and a *fairly reliable character* should be refused" (1953c, 263; emphasis added). The question concerning a "reasonable degree of education" is rather complicated. We'll return to it later. But the need for a reliable character can't be emphasized too highly. When he analyzed Dora, Freud assumed that his patients would "comply" with the treatment and behave honestly. Whatever else it conveys, the term *reliable character* implies a capacity for honesty and candor. Irregardless of the unconscious motives that comprise a neurosis, Freud believed that poor character couldn't be treated like a "symptom" that would, in time, be cured by analysis. Honesty is a prerequisite to treatment, not its consequence:

It must not be forgotten that there are healthy people as well as unhealthy ones who are good for nothing in life, and that *there is a temptation to ascribe to their illness everything that incapacitates them,* if they show any sign of neurosis. In my opinion a neurosis is by no means a stamp of degeneracy, though it may often enough be found in one person along with the signs of degeneracy. (263; emphasis added)

Psychoanalysis doesn't necessarily help liars or deceivers overcome their lying and deceptions. When we see the number of patients who are nowadays treated for character disorders—including the so-called narcissistic pathologies that include lying as a principal symptom—you have to wonder what these analysts discovered that Freud missed. Whether Freud was thinking of Dora when he wrote this passage—the same year the Dora case was published—we couldn't know. Many analysts today may have diagnosed Dora as narcissistic rather than hysterical. Some might have even refused to treat her "analytically," and others still claim that new techniques make such patients more amenable to psychoanalysis. But Freud was probably thinking about Dora in the following passage when he said, "Nor is the method applicable to people who are not driven to seek treatment by their own sufferings, but who submit to it only because they are forced to by the authority of relatives" (263–64).

The three other criteria for analyzability that Freud mentions chiefly concern diagnostic issues—the question of whether analysis is amenable to psychotics or those in crisis—and the question of age, because young and old patients may be unsuitable. However, psychoanalysis in modified forms is now commonly employed on children, psychotic patients, and a whole range of people who are increasingly depicted as "narcissistic" or "borderline," depending on the prejudice of the person making the diagnosis. It is still commonly accepted that people into their fifties are not suited for psychoanalysis. Implied in all of these criteria for analyzability is Freud's principal concern to distinguish the aims and methods of psychoanalytic treatment from the other therapies, all of which he called "suggestive." The reason it is necessary to determine a prospective patient's analyzability is because of what is endured by going through an analysis. For one thing, it is costly. Why would people undergo analytic treatment unless they expected to gain something from it? Psychoanalysis is aimed at changing the *person* who undergoes it. In contrast, Freud believed that suggestive therapies were incapable of bringing about the radical changes that a cure implied. This is one of the reasons why Freud advised against the expression of sympathy in psychoanalytic treatment, a common component of the suggestive psychotherapies.

Today there are many more suggestive therapies available than when Freud invented psychoanalysis. But we don't refer to them as "suggestive"—we call them *supportive*. If patients aren't suitable for psychoanalytic treatment—in other words, if they aren't analyzable—they may opt instead for supportive treatment. These therapies are far more popular because they rely on expressions of sympathy and because they aren't as demanding in terms of cost, commitment, and effort. Freud was concerned that some analysts might be tempted to modify their analytic principles for these essentially unanalyzable patients, while pretending to treat them analytically, with the implicit promise of a cure when one wasn't likely.

What are we to make of all the modified forms of psychoanalysis that have evolved since Freud's day? Many of them say they can successfully treat patients who were thought to be unanalyzable. This implies that, in spite of their modifications, they still promote the objectives of psychoanalysis: some form of cure. But many modified analytic therapies have also modified their aims. They "psychoanalyze" patients, it's true; but they don't presume the kind of outcome that Freud believed epitomizes analytic treatment. Any improvement, however temporary it may be, is called a success, particularly with so-called borderline patients. Consequently, many people ask whether these modified forms of treatment constitute a *psychoanalysis*. We even distinguish between psychoanalysis on the one hand and psychoanalytic-psychotherapy on the other. These distinctions are so complex that we sometimes lose sight of the basic point Freud is making throughout this paper: Are these patients, in our endeavor to help them, capable of being at all honest? If they aren't, what can we hope to achieve in the "treatment"? And can we genuinely call such a treatment "analytic"?—modified or no?

Another of Freud's criteria for analyzability, a reasonable degree of education, has sometimes been construed as an intellectual bias, suggesting that only people with a university education are suitable for analysis. Freud never actually spelled out what he meant by a "reasonable education," but it's doubtful he was advocating the kind of intellectual or academic gifts that lend themselves to overly conceptualizing one's problems. People seeking analysis should possess an inquiring mind and an openness to learning for its own sake. This suggests an ability to tolerate befuddlement, confusion and uncertainty. In other words, the patient should be "educable." Naturally, patients who appreciate the arts and literature would have interested Freud specifically because he was personally interested in these subjects. But Freud never advocated "prerequisites" of this kind. He believed, however, that anyone who seeks analysis should be alive to inquiry. Unlike the contemporary university student, the educated person in Freud's day wasn't especially "technically" minded. He was more likely to be grounded in the humanities, an increasing rarity in our age.

Freud advised against analyzing friends because it could jeopardize the transference. This advice, however, wasn't always followed by Freud. Many of his patients became friends and supporters during their analysis or after. Many analysts today praise Freud for his advice on this matter but condemn his actual behavior. But there isn't necessarily a contradiction between a "word of caution" on the one hand and expecting analysts to use their own judgment on the other. Freud had every right to experiment with his own rules and he did so all his life. It is remarkable how, if anything, Freud's views on technique became more relaxed as he got older. This is true of other analysts as well. Perhaps age breeds a degree of confidence and even indulgence that youth mistrusts. Freud was conservative with his advice and knew that many analysts would feel uncomfortable getting too close to their patients. But Freud was socially active and very charismatic. It isn't surprising that many of his patients were eager to support his ideas. Many of them continued to adore him after their analysis was over. Perhaps the more "unlovable" analysts are less likely to condone even a semblance of intimacy between themselves and their patients. But why should this become the standard for others to follow?

What about patients who are especially eager to start their analysis? Freud warns against being overly impressed by enthusiastic patients. They won't necessarily retain their enthusiasm as the analysis progresses, when they manifest resistances that, after all, are unconscious. One can never predict what form those resistances will assume or when they may appear. On the other hand, one shouldn't be put off by patients who are initially skeptical and even mistrustful. Freud believed that an absence of trust was "only a symptom like other symptoms and it will not be an interference, provided he [the patient] conscientiously carries out what the rule of the treatment requires of him" (1958e, 126). On the other hand, a patient's suspicions may overwhelm the analysis beyond repair. A concrete example was Freud's analysis of Joseph Wortis, an American psychiatrist whom Freud saw for six months in 1934 at the instigation of Havelock Ellis. Wortis even published an account of his analysis with Freud (Wortis 1954), which, unfortunately, was unsuccessful. According to Wortis's own account, he argued with Freud constantly, attacked psychoanalysis on theoretical grounds, and resisted the treatment throughout. Freud repeatedly urged Wortis to free associate but otherwise tolerated his obstinate behavior as something that he perhaps needed to get off his chest. Wortis never developed a positive transference and, perhaps for that reason, Freud didn't analyze his resistance to the treatment. This brief—ostensibly "didactic"—analysis went nowhere. Many today might ask why Freud didn't analyze Wortis's resistances, especially if mistrust is a symptom. But Freud would no more deprive patients of their suspicions than be misled by their eagerness. He believed that analytic patients had to place their faith in their own efforts from the start, and to base their success on the fruit of those efforts and nothing else.

Freud spent a good deal of time in this paper discussing time and money. The issue concerning time includes the length of each session, frequency of sessions, and the duration of treatment. He advocated daily contact except for Sunday. On the other hand, he thought that three sessions per week was reasonable when treating "slight" cases or when the treatment was well advanced. This implies a flexible attitude that is sorely lacking today. No one disputes the advantages of frequency, though the cost usually mitigates against it. Can a psychoanalysis be conducted two times a week, or even once a week? Four times a week is now a common practice in training institutes. In France and South America, three times a week isn't unheard of. Institutes that are not aligned with the International Psycho-analytic Association are considerably more flexible. At what point does it cease being psychoanalysis, in the sense that its aims have a chance of success? It's understandable that institutes require a more thorough arrangement with their candidates, but surely the frequency issue— like all the other recommendations—should accommodate the specific needs and abilities of each patient. Psychoanalysis is in danger of becoming obsolete because few can afford to pay for it. Two meetings a week isn't unreasonable given costs and restricted schedules. Obviously, more would be desirable—but is it essential? Only in the particular case can one say. As psychoanalysis is now merely one form of therapy competing with others, things have changed considerably since Freud's day. One mustn't forget that most of Freud's analyses lasted less than one year. Today, five to eight years is becoming the standard.

On the one hand, the analysts' livelihood should be considered. They have to earn a living. This is why Freud insisted on charging for missed sessions, a requirement that only the most dedicated patient accepts without protest. Many analysts, such as Frieda Fromm-Reichmann, say they could never charge for missed sessions. Should one be unyielding on this point or dispense with it entirely? If analysts charge for missed sessions only occasionally, patients will construe "forgiven" absences as a gift, a sign of the analysts' love. There is much wisdom in Freud's prescription but, again, like the other rules, analysts have to work it out for themselves and find the arrangement they can live with. They should avoid feeling guilty on the one hand or resentful of their patient on the other. Besides, the amount charged per session affects how frequently patients can afford to come and how easily they can bear unforeseen absences. The question concerning money can't always be isolated from how frequently the participants meet.

What about Freud's rationale for seeing patients daily? He said that "when the hours of work are less frequent, there is a risk of not being able to keep pace with the patient's *real life* and of the treatment losing contact with the present and being forced into by-paths" (1958e, 127; emphasis added). Freud's argument in favor of frequent contact belies the common misconception that it promotes regression and enhances "transference" phenomena. Freud simply wanted to stay in touch with the patient's "real life." Similarly, daily contact subverts the patients' expectation that analysis will be solely concerned with solving problems or improving relationships. This is one of the obstacles analysts encounter when seeing patients less often. Even with three-times-a-week arrangements patients tend to "catch up" on lost days—neglecting the present—or they simply ignore the absences, thereby neglecting their recent history. But this is a practical matter that can easily be worked with and "analyzed." These lapses may create obstacles, but they needn't compromise the opportunity to experience what a psychoanalysis is about, in its essence. Likewise, opportunities for resistance can't be eliminated or avoided however frequently one comes.

There's no doubt that frequent sessions often help patients feel more comfortable with the peculiar nature of psychoanalysis. "Free associating", which Freud emphasized more than most, is enhanced by increased frequency. Psychoanalysis is concerned with determining and attending to *unconscious* motivations. This requires a special frame of mind, one that involves reflective thoughtfulness and obstinate self-expression. Some find this task impossible to perform no matter how many sessions a week or how many years of analysis. Others take to it like ducks to water. In exceptional cases some patients achieve more twice or even once a week than others accomplish with relentless frequency. But the suggestion that people aren't genuinely "in" analysis because they're only seeing their analyst so often reduces the analytic experience to something numerical and even compulsive. This was never Freud's intention.

How long should analysis last? Freud says that "the question as to the probable duration of a treatment is almost unanswerable" (128). As we noted earlier, analytic treatments have gradually increased in duration since Freud's day. Now we expect analysis to last several years when Freud struggled against the modest requirement of several months! We should avoid, however, being too rigid or demanding when enlisting someone into a treatment whose objective, after all, is to become more reflective and accepting of limitations. Patients should always be warned that analysis takes a long time. How long? Longer than they want it to! It almost seems that each patient has a specific duration in mind at the outset. Whatever it is, it will be a conservative estimate. This is probably because each of us has our own limits. We endure deprivation so long, but we expect our eventual reward. As Freud says (see chapter 5), all patients expect to eventually be rewarded with their analyst's love. Sooner or later they realize this isn't likely to happen. That is when they will probably conclude they have had enough. But in fact, this is when their real work is cut out for them. Yet, this can't be explained at the outset. Patients have to *discover* what their limits are and, when they do, allow themselves to be struck by them. This is how "progress" is achieved. Ultimately, one's resistance to change will determine the treatment's duration. Yet, Freud only hinted at this problem in this series of technical papers (see chapter 20). It was only much later in his 1937 paper "Analysis Terminable and Interminable" (1964a) when he came to terms with the interminable manner with which time structures each analysis. As with Dora, irrespective of how little patients have achieved in their therapy, should they decide to discontinue the treatment Freud would readily "allow each one to break off whenever he [she] likes. But I do not hide it from him that if the treatment is stopped after only a small amount of work has been done it will not be successful and may easily, like an unfinished operation, leave him in an unsatisfactory state" (1958e, 129–30). Freud confessed that in his early years he tried to persuade his patients to continue with their treatments whereas later he couldn't get them to leave. Nowadays analysts frequently choose to interpret a patient's wish to terminate as resistance. If this fails to dissuade them, they may insist on two or three more sessions to "discuss" the implications of their decision. One has to question the analyst's motive for resorting to this ploy. Freud was remarkably tolerant of his patient's decisions, whatever they were. He didn't protest when Dora unexpectedly broke off her treatment, and history appears to suggest that he was right by not insisting she prolong her analysis beyond the point that she wanted to.

In the same vein, patients who want to be analyzed in order to cure one symptom but not others are wasting their time. Despite Freud's allusions to surgery and medicine he didn't believe that analysis could be used "surgically" in order to resolve an isolated problem. As with sexual impregnation, Freud believed that psychoanalysis sets forces in motion that, unlike science, can't be controlled or predicted. Happily married patients may divorce or contented scientists change careers as a consequence of the unforseen changes a psychoanalysis may unleash. Because it is solely predicated on determining the truth of one's situation—a truth that is, by definition, unconscious—no one can say what the nature of that truth will be, or where it might lead. This is why diagnostics didn't concern Freud the way they do so many analysts today. It wasn't intended to cure a specific *disease*. Psychoanalysis is concerned with the uneasiness we fall prey to as a consequence of denying the truths that determine our unique existence. The increasing tendency to split hairs over "differential diagnosis"—a different diagnosis and consequent technique for each analytic patient—is a far cry from the tolerant ambiguity that was epitomized by Freud. Even the length of a session wasn't sacred. If one hour wasn't enough, why not offer more?

Concerns over money tend to arouse, as every analyst discovers, the most extraordinary rationalizations and guile. Freud saw a parallel between our attitudes about money and sex. In effect, "money matters are treated by civilized people in the same way as sexual matters—with the same inconsistency, prudishness and hypocrisy" (131). He advocated a different tack entirely. We should be direct and to the point and avoid haggling over fees. Freud believed, however, that medical patients often assume doctors should work for nothing. The same attitude will insinuate its way into their relationships with analysts as well. We shouldn't be surprised to discover that this attitude is consistent with the symptoms that brought them into treatment in the first place. This is why it isn't wise to cater to these sentiments from the very beginning. Obviously, we don't have the benefit of interpreting such attitudes because the analysis is just getting started. As with so many things, we gain more with tact and directness than all the "analyzing" in the world could ever disclose. That was why Freud believed that patients should be charged for absences. It will encourage them to come regularly and protects analysts from the economic hardship that would follow if their patients only come when they feel like it. Patients need to acknowledge the reality of the analyst's situation. Why protect them from the fact that the analyst actually depends on their regular attendance? Analysts who wish they were omnipotent inevitably have a problem with this issue. They want to believe—and want their patients to suppose—that they're above the concerns of ordinary mortals. They even argue it might "damage" patients if they worried about—or felt responsible for—their analyst's livelihood. Freud believed this issue helps to make analysts more *real*. Protecting patients from the common necessities of life only encourages their narcissism. It also robs them of the knowledge that they are making a contribution to the analyst's existence, for which they deserve to feel a measure of pride.

Free treatment should also be avoided. Freud experimented with free sessions and discovered they usually increase resistance. This is because it takes the treatment away from the real world, where analysts and patients live. Freud wasn't above making exceptions, however, to patients who fell on hard times. Some of his followers were helped in this fashion. He even supported the "Wolf Man" when he lost his fortune. Ironically, Freud has been criticized for this by analysts who argue it is inherently wrong to give support to one's patients. It's even been suggested that this act of kindness precipitated the Wolf Man's brief psychosis! Yet, Freud didn't advocate such leniency in his technical recommendations. Instead, he warned against being gullible where financial benevolence was concerned. People who are poor are in turn probably poor candidates for analysis. They derive too much gratification from their pitiable condition to be sufficiently motivated to change it. This controversial prescription is nonetheless a basic premise of psychoanalysis, following the general rule of abstinence. If the patients' poverty is indeed a symptom and not merely circumstantial, one is advised against the hope that compassion will ever cure them of it. In any case, analysis is an expensive proposition—even twice weekly arrangements are costly. The would-be analysand needs to believe that it's worth the cost and find the means to pay it.

Of all Freud's recommendations, none have been followed more religiously than those concerning frequency of sessions and the recommended posture: the supine position, specifically devised to avoid eye contact with the analyst. Though Freud maintained this was merely his personal preference because he couldn't "put up with being stared at by other people for eight hours a day" (134), he also suggested that it helped "to prevent the transference from mingling with the patient's associations" (134). As a rule, analysts have taken this to mean that if a patient isn't using the couch then the treatment isn't a genuine psychoanalysis. This is a remarkably rigid interpretation of Freud's recommendation. Yet, classical technique—at least the kind that is administered to candidates in training—has generally followed this recommendation to the letter. Many theories have been offered since Freud's death defending this rule. They assume that, Freud's personal motives notwithstanding, he nevertheless intuited a fundamental principle that determines the analytic experience. The prevailing opinion suggests that without it the treatment won't necessarily realize its purpose. Even the unconventional theorist, Jacques Lacan (Schneiderman 1983), included a "linguistic" theory supporting the supine position—despite his alteration of nearly every other classical recommendation, including the length of the analytic hour.

The purpose of this rule was to induce patients into a state of reverie whereby free associations might come more easily, unimpeded by the kind of conversational dialogue that eye-to-eye contact encouraged. There are, however, other ways of avoiding eye-to-eye contact besides lying on a couch, while maintaining some sense of an ordinary, real relationship. Karen Horney (1987), for example, allowed her analytic patients to choose between the couch or the chair. Sullivan (Will 1992) never used the couch, choosing instead to position the chairs at right angles to avoid eye contact. Similarly, R. D. Laing (1977) abandoned using the couch soon after his analytic training, opting instead to situate the chairs at opposite ends of his consulting room, keeping eye-contact to a minimum.

Freud possessed such a strong personality that the couch was probably a relief to his patients. But other analysts become excessively remote when sitting behind their patients. Perhaps this recommendation suits some analysts more than others. One also needs to consider the personality of the patient. Some patients stare more than others and those who do can be unsettling. It might be less awkward to simply ask *all* one's patients to use a couch than to single out those who present a problem. But some patients get lost on the couch, dissociate rather than associate, and regress to such a degree that it undermines their analysis. Though many analysts apparently encourage "deep regression" in their patients and advocate the couch to promote it (arguing that without regression an effective transference won't develop), Freud never offered this rationale as a reason for using the couch. On the contrary, he believed that regression impedes analytic work. In fact, the use of the couch, as Freud conceived it, was supposed to make patients more *alert and responsive*—it wasn't intended to make them "crazier." We don't know how faithfully even Freud used the couch. He never mentioned it when reporting his analysis of Dora. He also made numerous references about some of his patients walking around the consulting room when they chose, with no apparent protest from him.

Yet, Freud admits that when patients resist the invitation to lie on the couch they should be refused. How does one reconcile this apparent contradiction? Perhaps Freud was concerned about the acceptance of the analyst's judgment rather than fidelity to a specific posture, per se. In other words, if analysts decide that the couch works best for them, then they should insist on the conditions that serve their interests. Another analyst could just as easily advocate a different arrangement, such as Sullivan's or Laing's. The peculiar nature of couch work, however, is more likely to enlist protest and analysts will have to decide for themselves how to deal with it. On the other hand, analysts shouldn't adhere to the use of the couch simply because they're "supposed to." Analysts should decide for themselves what works for them. The couch isn't a sacrament. It's supposed to enhance the sort of candor that isn't easy to perform even under the best circumstances. What is the essential vehicle of this type of candor? Freud advocated "free association," the best means by which the unconscious can be methodically and reliably disclosed. Yet, Freud devoted less than five pages to free association in his technical papers, surely a disappointment to those seeking an elaborate set of instructions. This is why the fundamental rule of psychoanalysis (one's *agreement* to free associate) is at the heart of this process. The rule is "fundamental" because, without it, Freud believed that the treatment wouldn't comprise a psychoanalysis. The rule concerning one's compliance with this process is relatively straightforward, yet difficult to execute. Why? This is how Freud explains the rule and its method of instruction.

> Say whatever goes through your mind. Act as though, for instance, you were a traveler sitting next to the window of a railway carriage and describing to someone inside the carriage the changing views which you see outside. Finally, *never forget that you have promised to be absolutely honest,* and never leave anything out because, for some reason or other, it is unpleasant to tell it. (135; emphasis added)

This analogy contains the essence of what free association entails. One might reduce it to the simple sentence, "say whatever goes through your mind." But doing so isn't so easy because of our tendency to edit what we say to others. Neurotics are less forthcoming than most due to the secrets that structure their neuroses. The part of this analogy that is particularly important is the relationship between travelers sitting by the train's window and the companions to whom they convey their observations—the relationship between patients and their analysts. The analogy also confirms that the fundamental rule and free association are not one and the same thing, though they are frequently cited interchangeably. Free association is the use of one's mind that each analytic patient is taught to adopt. But the fundamental rule concerns the patients' willingness to adopt it, their capacity for honesty and their agreement to speak their mind. This is why character plays a part in determining one's patients' capacity for analysis. Are they sufficiently honest to adopt the attitude that analysis requires? That is why analytic treatment rests on this rule. Yet, the concept of candor is vanishing from the analytic lexicon. Analysts today increasingly dismiss ethics—the foundation of Freud's "fundamental rule"—in favor of psychology. Whereas Freud emphsized the critical importance of candor, now we take inventories of our myriad defenses against self-disclosure. This was why Freud believed that "it is a bad sign if [one's patient] has to confess that while he [she] was listening to the fundamental rule of analysis he made a mental reservation that he would nonetheless keep this or that to himself" (138). It is better if patients can acknowledge their skepticism because by admitting it they're at least confiding that their suspicions exist.

What does it actually mean to free associate? Freud's conception of free association—*freier Einfall* in German, meaning literally, "free irruption" or "sudden idea"—is predicated on the notion that all of us are quite secretive about the thoughts that ordinarily occur to us. We're not accustomed to sharing most of these thoughts with anybody. When we confess something that really matters we carefully select what we say. We call this "discretion" but, actually, we simply don't want people to know what we're thinking. We worry about the effect that self-disclosure will have on others and what, in turn, they'll think about us. When we free associate, we undermine this type of censorship by disclosing things we ordinarily conceal. Naturally, the habit of censorship persists. Once we accept the "fundamental rule," we try to disclose our thoughts anyhow. Freud believed that by sharing the thoughts we are consciously aware of, unconscious thoughts will work their way to the surface as well, spontaneously and unexpectedly. Hence, free association serves a double purpose: (a) it engenders a relationship between analyst and patient that is founded on the principles of trust and candor; (b) it also provides a vehicle for gaining access to the unconscious, by utilizing one's unswerving participation in this endeavor.

How did Freud think of free association in the first place? It's usually attributed to Breuer's patient, Anna O., who described the method that he and Freud employed as a "talking cure." It is also credited to the writer, Ludwig Börne, who recommended writing down everything that came to one's mind as a device for learning how to write. But the notion of freely associating is actually more complicated than that. It is sometimes compared to confession. Yet, the type of disclosure it occasions goes much deeper than merely relieving one's burden of guilt. Freud believed that free associating, speaking freely, would open the door to *experience*. It helps to reveal the nature of earlier experiences we conceal from ourselves. The Socratic injunction, "Know thyself," is obviously a precursor to and influence upon this idea. Freud was thoroughly schooled in the Greeks, but there must have been an intermediary, someone closer to Freud's time who was famous for attending to his most personal, subjective, reminiscences. Anyone who is familiar with the essays of Michel de Montaigne, the sixteenth-century French philosopher, would have to suspect that Freud was acquainted with his writings and, perhaps, influenced by them. Actually, Montaigne wasn't a philosopher in the academic sense. Like Freud, he enjoyed ridiculing the philosophers of his day. But Montaigne was a thinker, a skeptic, and a classicist who was devoted to the Socratic injunction, a philosopher in the truest sense. Nearly all of his references are from the Greeks, many of whom, like Socrates, swam against the tide of convention. Montaigne even invented a modern literary form, the essay, which is notable for its predominantly personal style, rooted in autobiography and the writer's experience. Montaigne even became famous for his essays, his principal form of composition. His impact on Shakespeare has been documented and one recognizes his method of self-inquiry—a form of skeptic detachment—in the investigations of modern existential and phenomenological thinkers such as Nietzsche, Kierkegaard, Husserl, and Heidegger.

As it happens, the very last of his four-volume collection of essays (Montaigne 1925) is titled, *Of Experience*. In it, the seeds of the free associative method are sown. Freud didn't mention Montaigne specifically, but given his appreciation for the Greeks and Montaigne's notoriety we can assume that Freud was intimate with his writings. For example, in his essay on experience, written in the late sixteenth-century, Montaigne talks about gaining access to one's experience through memory:

> I should prefer to understand myself well by study of myself rather than of Plato. From my own experience I find enough to make me as wise as a good scholar. He who brings to memory the violence of his past anger, and how far that excitement carried him, sees the ugliness of that passion more plainly than Aristotle, and conceives a juster hatred of it. He who calls to mind the ills that he has incurred and those that have threatened him, and the trivial occasions that have moved him from one state to another, thereby prepares himself for future changes and for the examination of his condition. (1925, 4: 302; Ives's translation slightly modified)

This passage could serve as just as apt an instruction to free associate as Freud's railway carriage analogy. Allowing one's mind to wander of its own accord is essentially a *call to one's experience*. If we restrict ourselves to a summary of thoughts alone we would induce obsessions, "ideas" that are dissociated from one's affective experience. Experience itself would be effectively suppressed. Montaigne permitted his thoughts as well as his "natural inclinations to take their course" (303). He allowed his mind to wander, to see where it would lead him and what it could possibly disclose. He even claimed, "I study myself more than any other subject;

this is my metaphysic, this is my physic" (301). Where did his self-study ultimately lead? "The prolonged attention that I give to considering myself trains me to judge passably of others also" (305).

Could this injunction have offered the inspiration for the self-analysis that Freud embarked on when he wrote *The Interpretation of Dreams?* These quotations from Montaigne aren't isolated incidents; they're typical of his writings as a whole. In fact, virtually all his essays are free associations, musings about his life and his ails, his concerns and opinions which, together, reveal himself to himself as well as to us, his readers. His essays are free of jargon and speak in a way that is still unusual for the written word. This is probably because he valued the spoken word more highly than the written, which he felt, once penned, diluted the original. His essays are actually verbal expressions put to page, a style of "writing" that Freud imitated in his *Introductory Lectures on Psychoanalysis*. To free associate isn't, however, simply talking out loud; it's a verbal reflection, intended for someone's ears, for the purpose of disclosing oneself to another. If neurotics have lost touch with themselves because of the secrets they harbor, unburdening themselves of those secrets by giving way to the reminiscences of their experience can put them back in touch again—perhaps for the very first time. Some people are actually incapable of free associating. They simply don't want to know the source of their anxieties. Nor do they care to be reminded of their suffering. They simply want the bad feelings to go away. Others approach free association as a task, something that has to be mastered and "done well." They don't appreciate what might be gained by simply allowing their mind to wander, of its own accord, where it will. They feel that relinquishing control is a dubious proposition, at best.

Freud conceived of psychology as an ethical science. Because dishonesty occasions psychopathology, honesty and candor—the fundamental rule—is the principal path to its cure. This is a Greek conception of "psyche" that shows the depth of Freud's classical and philosophical roots. It provided the rationale for the fundamental rule and its critical role in analysis. Some patients will do almost anything to undermine the fundamental rule and protect their secrets. This is why resistance is axiomatic. But the extent to which it persists limits any progress the treatment might have, because resistance perpetuates the secretiveness at the heart of one's symptoms. However, we should always be cautious when addressing those resistances. Freud thought that the interpretation of resistance is a delicate matter. He suggested we hold back from doing so "until an effective transference has been established in the patient, a proper *rapport*" (1958e, 139). In other words, not until a spirit of collaboration has developed. Naturally, we can't force this to happen. It will (or won't) manifest of its own accord. The only thing analysts can do is to avoid becoming embroiled in their patients' conflicts, by exercising a measure of "neutrality" and the utmost "sympathetic understanding" (140).

Yet, neutrality was never a major concept in Freud's thinking or a guiding principle. It isn't even mentioned in Strachey's index to the *Standard Edition*. Nevertheless, it's become a basic term and has assumed the status of a sweeping principle. Laplanche and Pontalis include neutrality in their vocabulary of analytic terminology (1973, 271–72), though they acknowledge that the term, "which has become a classical definition of the analyst's proper attitude, is nowhere to be found in Freud's work" (271). They suggest, however, that the idea of neutrality epitomizes the technique that Freud outlined in the technical papers. According to Laplanche and Pontalis, Freud's counsel against "therapeutic ambition" (which he discussed in "Recommendations to Physicians Practising Psycho-analysis") demonstrates the efficacy of neutrality, where he advises analysts to adopt the demeanor of the surgeon. The rule against "educative ambition" is another. In neither case, however, does Freud invoke the word *neutrality*. The term apparently means different things to different analysts, though Laplanche and Pontalis insist that "in no way does it imply or guarantee a sovereign 'objectivity' in the person who exercises the profession of psycho-analyst" (271–72). They suggest that it simply pertains to the constraints against analysts imposing their moral values on their patients.

The only time when Freud specifically advocates the employment of "neutrality" is in "Observation on Transference-Love" (1958d), where the analyst's scruples assume critical importance. In his discussion about the effects of erotic transference Freud emphasizes the scrupulous manner with which analysts are called upon to behave. Whatever analysts do, they must deal with their patients' feelings honestly and not suppress any expressions of love that might arise, but neither should they give the impression that they invite them, either.

> Just as little can I advocate a middle course, which would recommend itself to some people as being specially ingenious. This would consist in declaring

that one returns the patient's fond feelings but at the same time in avoiding any physical implementation of this fondness until one is able to guide the relationship into calmer channels and raise it to a higher level. My objection to this expedient is that pycho-analytic treatment is founded on truthfulness. *In this fact lies a great part of its educative effect and its ethical value.* (164; emphasis added)

In other words, Freud insisted on total honesty with one's patients, an ethical—that is, moral—principle. When we respond to our patients feelings, whether they happen to be love or hate, we need to keep this in mind.

Since we demand strict truthfulness from our patients, we jeopardize our whole authority if we let ourselves be caught out by them in a departure from the truth. Besides, the experiment of letting oneself go a little way in tender feelings for the patient is not altogether without danger. Our control over ourselves is not so complete that we may not suddenly one day go further than we had intended. *In my opinion, therefore, we ought not to give up the neutrality towards the patient, which we have acquired through keeping the counter-transference in check.* (164; emphasis added)

Where in Freud's employment of neutrality does he *withhold* his moral position? In fact, he implores the use of morality as a positive—even essential—force in the treatment. Hence, one's ability to be truthful is an inspiration to the patient and lends to analysis "a great part of its educative effect and its ethical value" (164). Being neutral, in this context—the only context in which Freud uses this term—requires the highest ethical standard with one's patients. It means to act without guile. To act otherwise wouldn't be honest. Maintaining neutrality was never meant to suggest that analysts should keep their feelings—much less their morals— to themselves. They need to be true to their morals and use them for the benefit of their patients. This is how countertransference, properly speaking, compromises our capacity for honesty because, by it, we are tempted to compel our patients to serve *our* ambitions rather than theirs. As long as truthfulness is maintained, the confusion over whose interest is being served is less likely to corrupt the analysis.

How did Freud's conception of neutrality become so distorted (see chapter 24)? Perhaps because many analysts, including Laplanche and Pontalis, confuse it with "abstinence," an allied term that is, nonetheless, markedly different. Abstinence, which was introduced for the first time in the same paper as neutrality, involves the deliberate withholding of affection in order to avoid arousing or gratifying the patient's libidinal urges. In fact, the employment of abstinence—which Freud warned against carrying to extremes—may well elicit in patients those very demands which require their analysts to exercise neutrality. In other words, when one's patients encounter abstinence, some become more demanding than before. Analysts—now on the spot—may wish to compensate for their abstinence by becoming more devious or cunning with those patients, concealing instead of revealing what they think. In fact, neutrality compels us to be unreservedly frank, and to acknowledge what we suspect is happening—whatever the outcome.

How does this behavior bring about a cure? Freud offers the briefest remarks about this in his conclusion to this remarkably dense paper. Now he rejects the earlier notion that analytic cures depend primarily on understanding one's conflicts and emphasizes, instead, that resolution of transference is the heart of the matter. If we want to appreciate the specifically psychoanalytic conception of cure, we need to understand what motivates our patients to pursue treatment in the first place. "The primary motive force in therapy is the patient's suffering and the wish to be cured that arises from it" (1958e, 143). If not one's suffering, then what could motivate anybody to endure the humiliations every analysis entails? Yet, no matter how terrible one's suffering might be, "this motive force is not sufficient to get rid of the illness" (143). If it were, sympathetic concern would go a long way in obtaining relief. "Often enough the transference"—that is, the patient's attachment to his analyst—"is able to remove the symptoms of the disease by itself, but only for a while—only for as long as it itself lasts" (143). In this respect, as far as sympathy is concerned, psychoanalysis is no different from other forms of therapy that offer relief through the influence of the therapist's personality. The specifically analytic contribution to psychotherapy is distinguished by two critical factors: (a) one's desires are sufficiently freed to help combat resistances and, (b) through increased understanding, patients learn how to rally their efforts toward realistic—which is to say, realizable—aims.

> Thus the new sources of strength for which the patient is indebted to his [her] analyst are reducible to transference and instruction (through the communications made to him). The patient, however, only makes use of the instruction in so far as he is induced to do so by the transference. (143–44)

In other words, everything hinges on transference. Patients suffer in the first place because they are without love. Its absence prompts them to seek analysis, and continues to serve as the "motive force" that commits them to analysis. Because they long for love, they long for their analysts to love them. They, in turn, come to love their analysts and seek their direction. Once patients *can* love they are free, to leave and then lose what they had.

19

The Concept of Transference ("The Dynamics of Transference," 1912, and "Observations on Transference-Love," 1915)

Transference is the sine qua non of psychoanalysis, is it not? In his brief introductory remarks to the second of Freud's papers on technique, "The Dynamics of Transference" (1958a), Strachey notes that, despite its inclusion in the series, this paper is more theoretical in its tone than, strictly speaking, "technical." Why, then, did Freud include it? Perhaps he was simply preparing us for the papers that follow, before plowing into the specifically technical aspects of analytic treatment. Or perhaps its inclusion says something about the way Freud conceived the nature of technique, that it's more "theoretical" than we suppose.

Strachey's remark is typical of those analysts who insist on drawing a strict line between the technical and the theoretical. Freud struggled with these distinctions himself, but drawing a line *between* them was never his intention. As we saw earlier (chapter 9), the question concerning technique can't be reduced to mere notions of application. Like other intellectual activities, analytic technique occasions its theory, *practically*. This is because psychoanalysis is concerned with ideas, concepts, words, emotion, suffering. Where does the theoretical end and the technical begin when its technique embodies the very ideas that its theory ponders?

These distinctions are even more elusive when we turn to the concept of transference. How are we to handle it? Certainly not with our hands! For one thing, transference isn't even a phenomenon. It is a concept. We never actually *see* transference at work. It is an idea about something we observe and, in hindsight, experience. We see its signs and its symptoms, to be sure. But in order to label something someone says or does or feels as transferential we have to interpret it as such. And in that act of interpretation—an act of one's mind—we introduce the conceptual into the technical and prove the reliance of the latter upon it. When we speak of handling transference, what we are handling is conceptual. It would behoove us to understand what that means. Two of Freud's six technical papers on technique are specifically concerned with transference—"The Dynamics of Transference" and "Observations on Transference-Love," both of which I will address in this chapter. Even a third paper, "Remembering, Repeating, and Working-Through" (1958h), is essentially concerned with transference, including its temporal dimension.

When analysts are with their patients, they have to rely on their understanding of what transference is in order to recognize its signs when they arise. This is largely what analysts do. They *understand*. Transference requires understanding in order to be recognized. In turn, analysts hope to share their understanding with their patients, by helping them understand it too. Analysts hope they will come to recognize that what had previously been just a feeling or conviction is actually a rather complex affair that implicates their entire history of relationships with other human beings.

"The Dynamics of Transference" deals with the concept of transference and how it arises. No other concept in psychoanalysis is so widely discussed and so frequently misunderstood. Though Freud had dealt with the concept at length in his analysis of Dora, he uses this paper to explain its nature further, "theoretically," as Strachey would say. Freud sets about to explain what this concept means; not merely how it works but its aims. The introduction of this concept into our culture has changed the way we live. It arguably offers the most significant insight into the nature of love since the Greeks. Before Freud, our ideas about love were relatively simple, if naive. We were in touch with our feelings. We knew what we believed. I may not have known why I loved this person instead of that, but I knew who I loved and who I didn't. I couldn't control my feelings, but I knew what they were. Freud changed all that. He made things more complicated. I am no longer certain how I feel or what I believe. Even the things about which I am most certain may be open to doubt. In fact, often, the things about which I am most certain arouse the greatest suspicions. We no longer have direct, immediate access to the essence of our deepest and most significant beliefs. Now we have to think about them, and come at them, perhaps, from another angle.

Philosophers have always pondered the nature of certainty, the prevalence of doubt, the meaning of love, life, the hereafter. Asking those questions is what makes someone a philosopher. But not until Freud did we realize how central the problem of loving is to our existence, how dependant we are on it, how spiteful we can become without it. Not until Freud did we realize how difficult it can be, for most of us, *to* love, how frightened we become of it, how vulnerable it makes us, how readily we repress it. All of these—the pain, the fear, the longing—are implied in the concept that Freud called "transference," a word that pertains to love in its essence.

Freud's aim in his rather brief "Dynamics of Transference" is to articulate what transference is. From the first, in only the second paragraph, he establishes the dependence of the concept of transference on the phenomenon of love:

> It must be understood that each individual, through the combined operation of his [her] innate disposition and influences brought to bear on him during his early years, has acquired a specific method of his own in his conduct of his erotic life—that is, in the preconditions to falling in love which he lays down, in the instincts he satisfies and the aims he sets himself in the course of it. (99)

In other words, if we want to understand what Freud means by the concept of transference, we need to appreciate how all human creatures, in their own fashion, acquire a manner of falling in love with other human creatures, based on the interplay between innate predilections and the circumstances they inhabit. What Freud means to convey by the word innate doesn't refer to biological considerations as much as ontological ones. It is our nature, as human beings, to need love, in principle. We haven't a choice. Whether we love this person or another, we need somebody to serve as an object for our love, whether we like it or not. This is essentially a Greek idea, that love is something that all human beings need to express. We form impressions and convictions about love—its accessibility and inaccessibility—based on our experiences as we grow and mature. We develop expectations and apprehensions about love based on those experiences. Although our experience of love determines our developing attitude about it, that attitude is open to revision when we experience new circumstances. In other words, our developing attitudes about love aren't encased in cement, impervious to subsequent developments. On the other hand, whatever our experiences happen to be will determine our developing attitude about love. Because of our need for love we are driven relentlessly forward to meet persons whom we can love, and from whom we, in turn, can get love. But "only a portion of these impulses which determine the course of erotic life" become a part of our conscious concerns about love and our relationship with it (1958a, 100). Some of these impulses aren't conscious and, consequently, we don't think about them: "Another portion of the libidinal impulses has been held up in the course of development; it has been kept away from the conscious personality and from reality, and has either been prevented from further expansion except in phantasy or has remained wholly in the unconscious so that it is unknown to the personality's consciousness" (100).

All of us have certain preconditions for falling in love and those preconditions are laid down very early, though they're open to revision. But only some of our early impressions evolve and grow and become a part of our developing, conscious attitude about love. Other of our yearnings for love are held back. We only come to know about them through the emergence of "phantasies"—daydreams about people we are sexually attracted to—or they become repressed and we don't realize they exist. Consequently, "If someone's need for love is not entirely satisfied by reality, he [she] is bound to approach *every new person whom he meets* with libidinal anticipatory ideas; and it is highly probable that both portions of his libido, the portion that is capable of becoming conscious as well as the unconscious one, have a share in forming that attitude" (100; emphasis added). This comment is remarkable for two reasons. First, it emphasizes how prevalent our longing for love is. We don't single this person out and ignore the others. To the degree that we feel frustrated in our need for love, we approach every new person we meet with the hope of having our longing satisfied. The second point concerns the developing nature of what comprises "transference." Each of us develops an attitude about love that is a consequence of (a) our conscious experience of love; (b) our unconscious phantasies that we hold back and nurture; and (c) the frustrations we experience from our encounter with reality: the people we love and, in turn, are loved by.

This explains the universality of the transference with one's analyst—

and why there isn't anything unique about it, why "it is a perfectly normal and intelligible thing that the libidinal cathexis [i.e., our yearning for love] of someone who is partly unsatisfied, a cathexis which is held ready in anticipation, should be directed as well to the figure of the doctor" (100). In other words, our patients inevitably regard us as a potential source of love, not because there is anything necessarily special about us, but because we're simply being included along with the rest of humanity. The fact that analytic relationships are lengthy affords them the best opportunity to arouse these primordial longings and, more importantly, examine them. But what is it about this yearning for love and its manifestation in the relationship with one's analyst that is specifically "transferential," if it merely alludes, after all, to a universal phenomenon? What is it about transference that may become problematical, if it simply refers to the nature of love itself?

It's only natural that analytic patients develop affectionate feelings for their analysts because all patients are frustrated, somehow or other, in their capacity to obtain love. This is why they are likely to transfer their unfulfilled longing onto the analyst. In other words, all analytic patients—because they are in a state of inherent frustration—anticipate something is going to happen in their relationship with their therapist that will satisfy their longing for love. Although these strivings are frequently conscious, it is remarkable the degree to which we conceal their existence from awareness: "The peculiarities of the transference to the doctor, thanks to which it exceeds . . . anything that could be justified on sensible or rational grounds, are made intelligible if we bear in mind that this transference has precisely been set up not only by the *conscious* anticipatory ideas but also by those that have been held back or are unconscious" (100).

In order to grasp the subtlety of Freud's point we need to go back to his conception of reality and why our experience of it gives rise to phantasy in the first place. Reality frustrates our need to love and be loved. What do we do with that frustration? If we were without resource, perhaps we would accept reality more readily. After all, we wouldn't have a choice. But we have a choice: we withdraw from reality by harboring our unsatisfied longings, making them "unconscious." In turn, our longings for love find satisfaction in the symptoms that become vehicles for our unconscious phantasies. In time, we become committed to whatever symptom our phantasies occupy, *as though it were a lover.*

The problem with this solution is that the symptom engenders just as much anguish and frustration as the original object in reality. Now the symptom becomes the locus of our attention. But what, exactly, is being "transfered" onto the analyst? Not the neurosis itself because it remains intact and even arouses resistance against its removal. Nor is it the original object of desire, because analysts merely assume the function of that missing person as others have before them. Yet, some thing is being "transfered" from the original object onto the new one. What is it?

So far, all that Freud characterizes as transference is our inherent "yearning for love," the machinations of which are faithful to each individual's personality, which, because of its frustrated condition, is aimed at all of humanity. But the objects of those aims become sources of gratification in phantasy, not in reality. We include the analyst as an object of our phantasy life as a matter of course. But is this "transference" itself pathological? After all, it's due to our pathological condition—the original repression of desire—that we continue to feel frustrated and, in turn, find recourse in our symptoms. Because the symptom is, in effect, the current "object" of our affection, we're incapable of obtaining satisfaction from a real person. If, then, the analyst becomes an object of interest—the object of our longing for love—why should the transference become a vehicle of neurosis instead of a vehicle for cure? How, in turn, could transference become a vehicle of resistance if the impulse behind it is essentially healthy?

Let's return once more to Freud's distinction between phantasy and reality. As we know, this is the problem that every neurotic faces, the pleasures of readily available phantasies against the uncertain, elusive intimations of what can be achieved in relationships with others. Every relationship offers opportunities for both real gratification as well as a stimulus for one's phantasies. What sets neurotics apart is the degree to which their yearnings for love are unconscious, and the extent to which they are committed to satisfying those yearnings in phantasy. But what is neurosis? According to Freud, "An invariable and indispensable precondition of *every* onset of a psychoneurosis is the process to which . . . the portion of the libido which is capable of becoming conscious and is directed towards reality is diminished, and the portion which is directed *away* from reality and is unconscious . . . is proportionately increased" (102). In other words, it's the neurosis, rather than transference, per se, which is pathological. It's the neurosis, rather than transference, which compromises our relationship with reality—other people—and compels our withdrawal into erotic phantasies. As Freud discovered with Dora, she came to prefer her phantasies over the opportunities for real love that were ostensibly available. Resistance to analysis is a way of preserving those phantasies from which we derive pleasure. We resist their exposure and potential forfeiture. But the neurosis itself isn't transference. Transference pertains to the way neurosis seizes relationships and utilizes them to employ its unconscious aims. We need to distinguish between the aims of neurosis, on the one hand, and the transference feelings that service those aims on the other.

In order to appreciate how neurotic conflicts are able to insinuate their way into the transference and make use of it, we need to understand the nature of resistance and how transference may, without our awareness, become its vehicle. Freud discussed three sources of resistance in "The Dynamics of Transference." The first is the neurosis itself. Because neurosis is, by definition, the libidinal displacement of our longing for love onto a symptom that, in phantasy, is gratifying, we inevitably resist any effort to deprive us of that gratification.

> The analytic treatment . . . seeks to track down the libido, to make it accessible to consciousness and, in the end, serviceable for reality. Where the investigations of analysis come upon the libido withdrawn into its hiding-place, a struggle is bound to break out; all the forces which have caused the libido to regress will rise up as resistances against the work of analysis, *in order to conserve the new state of things.* (102; emphasis added)

In other words, our frustration with reality compelled us to regress into neurotic phantasies in the first place. Any effort to abandon those phantasies by reacquainting oneself with the relative harshness of reality is resisted. This is why neurosis, by its nature, is predisposed against its own destruction. But there is a second source of resistance that is even stronger than the preservation of neurotic symptoms. We also try to protect our neuroses from discovery. After all, the aim of analysis is, as Freud says, to "track down the libido" and make it accessible to reality. Consequently, the act of repression that gave rise to the symptom strives to protect itself by resisting the possibility of being discovered. Freud believed that "this is responsible for by far the largest part of the resistance" (103).

Once we understand how (a) neurotic conflict, and (b) the discovery of neurotic aims serve as sources of resistance to the work of analysis—in fact, the "analysis" of those very aims—we're able to appreciate how transference itself may serve as yet a third source of resistance. This is because *analysts themselves* are the vehicle through which the analysis is conducted. If, as Freud believed, the violation of the "fundamental rule" of analysis—to bare all—epitomizes resistance, we should remember that it is the person of the analyst who introduced that rule and continues to remind us of it.

But doesn't the transference of one's patients' longing for affection onto the analyst simply insure their status as welcome collaborators? How could the very impulse that serves as the agent of cure—the patient's positive regard—become a vehicle of resistance? After all, the transference, in and of itself, *isn't resistance.* Freud took considerable care to distinguish between the "mechanism" of transference—which he defines as "a state of readiness of the libido" (104), which seeks out and antici-pates gratification—and the role that transference assumes *in the treat-ment,* where it becomes a source of resistance to the treatment. In order to understand how transference may become a pawn of resistance we need to look further than transference itself, our "longing for love." In fact, we must learn to recognize two distinct forms of transference, "posi-tive" and "negative." Roughly speaking, the so-called positive transfer-ence occasions the patient's efforts to get well, whereas the negative serves to resist those efforts by taking a personal dislike to the analyst. But if transference, *in its essence,* is a "state of readiness of the libido"—a longing for love—then how can a "type" of that transference become its opposite, a transference of apparently hostile, even hateful feelings against that person? Wouldn't such a reaction be contrary to the essential motive force of the transference?

But Freud never said that the negative transference is comprised of hate, specifically. Borrowing a term from Bleuler he characterized the negative transference as one that elicits feelings of ambivalence (106). In other words, the negative transference, which "is found side by side with the affectionate transference" (106), is a reaction to the feelings of anticipation that epitomize its motive force. When our longing for love is "transferred" onto the analyst, we eventually encounter and take stock of the limitations imposed by the one-sided nature of this relationship. We reprise the old feelings of anguish and resentment that we experienced when we first turned away from an intolerably frustrating reality. Yet, why should the evocation of this familiar impasse arouse a negative attitude toward the analyst if we weren't threatened by the loss of something precious; unless we believed that someone—one's own analyst—was trying to deprive us of what is rightfully ours? This is when the negative transference is evoked, when we are threatened by *the potential loss of a symptom.*

This is why it's misleading to equate positive and negative transference with feelings of love and hate. The so-called positive transference is epitomized by our wish to get well, our obedience to the fundamental rule, the hope for a positive outcome to the treatment, our feelings of affection for the analyst, and a capacity to collaborate with him by adhering to the analytic attitude. The capacity to see this through occasions anguish and frustration. As long as those feelings don't serve the aims of resistance, they are entirely consistent within the scope of one's positive transference. On the other hand, the negative transference is epitomized by a withdrawal of our collaboration with the analyst. It engenders a sense of futility and despair about the outcome of treatment, for which the analyst is held personally accountable. Threatened by the loss of the symptom, we even suspect that the analyst is deliberately depriving us of what we long for the most.

If the negative transference isn't epitomized by hate, but by ambivalence, what is ambivalence? The commonsense notion that ambivalence is a mixture of love and hate is misleading, though it frequently elicits hatred "symptomatically." Ambivalence is simply the consequence of suppressing one's longing for love, manifested by an inhibition of libido. The emergence of hateful feelings is actually an attempt to resolve ambivalence by attacking the libido itself. This is why aggression is eventually aimed at the analyst, the person who, says Freud, is "tracking down the libido" with designs of liberating it. Consequently, the underlying conflict that gives rise to our experience of ambivalence is between *love and repression.* Even when Freud revised the pleasure principle by introducing the possibility of a "death drive" (see chapters 25 and 26), he refused to characterize his hypothesis of a self-destructive "instinct" as the epitome of hate and aggression, but instead as a flight from frustration.[1] If the negative transference isn't characterized, at the deepest level, by hatred, then *what* is transfered onto the analyst when we succumb to it? Freud doesn't spell

---

1. The collision between love and hate doesn't produce ambivalence, but guilt. See the following section on Freud's analysis of the Rat Man for a more detailed exploration of the relationship between ambivalence and guilt.

out the answer to this question for us. It may be helpful, however, to conceive of the term *negative,* not as synonymous with aggression, but referring to our tendency, in relation to others, to "negate" our most basic human impulse: the longing to love and to be loved by another person.

On the other hand, the negative transference isn't the only aspect of transference that serves resistance. On the so-called positive side of the equation, Freud distinguished between an "affectionate" transference—the vehicle for the patient's ultimate success—and the patient's "erotic" designs on the analyst. When we seek to determine what it is about transference, in any of its forms, that specifically serves resistance, we realize that the negative and erotic components share exactly the same aims: to obstruct the progress of treatment and so prevent the loss of the symptom. The negative transference attacks the analysis by becoming embittered against one's analyst, whereas the erotic transference achieves the same goal by "falling in love" with the analyst instead.

The crucial point to remember about the so-called transference resistance—whether negative or erotic—is how the analyst gains precedence over the symptom in the patient's preoccupations. This is what Freud alluded to when he conceived the "transference neurosis" (see chapter 20). Whether the analyst is blamed or idealized, the result is the same: the neurosis is protected against the encroachment of analysis. That is why the question of *what* is "transferred"? can't be reduced to a formula that is strictly comprised of "affects" and "ideas." At a deeper level still lies an underlying *purpose* that predetermines our affective experience. Perhaps it would be useful to conceive of transference resistance in general as a way of *utilizing* the relationship with one's analyst and the attitudes we form about him as a way of protecting our unconsciously gratifying neurosis. This is how transference—our intrinsic longing for love—functions as a vehicle for both success and failure. Our wherewithal to finally capitulate to that longing is constantly threatened, throughout the course of analysis, *by intimations of success,* by virtue of the gradual erosion of our unconscious phantasies and the consequent intrusion of reality:

> Thus the solution of the puzzle is that transference to the doctor is suitable for resistance to the treatment only in so far as it is a negative transference or a positive transference of repressed erotic impulses. If we "remove" the transference by making it conscious, we are detaching only these two components. . . . The other component, *which is admissible to consciousness*

and unobjectionable, persists and is the vehicle of success. (105; emphasis added)

This frequently repeated quotation contains a germ of insight into Freud's conception of transference that is often overlooked. Freud recognized three forms of transference in this paper: negative, erotic (positive), and unobjectionable (positive). There's been a lot of confusion about these distinctions, because the "unobjectionable" feelings that patients have for their analyst—the feelings that comprise their analytic attitude—are *also* transferential. But doesn't the very concept of transference suggest that these feelings aren't real, that they're unconscious, imagined, "transfered"? Some analysts (Lipton 1977) believe these feelings are real, implying that they're not actually "transferential" because they comprise the "real relationship" between the therapist and patient. Other analysts (Brenner 1979) suggest that Freud's allusion to the existence of "unobjectionable" transference feelings proves the virtual absence of a real relationship between therapist and patient, because it implies that the analytic relationship is essentially transferential through and through, no matter what type of transference it is. This view presumes that transference, by definition, is always unconscious and synonymous with phantasy. That is why it needs to be interpreted, not collaborated with.

But where, exactly, did Freud define transference in this way? He never said that transference wasn't specifically real, but that its aims were often "unrealistic." He suggested that transference is a compulsive repetition of our longing for love, a compulsion that we employ all the time, predominantly, but not always, unconsciously. This pattern—and the aims it fosters—doesn't become *less* real in analysis than it was outside it. As we've seen, there's nothing specifically pathological about transference itself. It becomes wedded to neurotic symptoms in order to further their aims, and that is where the pathological component resides.

Freud's characterization of yet a third form of transference, "which is admissible to consciousness and unobjectionable . . . and is the vehicle of success in psychoanalysis" (105), far from being "outside" of transference, actually epitomizes transference in its essence. It refers to that longing for love that was frustrated by reality and that, due to its extraordinary mobility, seeks *any means possible* to obtain satisfaction. Even the "pathological" becomes a resource for love's aims. By attaching itself to a symptom, our longing for love is held hostage by its phantasies, a source of gratification that subverts our relationship with the real. Yet, this same motive force, when separated from resistance, is capable, at any time, of becoming available to consciousness *and* reality. But why call this motive force, given its unobjectionable nature, a form of transference in the first place, if it occasions our capacity to face reality and come to terms with it? Why did Freud invoke the concept of transference to describe this phenomenon if it depicts those libidinal aims that are *potentially free* of unconscious, ulterior motives, unfettered by resistance and even serving as the motive force of the analytic attitude, one's "vehicle of success"?

In order to understand how Freud was able to use the same concept of transference to epitomize the basis of our inherently human condition, on the one hand—our longing for love—while serving our most pathological inclinations, on the other—inclinations that, by their nature, are opposed to love in its essence—we will need to return to where Freud started in his paper on transference, with his thoughts about the nature of love. If Freud believed that transference is both a creature of love and a vehicle for love's aims, then the ambiguity of his conception of transference is surely mirrored by the ambiguities inherent in love itself. Freud's conception of love, in spite of the convoluted twists and turns that characterize the presumed "forces" that drive it, is essentially a personal one. It is personal in the Greek sense that it lies at the basis of our humanity, and it is personal in the degree of cunning and deception we so readily employ in its service. Transference, as Freud conceived it, isn't a psychological term but an *ontological* one. It epitomizes human nature: an irresistible, insatiable longing, in everything we do, in every relationship we obtain, each day of our lives, for the love of another human being. Some may disagree with Freud and offer other motive forces that are, for them, more compelling. If so, then their conception of transference would be accordingly modified. These modifications tell the history of psychoanalysis since Freud, a dilution of love as the pivot of human relatedness. We disagree with Freud as we like, but we need to be clear what it is we disagree about. Freud's conception of transference is at the heart of this disagreement, but it is also the root of considerable confusion about Freud's clinical aims.

The essence of Freud's thoughts about the nature of love and its vicissitudes is spelled out in his paper on transference-love (see chapter 5). A feature of that paper concerns the problem of determining what it is that is specifically pathological about love. Freud concluded that all forms of love—transferential or otherwise—are the children of one's history. Love transforms us into temporal creatures because, by it, we succumb to mortality. We confront death and yearn, in our solitary existence, for someone to share our lives with. Without that someone, we become obsessed with reminiscences of our earliest experience of love when, frustrated, we turned away and tried to ignore it. When we "transfer" our hopes for love onto somebody new—the analyst—we actually *reincarnate* the need for love we had held in abeyance. Now it arouses all the dormant, "libidinal" yearnings that customarily demand expression. This is why the term *transference,* in and of itself, doesn't necessarily infer something pathological. It is a *creature of memory,* of love that persists no matter how much we resist it. The only thing we can honestly say that is pathological about love is its absence: our repression of its claims. The turmoil of love denied tells the story of every neurotic. Freud believed it was the only master whose tyranny we could never overcome. This notion about love, that, by its nature, it is tormenting *and* gratifying, was universally accepted by the Greeks. We witness its tragic ambiguity throughout Greek philosophy, mythology, and religion.

Easily the most extraordinary exploration of love in Greek literature is Plato's "Symposium," a brilliant summary of the extant theories of his day. At a dinner party attended by Socrates and several of his friends, a conversation ensues that ranges over a number of competing notions about love that were then entertained, virtually all of which are still retained in a variety of "updated" forms. Elements of nearly all these views found their way into Freud's theories about love, eros, sacrifice, life, death, devotion, compliance, jealousy, attachment. The arguments, all of which Socrates refutes, one by one, form a set of "hierarchies" of love, in ascending order, some baser than the rest—more narcissistic perhaps—whereas others are more noble and wise, even altruistic, suggesting *agape.*[2] The tension between "pathological" and "healthy" love is evident

2. The Greeks distinguished amongst three forms of love: *eros, philia,* and *agape.* Roughly speaking, *eros* referred to sexual love; *philia* to friendship; and *agape,* the highest form possible, was epitomized by grace, compassion, and charity (*carritas* in Latin). The three, though distinguishable, are not necessarily exclusive of each other. Yet, whereas it is possible to feel all three for the same person, Socrates believed that not everyone is capable of *philia* or *agape.* This point plays a central role in the structure of the *Symposium.*

The Catholic church subsequently adopted *agape* as the epitome of Christian love. Derived from Christ's teachings, it is essential to Christian theology. Its relationship to the Greek interpretation of *agape,* however, is obscure. The New Testament, for example,

throughout, not unlike the tone Freud adopts in his paper on transference-love. Eventually, everyone turns to Socrates and begs him to disclose his views about love, since he finds so much fault in theirs. On the spot, Socrates is called on to abandon his rhetorical style of always answering a question with a question—a style that epitomizes analytic behavior!— and give an answer that actually is an answer, a point of view that is *his*.

But again, with the slyness of a fox, Socrates manages to have it both ways: to answer, yet not reveal his position. He invokes instead the name of a former teacher, Diotima, "who was deeply versed in this and many other fields of knowledge, . . . who taught me the philosophy of Love" (Hamilton and Cairns 1961, 553). Diotima, he suggests, was his muse, the woman through whom Socrates came to grasp the meaning of love. The essence of her teaching was conveyed to him in the form of a myth, which Socrates repeats to his audience:

> On the day of Aphrodite's birth the gods were making merry, and among them was Resource, the son of Craft. And when they had supped, Need came begging at the door because there was good cheer inside. Now, it happened that Resource, having drunk deeply of the heavenly nectar—for this was before the days of wine—wandered out into the garden of Zeus and sank into a heavy sleep, and Need, thinking that to get a child by Resource would mitigate her penury, lay down beside him and in time was brought to bed of Love. So Love became the follower and servant of Aphrodite because he was begotten on the same day that she was born, and further, he was born to love the beautiful since Aphrodite is beautiful herself. (555)

Diotima explains to Socrates how love comes into being and, especially, its nature. Unlike Aphrodite, Love is neither god nor goddess. Neither is he a man, but something in between: a spirit. His parents are Resource and Need so, according to Diotima, it is "his fate to be needy; nor is he delicate and lovely as most of us believe, but harsh and arid, barefoot and homeless, sleeping on the naked earth, in doorways . . .

---

suggests that Christ introduced *agape* to mankind for the first time, implying an originality that the Greeks would have protested.

Freud didn't interpret love in this manner, though he did distinguish between transference-love (sexual love), on the one hand, and genuine or real love, on the other (see chapter 5), the latter of which approximates *agape*. His reformulation of the pleasure principle appears to combine the three forms of Greek love into one: *Eros*. However, his conception of *eros* wasn't rooted in sex, specifically. Though it included sexuality, it aspired to the highest possible love, including personal sacrifice.

always partaking of his mother's poverty" (555–56). Not a pretty picture, but it captures Freud's "driven" depiction of love, especially the insatiable insistence of its aims and its hunger. In the service of those aims, however, Love's best qualities emerge, born of Resource, his father: "But, secondly, he brings his father's resourcefulness to his designs upon the beautiful and the good, for he is gallant, impetuous, and energetic, a mighty hunter, and a master of device and artifice—at once desirous and full of wisdom, a lifelong seeker after truth, an adept in sorcery, enchantment, and seduction" (556).

Despite Love's lifelong searching, he never rests. He has his ups and downs, at times full of life and happy, but oftentimes sad and bereft. According to Diotima, "Love is never altogether in or out of need, and stands, moreover, midway between ignorance and wisdom" (556). If love is born of our acknowledgment that we have these needs to begin with, coupled with the resourceful determination to persist till we have it—but in *its* service, not ours—then whatever it is that we might construe as a pathological component of love would have to pertain to our denial of it: it's repression.

Some of us, like the Greek "gods" on Olympus, try to rise above our plight. We pretend we don't need love and live in denial. If we apply Diotima's example to Freud's thesis, the narcissistic individual comes to mind, one for whom love is less an object of devotion than a pacifier for his cravings. He can't recognize the beauty in others because he's so obsessed with himself. On the other hand, she describes those who lack the intelligence, resource or character to pursue love. They don't even know it exists, "and do not long for the virtues they have never missed" (556). In Freud's adaptation, this describes people who are so repressed they don't even realize that something is missing. They would be poor candidates for psychoanalysis and probably aren't likely to consider it. According to Freud, in order to be analyzable we have to at least yearn to bring our needs and resources together, by devoting ourselves to love's call. Anything less and our lives are no more than a lie, condemned to a solitary existence.

People come into analysis afraid to love but hoping to change. They entertain phantasies they aren't even aware of. Their notions about life and love are unrealistic, to varying degrees. The term *transference,* a concept, refers to the everyday phenomenon of love, in unconventional, complex ways. It serves to direct our understanding toward something that by its nature is enigmatic. If transference is a concept, however, that doesn't imply that the phenomenon it describes—our longing for love—is intrinsically imaginary or impersonal just because it's often resisted. Ironically, Freud has been condemned for being too real, too much *himself* with his patients. Psychoanalysis has embraced theoretical notions about transference since Freud's death that are increasingly impersonal. A shift in thinking has sought to found psychoanalysis on scientific principles. These principles (as we saw in chapter 8) conceive knowledge in predominantly abstract terms, so it's little wonder that the relationship between analysts and their patients should be conceived as something that isn't specifically personal either, or even real.

The idea of a real person being analyzed by a real analyst is disappearing with each successive generation of analysts. This epitomizes progress in the development of its theory and its technique. I believe this direction is mistaken. An appreciation of transference shouldn't lead to the disappearance of the *people* being analyzed. Rather, it should help to bring them into focus, where we discover they are human beings like ourselves. Increasingly, psychoanalysts construe the specifically transferential dimension of their patients' behavior as inherently pathological. Whatever one consciously experiences—ideas, feelings, beliefs—merely speaks to an unconscious motive that is determined by one mechanism or another. Once the pathological foundation for transference is made inherent, the way is open to interpret every feeling or sentiment as "transferential," in this bastardized sense. Similarly, the same can be said for the analyst, so that everything analysts experience refers willy-nilly to a yet-to-be determined unconscious motive or inclination. The person of the analyst and the patient disappears, because the analysis of a given individual's "psychic structure" demands we conceive of his person as a veil. This process of abstracting away the people who are being analyzed couldn't have been further from Freud's intention. If a cigar is sometimes just a cigar, surely a person is sometimes only a person. The concept of transference shouldn't be used to "deconstruct" the person who is analyzed, but to give them back their humanity, their purpose, even their idiosyncracies.

How did Freud actually *interpret* the transference? How did he go about *analyzing* the resistances? He doesn't say. Freud's principal concern, as we saw at the beginning of this chapter, was to insure that we understand what transference is, to avoid mistaking it for something else, or overlooking it altogether. We saw this style of instruction earlier in Dora's analysis, the poverty of concrete examples in what was, after all, a "technical" exposition. Then as now, Freud seemed to be saying: "Understand— and the rest will follow." What we do with that understanding, what we actually say or don't, is for us to determine. This goes against the grain of how psychoanalysis is now taught. These days, analytic instruction is more concrete, more precise, less ambiguous. It's even taught by rote, something that Freud would have hardly encouraged. In turn, Freud is criticized for not being sufficiently "analytic" in the way *he* conducted analysis. He is taken to task for not analyzing the resistances he took such care to uncover. Analyzing resistances—exploring their unconscious sources—didn't concern Freud the way it does analysts nowadays. Why? Freud didn't believe that analyzing the transference and its accompanying resistance was necessarily *therapeutic*. It's no wonder that proponents of "resistance analysis" (Gray 1982; 1986) hold a dim view of Freud's technique, when he virtually ignored their most valued intervention, the "analysis of defense." These technical innovations don't necessarily imply that psychoanalysis has advanced. Many analysts today simply disagree with Freud's methods. They have every right to, but we should admit that these criticisms are only disagreements and nothing more. Freud had his reasons. What were they?

His conception of transference should give us a clue. He conceived it in terms of erotism and the longing for love that every patient brings to analysis. Therefore, when attending to the transference, the analyst should simply be concerned with providing the time and space for these inclinations to become manifest and have their say. Freud explained in his paper "On Beginning the Treatment" (1958e, 141) that the aims of psychoanalysis will never be achieved by merely understanding why or how we struggle against our most basic needs. Its success depends on the confidences we share with each other. The patient's transference isn't served by dissecting its movement. We merely offer to become its target and its scapegoat. We agree to be the person for whom these yearnings come into being as they seek expression, knowing, given time, they will finally take their leave.

20

Working-Through ("Remembering, Repeating, and Working-Through," 1914)

Freud's paper on "working-through"—*Durcharbeitung* in German—is arguably the most subtle of his technical papers. It's remarkable that this pivotal concept should have been treated with such economy. In fact, the term is mentioned only twice in Strachey's index to the *Standard Edition*. It appears once in the paper we are now examining and again in an addenda to *Inhibitions, Symptoms and Anxiety* (1959a), published some twelve years later. The term crops up now and then in other papers, but this is the only publication in which Freud attempted to define what it means. Yet, he devotes a scant two pages to the task even in this context. More remarkable still, "working-through" has no precise definition. It is barely mentioned only at the very end of the present paper. Perhaps, for this reason, it stands out as one of Freud's most ambiguous concepts whose meaning continues to arouse considerable debate.

Freud begins this paper by reminding us about the importance of forgetfulness in the analytic experience. A great deal of the analysts' concern revolves around the task of helping their patients to *remember*. This would seem hardly worth emphasizing—after all, it epitomizes psychoanalysis—were it not for a special feature of remembering that is brought to our attention. When patients recall an incident in the course of their analysis that until then they had forgot, they invariably remark: "As a matter of fact I've always known it; only I've never thought of it" (Freud 1958h, 148). Freud even remarks that oftentimes a patient is disappointed "at the fact that not enough things come into his [her] head that he can call 'forgotten'—that he has never thought of since they happened" (148). Forgetting in this sense can't be equated with "amnesia" because it wasn't really forgotten in the first place. I simply hadn't realized its importance, it didn't matter to me until now, I didn't appreciate how I had felt about it, and so on. These accounts of having known all along what one presumably forgot reveal how important significance, relevance, and context are to the analytic process. Those analysts who accuse Freud of reducing transference to forgotten feelings while neglecting the here and now apparently skipped over this paper. Freud's conception of transference is less an account of how the past gains influence over the present as a depiction of the nature of temporality and its pervasive presence in our lives. Transference is already "here and now." But the concept of transference also compels us to remember the significance our histories employ on the present, including the relationship with one's analyst. This holds just as true for another form of memory in which the patient recalls incidents that never actually occurred: "phantasies." But these phantasies don't belong to the "past." They're coexistent with and inhabit every relationship we have. If our very notions about love and happiness are rooted in phantasies that help to salve our disappointments, they co-mingle with what's real in ways that are hard to decipher, and even detect. This is because phantasies are often disguised as memories. In this case they occasion an *anticipated* event that was longed for but never happened. When we're in a situation that reminds us of these unfulfilled longings, what we "recall" is simply a wish that never came true.

Freud's thoughts about transference contained an elasticity that is easily lost on the literal-minded. His thinking is no less subtle when he turns his attention to the notion of repetition, a concept he introduces in this paper for the first time. Another word for memory, repetition is a peculiar kind of memory in which "the patient does not *remember* anything of what he [she] has forgotten and repressed, but *acts* it out. He reproduces it not as a memory but as an action; he *repeats* it, without, of course, knowing that he is repeating it" (150). In other words, sometimes *behavior* is a type of remembering in the sense that, by it, we strive to recapture and achieve the longings for love we might have thought we forgot. If we resist acknowledging these longings by talking about them, we silently "act them out" anyhow. We see this happening in the course of analysis and realize something isn't being addressed. But in the same way that patients say they "knew" the repressed material prior to the moment it's recalled, we sometimes discover what we want by the way that we try to conceal it.

With the concept of repetition, we begin to appreciate how revolutionary Freud's notion of memory is. The "compulsion to repeat" is another expression of our longing for love. Repetition is simply our insistence on getting the love that eludes us. The purpose of analysis isn't to halt these pieces of behavior—of memory—but to bring them to our attention. Resistance, then, is our reluctance to admit what we already know, embodied in the acts that betray the truths we keep hidden. Now we see that transference is also a "repetition," because it is nothing more than the patients' efforts to gratify their longings through the developing attachment to the analyst. But these repetitions aren't restricted to the analyst. They implicate just about anybody who becomes available. In fact, according to Freud, "the greater the resistance, the more extensively will acting out (repetition) replace remembering" (151). In other words, if we resist the pledge to show ourselves in the space that analysis gives us, our needs for success, affection, and love seek circuitous means of expression. Like people who conceal they are angry, our longings spill out in frustration toward the person most likely to arouse them, the one who "reminds" us they're there. These feelings, reenacted onto the person of the analyst, aren't merely remnants of a forgotten past. As Freud says, "we must treat his illness, not as an event of the past, but as a present-day force" (151). These feelings are real. Our reluctance to acknowledge them, look at them, and recognize them as problematic inclines us toward the pathological. At the end of the day, our resistance against showing ourselves through language—by defying the fundamental rule—epitomized the resistance that Freud equated with neurosis. This explains how repetition, in turn, becomes a vehicle of one's desire. It harbors those wishes that continually reappear, however we try to hide them, like a hunger that won't go away till it's fed. "Repeating," according to Freud, "as it is induced in analytic treatment . . . implies conjuring up a piece of real life; and for that reason it cannot always be harmless and unobjectionable" (152). A psychoanalysis doesn't simply butt in to a life already predisposed; it intervenes and alters the equation of influences our patients now have to contend with. Before they were resigned and even content to indulge their neurotic suffering. Now something is expected of them; they have to account for their behavior and what they propose to do about it. Now they have to reckon with this "otherness" inside them, silent inclinations that pull them in contrary directions, the nature of which they are only beginning to grasp.

> He [the patient] must *find the courage* to direct his attention to the phenomena of his illness. His illness itself must no longer seem to him contemptible, but must become an enemy *worthy of his mettle,* a piece of his personality, which has solid ground for its existence and out of which things of value for his future life have to be derived. (152; emphasis added)

Freud goes to some lengths to emphasize the struggle that analytic treatment entails and expects from its analysands. Our life is soon overtaken by a task and a challenge we didn't anticipate. Before, we thought the therapist would "do all the work." Now, we realize we're in a little over our heads. The sacrifice, the toil, the labor were unexpected. The analyst, forewarned, should be prepared "for a perpetual struggle with his [her] patient" (153). This is hardly a "psychological" task, a matter of dotting i's and clarifying inconsistencies. It's more like a fight to the death in which all is risked and accounted for in our efforts to wrest free of our symptoms. But why should freedom require "courage"? Isn't it bad enough that we suffer? Shouldn't freedom from suffering be a sufficient motivation to endure the trials of analysis? Like Sartre, who built his entire philosophy around the fear of freedom, Freud realized how ambivalent we are about becoming emancipated. In fact, our fear of freedom is what prompts us to resist separation, and even attachment. The repetitive "solution" always pulls back and finds ways to defeat the fragile bond that creeps into relationships. These impulses, to the degree they're unadmitted, harbor acts of sabotage that help preserve the symptom at the expense of becoming attached to one's analyst. On the other hand, "if the attachment through transference has grown into something at all serviceable, the treatment is able to prevent the patient from executing any of the more important repetitive actions and to utilize his [her] intention to do so in *statu nascendi* as material for therapeutic work" (153).

Freud was determined to insure that whatever freedom patients brought with them at the start of therapy should remain intact. One's hard-won lessons should derive from mistakes committed and suffered, not from advice or prognostications. If we're fools, then we need the freedom to be fools and learn the lessons that only fools can learn. "One does not forget that it is in fact only through his own *experience and mishaps* that a person learns sense" (153; emphasis added). Freud's emphasis on the importance of getting in touch with one's experience—particularly the variety of experience that includes mistakes, mishaps and folly—reflects the value he ascribes to participating in the process of free association and adhering to the fundamental rule (see chapter 18). Here Freud emphasizes the efficacy of *succumbing* to experience, to live it, suffer it, and learn what only it can teach us. Montaigne (1925) described this lesson as learning how to play with one's thoughts and emotions. Similarly, Freud envisioned the relationship between analyst and patient "as a playground in which [transference] is allowed to expand in almost complete freedom and in which it is expected to display to us everything in the way of pathogenic instincts that is hidden in the patient's mind" (154). But if *play* can be expected to occur in a process that, by its nature, encounters resistance and obstinate rigidity, it's imperative that "the patient shows compliance enough to respect the necessary conditions of the analysis" (154). To the degree that these conditions are met, patients effect a special type of attachment to their analyst that subsequently becomes the focus of the therapy. In other words, the feelings patients have for their analyst become just as important as the therapy itself. Consequently, all of the conflicts typically experienced in their other relationships are repeated with the analyst. Once the analyst becomes that important to them, "we regularly succeed in giving all the symptoms of the illness a new transference meaning and in replacing [their] ordinary neurosis by a 'transference-neurosis' of which [they] can be cured by the therapeutic work" (154).

What is a "transference-neurosis"? Is it, as the term implies, a special type of neurosis? If so, then why does Freud refer to this new neurosis as an *artificial* illness and not the real McCoy? In fact, he admits that "it is a piece of real experience, but one which has been made possible by especially favorable conditions" (154). In other words, the transference-neurosis, despite its name, isn't a neurosis at all, but another edition of the "positive transference." The (misleading) term *transference-neurosis* simply refers to the attachment patients develop with their analyst in the course of their collaboration together, epitomized by the genuine affection that is elicited. But if it isn't a neurosis, why do we need to be "cured" of it? Why not let it persist, if it's gotten rid of the neurosis it's replaced? Because of the attachment itself. What can we *do* with it? Once they've developed such a high regard for their therapist, how can they say good-bye? The problem of separation has always plagued them. How will they handle it now? The transference-neurosis might just as easily have been called "termination neurosis" because the problem from which it derives concerns a relationship whose goal is its eventual completion. Every analysis has to end. To experience—and resist—such feelings of affection, dependence, reliance, devotion, and longing only to give it all up confronts analytic patients with a poignancy and depth of sacrifice that until now they have never been able to understand.

If the transference-neurosis isn't actually neurotic, the manner in which analytic patients embrace the magnitude of this very special attachment and, alternately, defend themselves against it invariably occasion all the neurotic inclinations in their arsenal. These tendencies need to be noted, confronted, and ultimately resolved. This is why the depth of one's transference—both in its neurotic and "positive" aspects—preoccupied Freud so. His analysis of Dora failed to develop the kind of positive transference Freud subsequently realized was essential to a successful outcome. She suffered "transferences," but did she develop a *transference-neurosis?* Apparently not, because her attachment to Freud never really developed. She kept him at arms-length and then, without warning, terminated the treatment. Even her unanticipated return elicited no feelings of regret or remorse, which was why Freud declined to resume her analysis. She simply failed to develop the kind of attachment that was vital for a fruitful prognosis.

Once a transference-neurosis has formed and the consequent attachment is sufficiently strong to reprise our most obstinate conflicts, then what? Freud conceived the work of analysis in terms of one's agreement to free associate, to speak with candor irrespective of the feelings aroused. Hence, the principal resistance to analysis is *loss* of candor. What if resistance persists, even after having been interpreted? Some of Freud's colleagues complained that interpreting a resistance didn't always make it disappear, as they had hoped. Sometimes resistance even grew stronger. The analysis would come to a virtual halt and seemed to get stuck. But Freud replies that

> this gloomy foreboding always proved mistaken. The treatment was as a rule progressing most satisfactorily. The analyst had merely forgotten that giving the resistance a name could not result in its immediate cessation. One must allow the patient time to become more conversant with this resistance with which he has now become acquainted, to *work through* it, to

overcome it, by continuing, in defiance of it, the analytic work according to the fundamental rule of analysis. (155; emphasis in original)

This brief remark comprises as exhaustive a definition of "working-through" as Freud ever gave. When he uses words like the "struggle" and the "effort" required to get through it, working-through conjures the notion of a battle that the analyst promotes and is even involved in, to help "overcome" the patient's resistances. Some analysts perceive an unanalytic dimension to Freud's work, epitomized by his conception of working through. Gray, for example, suggests that the terms "to 'work upon,' to 'overcome,' to 'deal with' the resistances, involve technical measures that are often different from those used in *analyzing* defenses" (1982, 630). Gray believes these terms reveal an implicit authoritarian dimension to Freud's technique. Rather than employing specifically analytic devices, he claims that Freud resorted to suggestion, even imploring his patients to simply abandon their resistances willy-nilly.

When we examine Freud's terms more closely, however, Gray's claims begin to look suspect. For example, Freud suggested that the analyst "must allow the patient time to become more conversant" (1958h, 155) with his resistances once they're pointed out to him. What does "becoming more conversant" mean? He presumably doesn't mean that the analyst should talk about the resistance more — what Gray refers to as "analyzing" it. He suggests, instead, that we allow the patient sufficient *time* to establish a relationship with it, to think about it, to dwell on it and allow the idea of it to sink in. This is what genuinely experiencing something means, to succumb to it, gradually, over time. Benefitting from experience by allowing it sufficient rope plays a critical role in Freud's conception of psychical change. The passage of time is pivotal if we want to permit experience to have its say. In an earlier study (Thompson 1985, 170–73) I discussed at greater length the nature of experience in Heidegger's conception of language. Like Montaigne, Heidegger describes experience in terms that are more evocative than how we customarily conceive it. Experience doesn't just happen, willy-nilly. We have to put our hearts into it and actually *undergo* our experiences, whether they pertain to language, suffering, thoughts, or a psychoanalysis. For example, in *On the Way to Language* (1971), Heidegger explains that "When we talk of 'undergoing' an experience, we mean specifically that the experience is not of our own making; to undergo here means that we endure it, suffer it, receive it as it strikes us and submit to it. It is this something itself that comes about, comes to pass, happens" (57).

In other words, experience is transformative. When I truly experience something I'm affected by it. It comes as a shock. Experience violates the familiar world I inhabit by forcing something unexpected into consciousness. Because experience is inherently unsettling, it's also revelatory. It reveals things I hadn't realized. We can even begin to approach our experiences with this in mind. This is why Heidegger believed we can prepare ourselves for undergoing an experience, purposefully, deliberately, thoughtfully. My experience is something I always have a hand in. The degree to which I willingly submit to my experiences determines how fully I experience. But because experiences are transformative, I tend to resist them and hold back. Sometimes I suppress my experience of something because it arouses anxiety. I may even repress the memory of experiences that I've had, in order to "forget" them.

If experience, by its nature, occasions change and arouses anxiety, we can appreciate how vital experience becomes to the analytic process, and why we resist it. Psychoanalysis advocates change. It exploits experience and encourages us to submit to whatever our experiences disclose. This was how Freud characterized the nature of compliance to the analytic process. The more we're able to "give in" to it, the more we'll get out of it. The positive transference is the first step, in effect, of undergoing an experience with psychoanalysis. The transference neurosis is an escalation of that experience, when we begin to *suffer* it. To experience something entails giving oneself to it, heart and soul. We succumb to the idea of it and the feelings that are aroused. Some of these feelings are painful and we resist them. We employ repression and a variety of resistances against anything that alerts us to them. Freud's characterization of "making the unconscious conscious" is only achieved by submitting to those experiences that, however painful, put us in touch with the deepest levels of our being. When we resist them, a part of our subjectivity is negated. We're unable to situate ourselves in history. We can't say who we are exactly. By undergoing an experience with our *self* as it unfolds, we inhabit our history and come to terms with it. We finally realize what our suffering and our existence are about.

This was what Freud meant by working-through. Our resistance to psychoanalysis occasions certain truths that, as they become known, overwhelm us. It takes time to accept something we've always been predisposed against. Even if we recognize a resistance intellectually when it's pointed out to us, we don't necessarily believe it. Truths aren't always easy to accept. We need time to become conversant with our resistances and the truths they keep hidden. We accomplish this, according to Freud, by plodding along with the analysis—free association—*despite* the resistances that inhibit our capacity for candor. In other words, Freud conceived of working-through as literally "working"—obeying the fundamental rule—"through" our resistance *to be* candid. It isn't as important to understand why we're employing resistance or where the resistance originated as it is to maintain our allegiance to the analytic process, however difficult it becomes. Rather than searching for explanations about the sources of resistance (by "analyzing" it), we strive to become more disciplined about our capacity for candor. Yet, resistance to candor is never finally defeated. When Freud talks about "overcoming" *(Überwinden)* resistances, he doesn't mean that we simply put them behind us. Instead, we *come to grips* with them. In the same way that overcoming a loss entails the acceptance of loss, overcoming a resistance implies an acceptance of our ambivalence toward suffering. Though Gray suggests that this attitude is unanalytic, it actually epitomizes the analytic perspective. We overcome our resistances and work through them by giving them the time and attention they require, by persisting in spite of hardships along the way.

Yet, how could Freud insist on *maintaining* candor when resistance is specifically employed to circumvent it? He recognized many types of resistance to uncovering the truth about ourselves. We know that transference may serve as resistance (Freud regreted that he hadn't interpreted Dora's transference to her sooner). Repression is another. Secondary gains also act as resistance, as well as the kind of guilt that forbids us from feeling deserving of a successful outcome to treatment. Virtually all so-called defenses can be employed as resistances, but only when they serve a specific purpose of subverting the fundamental rule of analysis. However much we resist this rule, in however many ways, the acknowledgment that it warrants our compliance is the only way out of neurotic impasse.

Ironically, criticisms like Gray's miss the essential point of Freud's conception of psychoanalysis. Despite his accusations of implied authoritarianism, analyzing resistances—relentlessly exploring their source—is even more so because it incites therapeutic ambition. Working-through implores us, thé therapists, to allow resistance its say and even persist, if need be, until it runs its course. In fact, "the doctor [analyst] has nothing else to do than to wait and let things take their course, a course that cannot be avoided nor always hastened" (1958h, 155). This paper, more than any that Freud wrote, explores the nature of time and shows how critical it is to the actual work of analysis, even more than its theory. The three concepts that comprise this paper serve to situate the significance of time in the analytic experience. "Remembering"- alludes to an existential conception of memory that transcends our conventional notions about the nature of cognition. It alludes to the manner in which Being takes hold of our histories and—with or without our compliance—"reminds" us of what really matters. "Repeating" shows how desperately we cling to our origins in spite of every effort to forget them. When we try to obliterate the past we only assault the cohesion of the present, because the past is so central to who I am. It can't be changed *or* forgotten. And finally, "working-through" shows how our experience of psychoanalysis entails a relationship with time. Because analysis is a process, it unfolds *in* time. How will we ever come to experience what we were unable to succumb to in the first place, if we don't let it be what it is?

Ultimately, psychoanalysis is a device, a contrivance that arranges for time to employ its effect on us. The couch, the inexorable yet arresting pace, the pregnant pauses that epitomize its odd conversational conventions, are all ruses that Freud devised to resurrect our neglected relationship with time. Remarkably few psychoanalysts have emphasized this temporal dimension to Freud's thought. Perhaps it took someone like Loewald, who studied with Heidegger, to recognize the philosophical dimension of Freud's most radical ideas. In a recent tribute to his work, Leavy examines how Loewald integrated his understanding of time, derived from Heidegger, into Freud's basic concepts. He notes, for example, "in 'Superego and Time', Loewald proposed that psychic structures are temporal in nature" (Leavy 1989, 238). And, "we learn that the past, although we think of it as fixed if we conceive it only objectively . . . is subject to influence by the present, as the psychoanalytic rewriting of history amply demonstrates" (238). Loewald's collected papers, a treasure-trove of "correct" psychoanalytic erudition, reveal an unexpected depth of philosophical reflection. In "Psychoanalysis as an Art and the Fantasy Character of the Psychoanalytic Situation" (Loewald 1980), Loewald—in a manner that is reminiscent of Heidegger's critique of science (see chapter 8)—depicts psychoanalysis as an art. The inherently existential element in his views are striking, especially in his references to the nature of time.

> The psychoanalyst, then . . . promotes that regression which conjoins the patient's experiential past (memories and fantasies) with his experiential present—the actuality of the analytic situation—so that they tend to become one. . . . In doing so, the analyst helps the patient to re-establish connections, links between these different facets of reality, links that give renewed meaning to memories and fantasy life and to the patient's actual life in the present. (367)

Terms like "experiential past" and "the actuality of the analytic situation" show the facility with which Loewald emphasizes the existential significance of these time-laden terms. Psychoanalysis isn't a "phantasy situation"—it's *real*. He goes on to suggest that "the resolution of the transference neurosis surely does not consist of removed repression or any ultimate relinquishment of recovered memories and fantasies, but of employing them, revived and made available for development and change in *the transference play, in actual living*" (367–68; emphasis added). Referring to "transference play"—an expression Freud alluded to in his paper on working-through—as another term for "actual living" dispels the common assumption that the transference isn't real just because it derives from a remote past. Loewald recognizes, as does Leavy (1980, 86–117), how one's conception of time can transform our understanding of Freud's concepts. That is because transference, repetition, memory, working-through, and regression are all concepts whose comprehension relies on our personal *experience* of time and the way it structures our existence.

Freud didn't actually discover the significance of the relationship between temporality and experience. He simply seized on it and made it an instrument of the analytic experience. Leavy points out that the relationship between one's personal history and one's experience was appreciated as early as Hippocrates, if not earlier.

> At least as early as Hippocrates' time, it was recognized that human nature is not limited to that which can be observed by the examination of the body. Human nature is historical, and the first part of the examination, then as now, consisted of a history, an *anamnesis* as it is still called, which means a calling to mind of a person's past. Nor did Hippocrates make this *anamnesis* just a listing of earlier symptoms or earlier diseases; *it is also an*

account of his experiences, so far as they are thematically pertinent. (1980, 8; emphasis added]

Without this understanding, Freud's concepts can become confusing. Sometimes his own concepts—the products of a relentlessly fertile mind—betray him. The structural model, which only emerged some seven years after the "technical papers" were written (*after* all his major cases were published), was meant to show the diversity of what we ordinarily call "subjectivity." The tripartite structure was intended to help the analyst appreciate the immense subtlety with which unconscious inclinations emerge throughout the course of analytic treatment. As a concept, however, the structural model was a failure. It had virtually no impact on Freud's technique. Even his final technical paper, "Analysis Terminable and Interminable" (1964a), added nothing in the way of alterations in his technique as a consequence of the newer, tripartite structure. On the other hand, this conceptual shift has caused immeasurable damage. Instead of encouraging analysts to develop an appreciation of the unbeknownst motives that structure one's *being,* it has virtually reduced our unconscious to "mechanisms" that simply govern the mind. The difference is remarkable. In its wake, the structural model has led to the development of increasingly conceptual, impersonal theories that require de-personalized techniques to complement them. Because Freud set this in motion, his name lends credence to their legitimacy—while he is condemned for not having followed them himself! (see chapter 24).

This was why Freud's efforts to translate his conception of resistance into the framework of the structural model weren't always successful. In *Inhibitions, Symptoms, and Anxiety* (published in 1926) he proposed that three types of resistance—transference, repression, and secondary gain— are governed by the ego, but that two others—the employment of guilt and the repetition compulsion—are governed by the superego and id respectively (1959a, 160). This outline is remarkable because of Freud's refusal to equate resistance with "ego defenses," even this late in his career. The so-called id defense—repetition—for example, can only be resolved by *working through* one's resistance, because that specific form of resistance doesn't actually derive from the ego. Consequently, any attempt to analyze a form of resistance that, instead, derives from the id would be futile. This qualification has been dismissed by proponents of "defense analysis" who, like Gray, mistakenly equate (the ego's) defenses with (all forms of) resistance. On the other hand, Freud's efforts to integrate his earlier conception of resistance into a structure as convoluted as his tripartite model only goes to show how confused we are liable to get if we take his speculations too literally.

Freud didn't have tricks up his sleeve. He never thought of himself as a particularly clever analyst. Hence, he is frequently depicted as having been ineffectual. Each time a young gun comes up with a newer theory or technical innovation, he claims to have done work that is "better" or more "effective" than Freud's. More effective to what end? Newer analytic theories and the techniques they employ don't always imply progress. Often, these innovations are a tribute to analytic hubris. Sometimes the acceptance of limits—ours as well as our patients'—is all we can do. Isn't that, in fact, what it's about?

V

THE RAT MYSTERY

When you hear of Freud's influence today it's almost always in association with his treatment of hysterics. Nearly all his early patients were diagnosed as suffering from hysterical symptoms. When he inaugurated his medical career Freud hoped to achieve notoriety by breaking new ground in the treatment of this heretofore "incurable" illness. We sometimes forget, however, that Freud's theoretical formulations about obsessional neurosis represented an even more original contribution to psychiatry than his work with hysterics. While the phenomenon of, and the actual term for, hysteria has been around since the Greeks, Freud was the first to demarcate obsessional neurosis as a nosological entity worth special attention.

Though Freud only finally gained a wide degree of attention for his theories about obsessionality with the publication of the "Rat Man's" analysis in 1909, he isolated obsessional neurosis earlier still in an 1894 paper titled, "The Neuro-Psychoses of Defense" (1955). Laplanche and Pontalis note that "since that time the specificity of obsessional neurosis has become a more and more certain tenet of psycho-analytic theory" (1973, 282). While Freud was the first to isolate obsessional neurosis nosologically, he wasn't the first to confront it as a phenomenon. Janet, for example, included some of its features under his diagnosis for "psychasthenia," though it hardly presented as clear a picture as we have now come to recognize under the rubric, obsessionality. Outside the medical community, also, obsessional character types have been noted and described, especially in literature and philosophy. Michel de Montaigne, for example, in his seventeenth-century essay "Of Experience," was obviously describing the obsessional character when he said that men do not recognize the natural disease of their mind: it does nothing but ferret and search, and is incessantly beating the bush and idly obstructing and impeding itself by its work, and stifles itself therein like our silk-worms: *like a mouse in a pitch-barrel* [Erasmus]. It thinks that it beholds far off I know not what glimmer of light and fancied truth. But while the mind hastens there, so many difficulties block its path with obstacles and new quests, that they turn it from the path, bewildered. (1925, 4: 294)

Today, obsessionality enjoys a privileged status in the corpus of analytic literature and theory. Side by side with hysteria, the two very nearly comprise the entirety of what we have come to identify as "the neuroses." Yet, outside the analytic community the neuroses have all but vanished, displaced by the American Psychiatric Association's emphasis on a plethora of pathological disorders, a litany of literally hundreds of diagnostic entities that have actually abandoned Freud's painstaking efforts to distinguish between the neuroses and her close cousin, the psychoses. Now, even within the analytic mainstream, attention has increasingly shifted to an area of psychopathology that replaces the distinction between neurosis and psychosis with new nosological categories that essentially obfuscate the two with a hybrid: the so-called narcissistic and borderline conditions.

The training of psychoanalysts, however, is still preoccupied with the treatment of what is customarily called the "classical" pathologies, hysterical and obsessional neuroses. When we look for distinctions between obsessionality and hysteria in the literature, we often find that the latter is depicted as the "feminine neurosis." This doesn't imply, however, that only women are hysterics, though at one time this was commonly believed. Nor does it suggest that obsessionality is the "male" neurosis. It is remarkable, however, when formulating the etiology and symptomatic expression of an individual's neurosis, the degree to which gender identification and sexual symptomatology figure into his or her diagnosis, whether the one or the other. At the same time, whether a person is diagnosed as suffering from a hysterical neurosis or an obsessional one, everybody possesses elements of both, so differential diagnosis isn't that simple. It is remarkable, nevertheless, the preponderance of masculine features we typically note in women who are diagnosed the obsessional type, and the feminine features that figure so prominently in men with whom we identify the hysterical character. The more we associate either of these neuroses with characterological aspects of the personality, the more "genderized" the diagnosis becomes.

But does diagnosis, itself, really make much sense, anyhow? It was Freud himself who established the elaborate and enormously complicated diagnostic criteria that now serve as the foundation for contemporary psychoanalytic nomenclature. In fact, it's hard to imagine what a psychoanalytic treatment would look like without its customary diagnostic presuppositions. But Freud tended to paint his canvas with broad strokes and, as we know, when it came to making distinctions—whether between one form of neurosis and another, or between vast regions of pathologies, the neuroses and psychoses—things became distinctly ambiguous. It's ironic that the analytic community, in its evolution since Freud, has become increasingly intolerant of those ambiguities, an aversion that is itself sometimes associated with obsessionality!

And what would Freud make of the "newer" pathologies that have recently emerged, the narcissistic and borderline conditions? More and more it seems that every neurotic, on closer examination, is a closet narcissistic or borderline type. Increasingly, neurosis, as an entity for treatment, is disappearing. It seems that the only place we are sure to encounter a hysteric or obsessional neurotic is amongst analytic candidates in training—both the patients being treated *and* their therapists. What accounts for the gradual disappearance of the typical, classical neurotic in contemporary analytic literature? Perhaps the following observations will prove suggestive:

1. Our Western culture—particularly American culture—seems to be fascinated with the concept of narcissism. Its features are easily recognized in virtually all neurotics, but until recently they hadn't seemed as prevalent, nor did they appear to be specifically "pathological." Freud, for example, refused to equate lying or other aspects of poor character—typical features of these newer pathologies—with psychopathology, per se; nor did he believe they were treatable. While this diagnosis is becoming increasingly fashionable, it's acknowledged that its curability is dubious at best. Nonetheless, its newfound acceptance in the analytic community as a treatable diagnosis conveniently opens the door to thousands of previously "unanalyzable" patients.

2. More and more, the typical candidate for analytic training is identifiable as an "obsessional type": serious, determined to succeed, dedicated to a mission, self-sacrificing, humorless, resourceful, studious. Many of the features that characterize the development of psychoana-

lytic theorizing, writing, and technique since Freud's death could be viewed in terms of values that are consistent with those of the obsessional character: (a) aloofness and detachment in technique, characterized by increasing emphasis on the prevalence of neutrality and abstinence (and the colorless reinterpretation of their original meaning); (b) the gradual elimination of the personal dimension of analysis—a typical obsessional fear in *any* relationship; (c) the neglect of emotion in analytic theory and in the analyst's behavior, consigning its manifestation to exclusively "unconscious processes" in the form of transference and countertransference (even the analytic term *affect* demonstrates the uneasiness with this phenomenon); (d) the increased rigidity in training curricula, reducing study to standardized norms that are easier to transmit, yet more complex in their conception; (e) the increasing emphasis on the so-called scientific aspects of the analytic relationship as well as the technique that is supposed to contain it; (f) the increased efforts to isolate "pure" psychoanalysis from techniques that are said to dilute it—specifically those that expose the personality of the analyst; (g) the inexorable increase in the amount of time that is required to complete analysis, suggesting an obsessional preoccupation with perfection; (h) the growing pessimism in the literature concerning the possibility of a structural change in one's personality, epitomized by the bias against treating psychoses; (i) and finally, the tendency to decry experimentation in the development of analytic technique in favor of fidelity to established orthodoxy, perpetuating "correct" analytic behavior.

3. Analysts who exhibit hysterical—or histrionic—personalities rarely assume the mantle of training analyst. Sandor Ferenczi, Wilhelm Reich, and Jacques Lacan are notable examples of once-prestigious training analysts who fell from the graces of the International Psychoanalytic Association. All exhibited marked hysterical personalities. Today, it would be extremely unlikely that any of them would have ever become training analysts in the first place.

This brief list of obsessional—that is, rigid—bias in the analytic community serves as a provocative backdrop to Freud's treatment of obsessional neurosis and the analytic community's response to it. The analytic "culture" of today, as we know it, has incorporated many of the common features of obsessional character. This bias is so commonplace in the culture at large that Hans Loewald even referred to it as the "normal neurosis" (see chapter 2). Perhaps, for this reason, one is inclined to favor other diagnoses to treat when this one is so close to home.

Meanwhile, psychoanalytic teachers and their candidates in training feel increasingly attracted to theories and techniques that suit the kind of person who wants things neat and tidy, devoid of ambiguity, taught in rotelike fashion. In turn, Freud's behavior must seem astonishing to many young analysts who are confounded by his relatively loose technique and the degree to which he shared his personality with his patients. Given the manner in which they're taught, his behavior surely comes off as unanalytic. It's ironic that Freud's treatment of obsessionals—exemplified in his analysis of the Rat Man (and later, the Wolf Man)—occasions a loosening of analytic technique, incorporating unabashedly freewheeling interventions. Apparently, Freud believed that obsessionals, of all people, could benefit from a relaxation of technique, something less than total abstention, where neutrality wasn't applied to every single facet of the treatment. While a preponderance of such behavior with hysterics may be construed as seductive, Freud apparently believed that overt demonstrations of kindness, generosity, and compassion were useful in the treatment of obsessional patients.

Freud began his analysis of Ernst Lanzer in October 1907, two years after the publication of Dora's analysis. He called Lanzer "the man with the rats" in deference to one of his more bizarre obsessional symptoms. The publication of this case was intended to complement his exposition of Dora, only now it would articulate Freud's understanding about the nature and treatment of an obsessional neurotic. In fact, according to Jones, "Freud expressed his opinion that for the study of unconscious processes the investigation of this neurosis was more instructive than that of hysteria" (1955, 2: 262). Jones was obviously impressed with Freud's account of the case, when he said that "Freud's analytic powers showed at their best in his unraveling of this case. His delicate and ingenious interpretation and elucidation of the most torturous mental processes, with their subtle play on words and thoughts, must evoke admiration and were hardly surpassed in any other of his writings" (263).

Jones is frequently accused of acting as Freud's apologist, of having always colored his mentor in a favorable light, of offering opinions that were highly subjective. But his assessment of Freud's remarkable presentation of Lanzer's analysis has never been contested, even by those who believe that its conclusion was less successful than Freud claimed. Its manner of composition and use of the material was a masterful tour de force. Of his five major cases (Freud didn't actually treat "Little Hans" or Judge Schreber), Freud's treatment of the Rat Man was the only one that he believed was an unqualified success.

Peter Gay, whose impressive biography is less prone to accusation of bias in Freud's favor, also concurs that his treatment of the Rat Man should be acknowledged as an astonishing achievement:

> Freud's account remains exemplary as an exposition of a classic obsessional neurosis. It brilliantly served to buttress Freud's theories, notably those postulating the childhood roots of neurosis, the inner logic of the most flamboyant and most inexplicable symptoms, and the powerful, often hidden, pressures of ambivalent feelings. Freud was not masochist enough to publish only failures. (1988, 267)

Unfortunately, Lanzer died just a few years after the analysis was terminated while fighting in World War I. We have no way of knowing if he would have suffered relapse had he lived longer, as some have conjectured. Others suggest that the analysis wasn't "deep" by today's standards and amounted to little more than a psychoanalytic "psychotherapy." Freud, however, never wavered from his assessment that the treatment was a shining demonstration of his clinical technique. Yet, the case is extraordinarily complex, so much so that Freud was concerned no one outside his inner circle could follow it. According to Gay,

> the material the Rat Man scattered with such abandon—material strange, copious, apparently pointless—threatened to elude Freud's control. He complained to Jung as he was completing his case history, "It is very hard for me, almost surpasses my arts of presentation, will probably be inaccessible to anyone except those closest to us." (264)

Even Jung was baffled by the case, and he complained to Ferenczi that Freud's paper, while wonderful to read, was nonetheless, "*very hard to understand*. I will soon have to read it for the third time. Am I especially stupid? Or is it the style? I cautiously opt for the latter" (264).

With all its bravura of complicated temporal connections, linguistic ellipses, and symbolic associations that challenge the imagination, it would be misleading to assume that the success of Lanzer's treatment—

as with any other—rests on the solution of puzzles or the ultimate "conquest" of the unfathomable. Of all Freud's cases, nowhere does the simplicity of his technique come through with such clarity. In Gay's words, "The point was not to set about rationally solving the puzzles that the Rat Man had set, but to let him pursue his own path—and to listen" (264).

21

The Cruel Captain

As he did with Dora, Freud reminds us in a brief introduction to his 1909 *Notes Upon a Case of Obsessional Neurosis* about the need for absolute confidentiality between analysts and their patients. Many details about patients' lives must be omitted to protect their anonymity. On the other hand, analysts shouldn't stoop to deliberate distortion of the patient's life, for analysts will run the risk of reducing their report to a fiction. It's better to omit material and live with the gaps created than to deliberately mislead and, therefore, deceive one's readers. Honesty always weighed heavily in Freud's conception of the analyst's behavior—with his peers as well as his patients. Perhaps this was why Freud chose the obviously pseudonymous "Rat Man" rather than another common name—such as Dora—with which to introduce this patient to his readers.

When turning to the treatment of obsessions, Freud warns that severe cases are virtually impossible to cure. Even moderate cases aren't that easy to understand. When we try to gain access to its meaning it is helpful to think of obsessional neurosis as a counterpart to hysteria because "the language of an obsessional neurosis—the means by which it expresses its secret thoughts—is, as it were, only a dialect of hysteria" (1955c, 156–7). This is because the dialect of each serves the same end, to conceal the hidden device of one's suffering and, by that concealment, protect it from discovery.

Ernst Lanzer—the Rat Man—introduced himself to Freud on the first day of October in 1907. He was twenty-nine years old and had only recently completed his law degree with difficulty. He was unmarried, though in love with a young woman, and fresh from military maneuvers in the Austrian army where he served as a reserve officer. He had suffered from obsessions since childhood but more recently they had gotten worse. He was haunted by the fear that something awful would happen to the two people whom he loved the most: his father and his girlfriend. He was seized by occasional impulses to slit his throat with a razor, yet he wrestled with guilt-ridden prohibitions against all sorts of other, seemingly trivial, activities. He felt his life had been wasted. He was hopelessly unhappy. He had only just lost his virginity at age twenty-six and felt his sexual life was unsatisfactory, even "stunted."

Freud, nonetheless, recognized in Lanzer a most remarkable young man. Clear and intelligent, he was a worthy candidate for psychoanalysis. He would prove to be the favorite of the analytic cases Freud published. Once Lanzer was accepted as Freud's patient, he began to talk about his childhood. He had been fond of a young governess, Miss Peter, who, when he was six, let him crawl beneath her dress and fondle her genitals. He loved to look at her naked body when he went with the governess and his sisters to the Baths. A subsequent governess, Miss Lina, came later, and she invited him to look and fondle her as well. He experienced erections and even complained to his mother about them. But he didn't tell his mother that what prompted his erections to occur were his secret activities with Miss Peter and Miss Lina. He subsequently became convinced that his parents could read his mind, the first indication of obsessive guilt that would gradually grow worse. He felt compelled to look at women, then suffered premonitions that his father would die. Even now, in his analysis with Freud, he was tormented by the persistent obsessive idea that some awful fate awaited his father, even though he was already dead!

Lanzer's obsessional neurosis had originated in childhood, at the age of seven. Every time the young Lanzer experienced an urge to see a girl undressed, he was gripped with the fear that something terrible would happen. Freud translated this vague premonition into a more direct statement: "If I have this wish to see a woman naked, my father will be bound to die" (163). Freud believed that all obsessions contain a superstitious component prompting fanatical contortions that are intended to ward them off. This "superstitiousness" helps to explain the obsessional's phantasies, lending this neurosis its irrational character. Another component of Lanzer's irrational beliefs was contained in his delusional conviction that his parents could read his thoughts. Freud reassures us, however, not to be alarmed by such symptoms. They're not at all uncommon in the secret lives of one's patients. Each delusion contains a meaning that, if we persist, can be uncovered.

On the second day of his analysis Lanzer recounted a horrible story that would play a crucial role in his treatment and earn the nickname that made him famous. While on maneuvers with his regiment he lost his eyeglasses but didn't want to hold the troop up by looking for them. Later he wired for new ones from his optician in Vienna. In the meantime, he was sitting one day with two officers, one of whom was a Czech captain who was known to be sadistic, even cruel. The captain proceeded to tell him about a form of punishment he had heard was used in the East. With obvious distress, Lanzer stopped his story, but continued at Freud's urging. The torture consisted in tying the criminal up and placing him face-down on the floor. Next, a pot containing some rats was turned upside down and placed on top of the prisoner's naked buttocks, the idea being that one or more of the rats would bore its way into the prisoner's anus. Lanzer, however, wasn't able to provide this last detail of the "rat torture." Freud had to finish it for him. He noticed that while Lanzer was telling his story, however, "his face took on a very strange, composite expression. I could only interpret it as one of *horror and pleasure of his own of which he himself was unaware*" (166–67).

Continuing with his story, Lanzer told Freud that when he heard the gruesome details of this torture described, the idea had flashed through his mind that something of the sort was happening to someone he loved. On further prompting, he admitted that this certain "someone" was his girlfriend. Freud surmised that the "idea" that had flashed through his mind was in fact a *wish,* but Lanzer protested. He insisted that the thought of it was absolutely repugnant. Then he admitted that his father was also an object of this fantasy. Seeing as how his father had been dead for many years when Lanzer had heard this story recounted, this part of his story was stranger still. At this point, Lanzer's story took an unexpected, even mind-boggling, turn. Later that evening, the "Cruel Captain" gave him a packet containing the glasses Lanzer had ordered. Then the captain instructed him to compensate "Lieutenant A," who had paid the charges on his (Lanzer's) behalf. When given this command, however, the thought flashed through Lanzer's mind that, in fact, he mustn't repay the debt to Lieutenant A because, if he did, his premonition that rats might penetrate his father's and his girlfriend's anuses would come true. But then a contrary command came to mind which told him: "You *must* pay back the money to Lieutenant A." What could he do? When he proceeded to repay Lieutenant A the money, he was shocked to discover that—contrary to the captain's account—he (Lieutenant A) hadn't been involved in the payment for the glasses, after all. Lieutenant A said it was Lieutenant B, not he, who paid the charges. Remarkably, Lanzer didn't feel particularly confused about the conflicting reports. Instead, he felt dismayed. This is because he was upset that the vow he made to himself earlier to repay Lieutenant A the money could no longer be obeyed, because it wasn't Lieutenant A who had loaned it to him in the first place. He wasn't concerned to simply compensate whomever it was who had paid for the glasses. He was preoccupied instead with *obeying his vow* to repay Lieutenant A, whether or not he owed him the money!

In order to repay the debt (to Lieutenant B) and at the same time obey his vow (to Lieutenant A) Lanzer arrived at an ingenious scheme. He would go to the post office with both Lieutenant A and Lieutenant B. Then he would instruct Lieutenant A to pay the post office clerk who, in turn, would give the money to Lieutenant B. Lanzer would compensate Lieutenant A for the money he had just paid the clerk thereby fulfilling his "vow," while insuring that Lieutenant B also got his money. We needn't go into the convoluted series of events that followed Lanzer's plan to bring all the parties together at the post office. They included a variety of obsessional fears, bouts of ambivalence, second thoughts, and panicked behavior. At the end of the day Lanzer failed to carry out his original plan to go to the post office with Lieutenant's A and B—he was simply too embarrassed to enlist them into his hair-brained scheme. Instead, he enlisted the aid of an old chum from Vienna, whom Lanzer trusted, to accompany him to the post office. With the help of his friend, Lanzer went to the post office and then paid the money to the clerk, a young lady who worked there. What in the world, Freud must have thought, was Lanzer doing? Why did he neither fulfill his vow to repay Lieutenant A nor satisfy his real debt to Lieutenant B? Freud then realized that Lanzer had been deceiving him. He had owed the money to the clerk who worked there, the woman, all along. The befuddling "debts" to Lieutenants A and B had been an invention! Lanzer admitted that he had known all along the debt had been paid by the post office clerk, because yet another captain had told him so before the "Cruel Captain" had relayed to him the erroneous information. In other words, he had known the true story *before* making his vow to repay Lieutenant A the debt (that in fact he didn't owe him). Freud was even more surprised by Lanzer's apparent deception—even if it was a "lie by omission"—than the obsessions themselves. Lanzer had known the truth all along, but disregarded it when making his absurd vow; and now again, when telling Freud his "story." Lanzer's neurosis harbored a tendency to avoid the truth, belying the apparent compliance he offered on the surface. Apparently, Lanzer himself wasn't all that clear what the truth was. It was "there" in his consciousness (it, in fact, had not been repressed), but then he simply ignored it when his obsessions arose. Repaying the debt to the clerk, however, didn't appease the obsessions. He considered consulting a doctor to ask him to write a letter that would "certify" the payment to Lieutenant A was part of his treatment, for the purpose of placating his symptom. When Lanzer accidentally chanced upon one of Freud's books (*The Psychopathology of Everyday Life*) he decided to look him up. He subsequently abandoned his original plan and opted instead for a course of analysis.

As the treatment continued, it became obvious that Lanzer was still quite troubled over his father's death. Suffering from a lengthy illness, the night his father passed away Lanzer had fallen asleep. He was understandably upset when he learned that his father had called out his name just before dying. His guilt was so overwhelming that he tried to deny that his father's death was even real. This was manifested in his anxiety that his father's death was imminent, as if he was still alive. Why did Lanzer feel so guilty when he was obviously blameless in his father's death? Freud proposed that the source of neurotic guilt is always unconscious. One must determine the actual source of guilt—which is hidden—and come to terms with it. Lanzer's guilt, the meaning of which had been repressed, had in turn given rise to the obsessional symptoms that now consumed all his energy.

The theme of his father's death was the pivot round which Lanzer's neurosis ultimately revolved. Freud interpreted Lanzer's fears about his father's death as disguised wishes. Lanzer protested, however, that this couldn't be. Freud suspected, in spite of his protestations, that Lanzer had repressed hateful feelings for his father that he couldn't bring himself to acknowledge. His symptoms were a form of self-punishment, permitting him to cope with his latent hostility. From a technical standpoint, Freud's advocacy of a specific interpretation—despite Lanzer's resistance—wasn't intended to convince him the interpretation was indeed "correct." He simply wanted to unearth the repressions and expose them, helping Lanzer to become acquainted with their existence: "It is never the aim of discussions like this to create conviction. They are only intended to bring the repressed complexes into consciousness, to set the conflict going in the field of conscious mental activity, and to facilitate the emergence of fresh material from the unconscious" (181).

Fresh clues about the source of his hatred came to light when Lanzer acknowledged he had felt pulled between his love for his girlfriend and his loyalty to his dying father. Six months before his father's death he had fallen in love, but because he hadn't any money he wasn't in a position to marry her. Then he got an idea: his father's death could make him rich enough to get married (179). But he fought against this "wish" with the countervailing idea that he mustn't be allowed to inherit the money after his father died. This spontaneous recollection confirmed Freud's suspicion that Lanzer had at one time believed his father was an obstacle to obtaining the woman he loved. Anyone is liable to entertain such phantasies without taking them at all seriously. Although we sometimes covet our parents' wealth, we don't necessarily wish they would die to obtain it. Lanzer's phantasy convinced Freud that the source of his guilt must have originated earlier still. Perhaps these feelings were first elicited at an age when his fidelity to his father wasn't as strong, when he loved someone else even more.

22

The Rat Mystery

Freud categorized Lanzer's obsessions into several groups, most of which referred to the chronic ambivalence he felt about his girlfriend: (a) He was obsessed with the idea that something would happen to her and felt compelled to protect her from harm; (b) he was compelled to count the time between a flash of lightning and its subsequent thunder; (c) he told Freud he had removed rocks from the road that he was certain his girlfriend's carriage would run over—then he felt obliged to replace the rocks, because removing them in the first place had been so absurd; (d) finally, he divided words into syllables, and tried to elicit the meaning of each one as though his native tongue was no longer intelligible.

Freud traced each of these obsessions—protecting, counting, obligation, understanding—to Lanzer's relationship with his girlfriend. He derived two principal conclusions about them: (a) they centered around an unconscious impulse to protect his girlfriend from harm; (b) the harm from which she needed protecting was Lanzer's own hostile feelings. Counting between lightning and thunder would somehow delay the imminent harm he might cause her. His "obligation" to replace the rock in the road was intended, not to protect her, but to upset her carriage. The need to question what others were saying was symptomatic of the chronic doubt that haunted him. His incessant study of what people were saying suggested he couldn't believe them. Freud took this to mean that Lanzer couldn't believe that his girlfriend loved him. These incessant doubts apparently accounted for his ambivalence about marriage. In fact, this ambivalence caused every one of his compulsions. This observation also provided Freud with a way of distinguishing between hysterical and obsessional neuroses in the broadest terms:

> What regularly occurs in hysteria is that a compromise is arrived at which enables both the opposing tendencies to find expression simultaneously—which kills two birds with one stone; whereas here each of the two opposing tendencies finds satisfaction singly, first one and then the other, though naturally an attempt is made to establish some sort of logical connection (often in defiance of all logic) between the antagonists. (1955c, 192)

This doesn't suggest that ambivalence is unique to obsessional neurosis. It is a feature of all neuroses, including hysteria. Dora's ambivalence about her father, for example, was more subtle. She denied her love for him altogether, while displacing that love onto her symptomatic dependence and infirmity instead, killing, as Freud says, two birds with one stone. Lanzer's ambivalence was more blatant. It lurched from one extreme to the other. He obeyed his father but defied him; he loved his girlfriend but mistrusted her. In fact, Lanzer still held a grudge from ten years earlier, when he had proposed to her and she rebuffed him. "Since then he had to his own knowledge passed through alternating periods, in which he either believed that he loved her intensely, or felt indifferent to her" (194). But why did Lanzer's mother play such an insignificant role in a neurosis that sought refuge in the woman he loved? His mother came from a wealthy family, and because of their means her father had taken his son-in-law—Lanzer's father—into the family business to insure a comfortable living. Before meeting Lanzer's mother, however, he had fallen in love with another woman whose family was not wealthy. As it happened, he eventually opted to marry the wealthier woman. After his father's death, Lanzer's mother arranged for her son to marry the daughter of one of her cousins, on the condition that Lanzer complete his studies. Like his father before him, he would be insured a prosperous future through family connections. And, like his father, he was already in love with another whose family had little to offer.

But unlike his father, Lanzer couldn't bring himself to choose between the two women. Instead, he "chose" a neurosis. He developed symptoms that incapacitated his ability to work. Consequently, he was unable to complete his studies, the precondition to marrying the woman his mother had selected for him. Lanzer was unwilling to follow in his father's footsteps and marry his designated bride, but he couldn't bring himself to boldfacedly reject what had been assigned to him. He took the only way out: the neurotic "solution."

Yet, Lanzer's procrastination disguised the real conflict that survived unconsciously: his ambivalence about his father. That was why he could neither openly defy nor give in to his parents' authority. What was the basis of this hostility that he couldn't bring himself to acknowledge? Freud believed "there can be no question that there was something in the sphere of sexuality that stood between the father and son, and that the father had come into some sort of opposition to the son's prematurely developed erotic life" (201). Lending support to Freud's suspicions, Lanzer revealed that some years *after* his father's death, when he lost his virginity, the idea spontaneously occurred to him: "This is glorious! One might murder one's father for this!" (201). Lanzer was convinced that his father stood in the way of his sexual emancipation. But why? We don't actually know. Lanzer recovered from his neurosis before Freud could discover the answer, concluding that "the therapeutic success of the treatment was precisely what stood in the way of this. . . . The scientific results of psycho-analysis are at present only a by-product of its therapeutic aims, and for that reason it is often just in those cases where treatment fails that most discoveries are made" (207–8n.).

Despite this gap in the case, Freud was able to obtain a number of clues about Lanzer's relationship with his father. For example, he discovered that Lanzer had developed a fear of his father at an early age due to a bizarre incident—when he was three or four years old—during which his father gave him a beating for having bitten one of his friends. While he was being spanked, Lanzer had flown into a rage and, not yet knowing curse words, called his father everything he could think of: "Lamp! Towel! Plate!", and so on. His father was so shocked at this outburst that he remarked: "The child will be either a great man or a great criminal!" (205).

Freud suspected that Lanzer had never forgiven his father for the spanking. After that incident, he developed a cowardly demeanor, though his father never threatened him again. His rage had been so powerful that from that moment on he became afraid *he would kill the father he loved*. In fact, not until Lanzer developed a negative transference with Freud did they reach this turning point in the analysis. It culminated in the solution to the "rat mystery" and the remission of Lanzer's neurosis. Though he resisted the notion that he harbored any animosity toward his father, he began to experience hostility against Freud in his dreams, phantasies, and associations. He became convinced that Freud wanted him to marry his own daughter, whom Lanzer insulted and ridiculed. He even avoided lying on the couch because he feared that Freud would beat him. He was actually afraid that Freud might terminate the treatment because of his mounting aggression. Freud's response, however, was benign and tolerant. Lanzer expected rejection and punishment, but he got compassion and sympathy instead. Freud apparently didn't even protest his rejection of the couch. He felt—and expressed—concern and understanding. Freud fed Lanzer when he was hungry and sent him postcards when he was away. He was anything but the punitive "father" Lanzer feared he would be.

Now a mass of material was unleashed that brought the treatment to a close. Freud concluded that Lanzer had transfered his fear of his father onto the "Cruel Captain" when he was instructed to repay Lieutenant A the (nonexistent) debt. Lanzer's father had served in the military himself and earned a reputation as something of a gambler (*spielratte* in German, literally "play-rat"). When he lost some money at cards a friend had generously covered his debt. His father, however, had never managed to repay the money in spite of his efforts to do so. Lanzer was ashamed of this seeming blemish on his father's character. When the "Cruel Captain" instructed him to repay Lieutenant A the debt which in fact he did not owe, it reminded him of his father's debt, which he also did not owe, but for which he felt guilty, nevertheless.

Then Freud learned that something had happened at the post office that Lanzer had omitted. When he visited there the first time—before ordering his new glasses—he had met yet a second woman who worked in the office above. He felt attracted to her and she, in turn, had flirted with him. To make a long story short, he couldn't choose between the two women who worked there. It reminded him of the conflict that he'd felt earlier between his girlfriend and the woman his mother wanted him to marry, and the two women between whom his father had felt torn. His neurosis then seized on the confusion of identities (between Lieutenants A and B) that the Czech Captain had created. He subsequently devised his complicated scheme on the train journey in order to get the two lieutenants together: a symbolic way of having *the two ladies.*

The solution to the rat torture now came to light. According to Freud, "The idea of the punishment carried out by means of rats had acted as a stimulus to a number of his instincts and had called up a whole quantity of recollections" (213). Upon hearing the "Cruel Captain's" account of the torture, all sorts of symbolic associations had been unleashed explaining the compulsive nature of his obsessions and his transference with the Captain. The word *rats* (*ratten* in German) aroused Lanzer's latent anal erotism from his childhood. By extension, it stirred up his fixation with money, which had played such a critical role in his efforts to acquire it. The Captain's "order" to pay Lieutenant A the postal charges had brought to mind his father's unpaid gambling debt to the friend who had covered his losses. As we saw earlier, the German *Spielratte*—a colloquial expression for a gambler—had flashed into Lanzer's mind when he heard the Captain recounting the rat torture. He produced a chain of associations between "rats" and "worms"—and by extension, "penises"—all alluding to the spanking incident with his father. Even a story by Ibsen— *Little Eyolf*—which featured a "Rat-wife," figured into Lanzer's memories of his childhood at a time when he had actually identified with rats. And don't forget that when his father spanked him it was for having bitten someone with his teeth!

The elaborate interplay between Lanzer's obsessions and the compulsive behavior they elicited is typical of how obsessional neurosis becomes manifest. Unlike hysteria in which one's "obsessions" are effectively repressed, Lanzer was fully conscious of the ideas that compelled him to obey or resist. But he couldn't put the myriad components of his compulsive acts together, because he had unconsciously isolated the one from the other. His consequent confusion was a form of "not-knowing"—a failure of reflection—that epitomizes the obsessional thought process in its essence.

Freud concluded that the cruelty Lanzer noted in the Czech officer reminded him of the humiliation he experienced when his father had spanked him. The hatred that was unleashed toward his father when he was punished was subsequently displaced onto the Captain. Though he knew the Captain was mistaken when he said that Lieutenant A had paid his debt, he opted to obey his command to the letter, knowing he couldn't genuinely do so. This must have been a repetition, Freud believed, of how the young Lanzer had felt when he was being spanked. He would "obey" his father to the letter, but hold something back as he had done with the Captain. His ostensible act of obedience to an authority whom he hated allowed Lanzer to obey and defy simultaneously. Because he was unable to defy his father's authority, his suppressed anger had no other recourse than the symptomatic solution his neurosis handily provided.

23

Guilt and Truth

Freud's solution to the rat torture led to the disappearance of Lanzer's rat fixation and its accompanying obsessional symptoms. Yet, Freud was reluctant to conclude that the spanking incident, in and of itself, had "caused" his neurotic condition in the first place. There are other elements of the case that hint at possible explanations, though Freud himself doesn't appear to have taken them into account. For example, he failed to exploit the theme of the naked buttocks that proliferated throughout Lanzer's accounts of his childhood, culminating in his encounter with the "Cruel Captain." Freud concurred that the spanking incident had unleashed such fury against Lanzer's father that it surely made an indelible impression. But he didn't attribute to this incident the specifically erotic etiology that was subsequently manifested in his symptoms. Remember that soon after the spanking incident, the young Lanzer became attracted to the naked buttocks of his governess, Miss Peter (when he was four or five years old). His obsession with bare buttocks apparently began immediately after he was spanked. When he was six, his fascination with buttocks survived the departure of the first governess and persisted with Miss Lina, her replacement. By now, he was tormented by feelings of guilt and convinced his parents could read his mind. A connection had been established in his mind between the governess's sexually alluring buttocks and *his*, which his father had spanked. Subsequently, whenever he was sexually aroused he became anxious.

When Lanzer first heard the "Cruel Captain's" account of the rat torture, inflicted on the naked buttocks of the prisoners, he was panic stricken. Upon telling Freud of this episode, he actually called Freud his "Captain" and couldn't complete the story. Lanzer's sexual fantasies about naked buttocks were obviously linked in his memory to having been spanked himself. But this never came out in the analysis. Yet, he was cured without this crucial point having been made. How was this possible? Lanzer was cured in spite of this mystery having never been solved, ironically—due to the cure—because the success of the treatment led to its termination. As with Dora, Lanzer's analysis was abandoned just when events were unfolding toward a potentially decisive resolution. But in his case the termination was the consequence of having been cured, despite the incompleteness of his analysis. What does this tell us about the nature of the analytic "cure"? What accounted for his remarkable recovery, if not the ultimate solution to his condition? Is one's understanding of why a person becomes neurotic an aid to recovery, or merely a complement to it that is valued more highly by the psychoanalyst? If "solutions" aren't necessarily decisive, what is?

The answer, according to Freud, was the resolution to Lanzer's transference, to the degree it was possible given the length of his treatment. In other words, Lanzer's cure was the direct consequence of resolving his negative transference with Freud. We see this point emerge three years later as a guiding principle in "The Dynamics of Transference" (1958a), and later, in "On Beginning the Treatment" (1958e). There, Freud emphasizes how analysis obtains its cure through the transference, not "intellectual" understanding. In fact, the need to "understand" everything to the "*n*th" degree was one of Lanzer's obsessional symptoms. Freud confessed that abandoning this point of view was a major shift from the way psychoanalysis had previously been conceived in its earliest days.

What is "transference"? According to Freud, "a proper rapport with one's patient" (1958e, 139). But isn't the negative transference a breakdown in that rapport? Not necessarily. In Lanzer's case, it was due to his positive regard for his analyst that he was able to permit his negative transference to emerge in the first place. Otherwise, he might have continued to suppress those feelings, as was his custom. That doesn't mean his negative feelings, when they finally arose, were of little consequence. The transference was so powerful, so irrational, that Freud called it delusional. Lanzer began to fear what (he thought) Freud might do if he discovered the terrible things he was thinking. In fact, Freud's ability to accept Lanzer's paranoid accusations without protest gave his patient the freedom to allow those thoughts and feelings their say. The freedom to *feel* hateful when one does, and to *be* hateful when one is gives us the opportunity to experience ourselves as we are. In this lies the path to our quest for sanity: the acceptance of ourselves by another. Once Lanzer was convinced that Freud's acceptance of him was "unconditional"—that he didn't have to be a certain way to win his approval—there was nothing more he needed to "understand." His puzzles required no further solution.

Yet, puzzling together over the intricacies of Lanzer's neurosis comprised a significant part of their collaborative work, allowing for a context through which their rapport could evolve. On the other hand, it was Freud's capacity for compassion and his unusual interest in the details of Lanzer's suffering that provided the much-needed foil against his (Lanzer's) incessant doubts, uncertainty, and mistrust. Even Lanzer's attacks on Freud's daughter failed to arouse his disfavor. Freud's patient understanding helped Lanzer accept the inherent safety of the situation, despite his emerging hostility. Freud had succeeded in instigating, in effect, a "cure through love" and with it a turning point in his own thinking. Freud's growing appreciation for the significance of transference—another word for "love"—was the key to the Rat Man's successful termination. He realized that the efficacy of psychoanalysis isn't based on the relative "understanding" of one's plight. It is based on one's capacity for love, embodied in the transference situation where patients enjoy the freedom to simply *tell the truth* to another person. We can see why Lanzer was his favorite patient. He demonstrated to Freud that nothing is more imperative to the psychoanalytic experience than the rapport that passes between the two participants. In other words, by shifting the goal of analysis from the search for solutions to the resolution of transference, the analyst's behavior shifted from determining causation to instilling rapport.

Lanzer employed a considerable degree of intrigue, deception, and subterfuge to disguise the details of his past. This was a form of resistance, but Freud didn't interpret it as such. Why? Lanzer believed he couldn't let anyone know what he was thinking. This is a common feature of obsessional neurosis. It parallels a similar theme that emerged in Freud's analysis of Dora. She couldn't let anyone know who she loved. Unlike Dora, however, Lanzer sought to be candid and cooperated with the treatment, but he twisted events in his mind so that the "truth" was hard to obtain. Instead of analyzing Lanzer's resistances, Freud decided to wait and give the truth enough time to emerge of its own accord. Similarly, when Lanzer developed a negative transference and even questioned Freud's intentions, Freud decided against analyzing the transference as a form of resistance. In fact, Freud's seeming indulgence of Lanzer's behavior was the catalyst for his subsequent recovery. Because Lanzer was so anxious that his thoughts might be discovered, Freud didn't want to appear confrontational. He allowed Lanzer the time he needed to work through his feelings and overcome his suspicions. In other words, it was the opportunity that Freud gave Lanzer to reveal himself over time and, in turn, Freud's ability to elicit those revelations in the first place that finally cured his neurosis. This is why the specific "truths" that Lanzer concealed, in and of themselves, weren't that important. Rather, it was his propensity to hide things in principle that gave rise to his neurotic conflicts.

Lanzer's inability to trust his feelings epitomized the most prevalent theme that emerged during the course of his analysis, the relationship between guilt and truth. In the theoretical portion of Freud's account of the analysis, he went to some lengths to explore the remarkable capacity for uncertainty and doubt that characterizes obsessional neurosis and, by extension, its relationship to guilt. Like Dora, Lanzer became convinced at a very young age that he had to hide the truth and hide from the truth because it was dangerous. His greatest fear was that people would learn what he was thinking because, if they did, they would uncover the terrible secret he was hiding: the hate he felt for his father.

He couldn't tolerate any hint of resentment for the father he so adored, so he repressed it. He became secretive and engaged in intrigues, which he used to displace his aggression onto seemingly unrelated events. He was consumed with uncertainty and inhibited his aggression so successfully he assumed the affect of a coward. A coward is someone who lacks courage; literally, a person who *can't love*. As Freud explained, "The *doubt* corresponds to the patient's internal perception of his [her] own indecision, which, in consequence of the inhibition of his love by his hatred, takes possession of him in the face of every intended action. The doubt is in reality a *doubt of his own love*" (1955e, 241; emphasis added).

According to Freud, Lanzer used his doubt and uncertainty to protect himself from reality, a reality whose implications he could barely tolerate. Freud observed that "the creation of uncertainty is one of the methods employed by the neurosis for drawing the patient away from *reality* and isolating him from the world—which is among the objects of every psychoneurotic disorder" (232). In other words, Lanzer's chronic sense of doubt was a manifestation of his guilt toward his father. Freud elaborated his theory about guilt later in *Totem and Taboo* (1958i), but the essence of those views is contained in his critique of Lanzer's pathological conflicts.

Guilt and ambivalence are closely related, but obviously they are not the same. Dora was ambivalent about her relationship with her father but, unlike Lanzer, she didn't experience any guilt as a consequence of her contempt for him. This is made clearer by the way Freud conceptualized the relationship between the two. Ambivalence is the consequence of the conflict between love and repression. Dora loved her father, but she repressed it because it frustrated her so. Consequently, she was ambivalent about the nature of her attachment to him. She loved him but convinced herself that she didn't. On the other hand, Lanzer loved his father, but hated him, too. He never actually denied—as Dora did—that he loved him. In his case, it was his hostile feelings that became unbearable, not his affection. As a consequence of repressing his hatred, he experienced guilt, and because of that repression, he couldn't determine its source. Unlike Dora, who paraded her aggression like a badge of honor, Lanzer suppressed and, then, denied its existence.

In general terms, hysterics repress their libido, whereas obsessionals tend to suppress their hostility—for the person they love. We find elements of both in everybody. Each prompts degrees of ambivalence that are discernable in every neurotic, both the kind that occasions guilt and the kind that doesn't. It is nevertheless impressive the degree to which we notice the prevalence of repression in hysterics and "reaction formation"—epitomized, for example, by the exaggerated sense of Lanzer's devotion to his father and protectiveness of his girlfriend—among obsessionals. This is why Lanzer's analysis crossed a major threshold when he could feel and acknowledge his ambivalent hatred for Freud. He transferred onto Freud the hostile feelings that he unconsciously harbored against his father. Once he could be truthful about how he felt—and could see there was nothing wrong with having those feelings—his guilt disappeared. Guilt, which is typically caused by hating the person we love, is also the consequence of *being untruthful* with ourselves. On the other hand, just because Dora didn't *feel* any guilt doesn't mean she was immune from it. Why else would she punish herself with so many symptoms? All neuroses are the consequence of turning one's back on the truth. When we deny the truth about whom we desire, we try to compensate for it by seeking solace in a symptom. But that symptom is also a way of atoning for our sins. Sometimes it achieves its aim so successfully we're reconciled to it. Having denied the truth about his hate for his father, Lanzer sought to punish himself for it. Yet, as long as he denied his true feelings, no amount of atonement could entirely appease the enormity of his guilt. When this constellation of feelings was transferred onto Freud, he was finally able to purge them and transcend his tormenting obsessions.

A few years later, when Freud revised his theory of anxiety in light of the structural model, the investigation of unconscious guilt became a feature of every psychoanalysis. Freud even introduced a new psychical agency—the superego—whose principal function was to arbitrate our moral conflicts. The function of truth came to the fore in this new model. Whereas previously guilt had been the consequence of *denying* reality (as with the Rat Man), now it is the consequence of *serving* reality so compliantly that we deny our true feelings. Consequently, guilt is caused by denying *truth,* not reality specifically. If there was one advantage to Freud's new model, it was probably this more sophisticated conception of guilt. We become guilty for hating the person we love; but more to the point, we are guilty for complying with circumstances we don't genuinely accept. With this reformulation, Freud abandoned an exclusively libidinal conception of guilt and replaced it with one that was inherently existential.

24

"Classical" Technique—and Freud's

After terminating his analysis with Freud, Ernst Lanzer became engaged to and finally married the woman he had courted for so many years. They settled into a life of domestic contentment and he resumed his professional career. With his incessant worry, procrastination, and self-doubt behind him, he embraced a way of life that had previously seemed inconceivable. He was happy. We can't say whether his contentment would have lasted. We don't know if, in time, he would have suffered relapse. As tragedy would have it, a few years later he was dead, a victim of the Great War that indifferently consumed Europe's youth. In spite of Freud's claims, an extensive literature has developed that is increasingly critical of Lanzer's analysis. Generally, these criticisms have focused on the relative absence of neutrality in many of Freud's interventions. Even if the analysis was a qualified success, it succeeded for all the "wrong" reasons. Some are skeptical about the degree to which Lanzer was actually cured. How thoroughly was he analyzed? Discrepancies are noted between Freud's conduct of the analysis on the one hand and his own recommendations concerning analytic technique on the other. If Freud's technical papers depict classical technique as he envisioned it, was his actual behavior appropriately classical, or did he neglect his own recommendations? I would like to briefly summarize the most frequently expressed criticisms of Freud's treatment of Lanzer and examine them in turn.

One of the unique aspects of the Rat Man case concerns the discovery after Freud's death of surviving process notes that he customarily destroyed after each case was published. Strachey included them in an appendix to Freud's official report in 1955 (Freud 1955e). They have been the source of constant debate ever since. Is Freud's report faithful to the notes he never intended for publication? What do they reveal that was omitted from the report itself? The case notes raise many questions and add extensive material to what Freud initially reported. They have been used, however, to embellish criticisms that had already been raised even before their discovery. For example, Kris (1951, 17), in 1949, accused Freud of "intellectual indoctrination" in his treatment of the Rat Man and of systematically neglecting the transference. In "The Transference Neurosis of the Rat Man," originally published in 1952, Kanzer maintained that Freud treated his patient "brutally" by insisting that he relate the story of the rat torture, ostensibly against his will (1980, 139). He even accuses Freud of incorrect analytic technique by allowing Lanzer to rise from the couch during his sessions. Once the case notes became available, however, attacks shifted to Freud's "extra-analytic" behavior with Lanzer. Specifically, Freud mentions in one of his notes that he had given his patient a meal when he was hungry. On another occasion, he had sent Lanzer a postcard during a break in the treatment. On yet another occasion, Freud loaned Lanzer a book. In "The Misalliance Dimension in the Case of the Rat Man," Langs identifies this type of behavior as "deviations" from strict analytic neutrality (1980, 215–16). When he contrasts Freud's behavior with contemporary standards of technique, Langs says that Freud repeatedly violates the "analytic frame":

> There are inherently sound safeguards in the specific tenets which constitute today's ground rules and boundaries—the frame—of the psychoanalytic relationship and situation. The sensitivity of the Rat Man to alterations in this frame, which to some extent was not that of Freud at the time, appears to support such a thesis. (223)

In other words, Freud's expressions of encouragement and support are violations of what Langs—and a great many analysts with him—understands by the term *neutrality*. Any such violation impinges on the analytic "frame," a concept that Freud, incidentally, never used. Another example of violating the frame is Freud's gesture to feed the Rat Man a meal—a practice that, according to Jones, was not at all uncommon. But Langs claims that: "the feeding provided obvious transference gratification and was the basis for a sector of misalliance which disturbed the Rat Man to some extent, although he participated in and accepted gratification from it" (227).

Langs echoes the sentiments of an increasing number of analysts who insist that almost any gesture of kindness or concern "endangers" the analytic frame by unnecessarily "gratifying" the patient. He even goes so far as to suggest that "the feeding, as this material indicates, was seen in part as a dangerous homosexual seduction and attack, to which the Rat Man reacted with great mistrust and rage" (227). Freud then compounds his "mistake" by giving Lanzer a book to read, another act of "homosexual seduction" because, "in his fantasies, the Rat Man felt that Freud was behaving like a prostitute—or using his patient as one—and was attempting to seduce him" (228).

In a more recent study of the Rat Man, Mahony agrees that Freud's analytic behavior is somewhat less than "analytic" by current standards. He says that "the very absence of detailed transferential interpretations, both as to what Freud specifically represented and as to what was the Rat Man's immediate reaction, fuels the doubt that Freud persistently focused on clarification and dissolution of the transference neurosis" (1986, 89).

In basic agreement with the arguments expressed by Kris, Kanzer, and Langs, Mahony believes that Freud's depiction of Lanzer's analysis gives us a "picture of Freud as frequently intrusive, reassuring, and seemingly more drawn to genetic interpretations and to reconstruction of past events than to the current interplay in the clinical situation" (90). These criticisms of Freud's excessively "involved" behavior with the Rat Man are in stark contrast to his apparent aloof manner with Dora (see chapter 15). Mahony acknowledges this seeming contradiction in his criticisms about Freud's technique, but arrives at the conclusion that "if Freud was a prosecutor with Dora, he was a befriending educator to Lanzer" (95). Apparently, ideal analytic behavior—determined by the current emphasis on neutrality—would strive to tow a line somewhere between Freud's alleged excesses.

Mahony attributes Freud's "incorrect" technique to his countertransference. He couldn't help it. After all, he had never been analyzed himself. In Mahony's estimation, Freud's "clinical practice was affected by his impatience, his theoretical preoccupations, his use of suggestion, and his patriarchal attitudes" (98). Besides, Freud "talked too much" and was aggressively helpful, presumably succumbing to therapeutic ambition. Mahony also objects to an occasion during which Freud asked his patient to produce a photograph of his girlfriend in order to help Lanzer overcome his reluctance to talk about her. Mahony sees this request as "a direct, intrusive demand" that elicited a "violent" reaction (115). Seconding Langs's objection to Freud's having sent his patient a postcard, Mahony adds that "like the ejaculation, Freud's intimate postcard was felt to be premature" because he had signed the card: "cordially" (118). Overall, Mahony feels that Freud failed to interpret Lanzer's transference and instead committed a number of unconscious gestures whose effect was undesirable. Virtually all of Freud's acts of encouragement and kindness are interpreted as signs of "overinvolvement" and countertransference "intrusiveness." Even if we allow that Freud committed these gestures deliberately and with what he believed was good reason, Mahony perceives signs of unanalytic behavior nonetheless.

Actually, the only thing the process notes prove is that Freud's behavior with Lanzer was even more spontaneous than we had already concluded from the official report. Although the meal, the photo, the postcard, and the book weren't mentioned in the published case, none of these gestures are inconsistent with the cordial and reassuring manner with which he treated Lanzer throughout the analysis. Freud's critics point to the breach of neutrality as the main justification for their disapproval of his behavior. But Freud hadn't even used the term *neutrality* until 1915 in the last of his technical papers, "Observations on Transference-Love." Given the nature of these criticisms, one would have thought that this concept introduced a marked departure concerning the nature of the analyst's conduct with his patients.

In fact, neutrality hardly stood out in Freud's mind as a principal concept. As we saw earlier (chapter 18), the only time he used the term was in reference to handling the erotic transference. Freud used neutrality to suggest that the analyst should neither encourage nor discourage his patients from "falling in love" with him but, instead, should simply accept whatever feelings they happen to experience. He even warned analysts against pretending to care for their patients when they don't, and to hold those feelings in check when they do. According to Freud, "Our control over ourselves is not so complete that we may not suddenly one day go further than we had intended. In my opinion, therefore, we ought not to give up the neutrality toward the patient, which we have acquired through keeping the counter-transference in check" (1958d, 164).

Contrary to common wisdom, Freud never applied his notion of neutrality to every component of the analyst's relationship with his patients. Its application was narrow. Yet it has gradually assumed a significance in the eyes of contemporary analysts that dictates virtually every intervention. By today's standards, Freud was never "neutral"—nor did he ever advocate such a stance, so how could he have ever broken this "rule"? In practice as well as in word, Freud never regretted spontaneous gestures of support and encouragement. Instead, he emphasized the need to express sympathetic understanding and to employ one's *human influence* in order to elicit the optimal attitude—a "positive transference"—in one's patients. Even in his discussion of abstinence—which many analysts confuse with neutrality—Freud advised against withholding "everything that the patient desires, for perhaps no sick person could tolerate this" (1958d, 165).

It's true that Freud condemned suggestive (i.e., supportive) therapies. He believed that support alone rarely cures a neurosis. But he never claimed that psychoanalysis should be devoid of the analyst's support, epitomized in those very gestures that are now condemned in his treatment of the Rat Man. Laing (1967, 35–49) used the term *mystification* to characterize a situation in which one person attributes to another a point of view that, in fact, that person doesn't hold. It is intended to persuade people to believe something that they don't. If exercised relentlessly, people who are subjected to mystification don't know what they believe; eventually, they may even become psychotic. Freud is dead, so we can't mystify him in the way that Laing demonstrated occurs in some families. But the act of attributing to Freud attitudes about analytic technique that he himself never held is common practice. First, Freud's name is used to legitimize a technique, such as neutrality, and to label that technique as "classical" because Freud thought of it first. Then, when there is no evidence in Freud's clinical cases to support such a thesis, he is accused of not having obeyed his own rules!

In a famous study of Freud's technique, Lipton (1977) notes that many analysts today accuse Freud of violating the tenets of classical technique in his analysis of the Rat Man. But they also insist that Freud altered his technique later and eventually adopted what we now characterize as the classically neutral analytic stance. There isn't a shred of evidence to support this claim. Actually, Freud's behavior with the Rat Man was typical of his treatment of patients throughout the remaining thirty years of his career. In fact, his analysis of Lanzer is consistent with all of the recommendations Freud introduced in the "technical papers," which he began constructing immediately after Lanzer's treatment ended in 1909 and completed six years later.

Lipton shows how analytic technique changed dramatically, however, after Freud's death. These changes, which had already started prior to the publication of Kris's paper (1951) where he openly criticized Freud's treatment of the Rat Man, reveal an increasingly rigid interpretation of analytic neutrality. Yet, these changes are characterized as inherently correct, *classical* analytic technique. Lipton suggests that this newer technique should be called "modern" because, (a) it differs from Freud's technique, and (b) it is an innovation of Freud's conduct and presumes to be an improvement of it. Lipton defends the technique Freud employed with the Rat Man because the analysis was successful, not simply because it was Freud who performed the treatment. In his examination of the divergences in analytic technique since the 1950s, Lipton argues that the absence of spontaneous, supportive gestures, justified by a more expansive interpretation of neutrality, seems to characterize this newer technique in its entirety. He suggests that Freud separated his technique from his personal relationships with his patients, whereas today the entirety of the analyst's relationship with his patients is determined by his technical behavior. Freud felt free to feed his patients if he liked, or send them postcards, or loan them books, because he didn't believe these kinds of gestures compromised narrower technical considerations. Adverse reactions could always be analyzed later. There is considerable evidence to support Lipton's contention that Freud recognized a "real" or "personal" component to his relationships with his patients, distinct from the so-called transferential and countertransferential considerations (we examined this subject in detail in chapters 19 and 20). For example, Freud's characterization of the "unobjectionable transference feelings" are usually depicted nowadays as real, actual, or nontransference feelings of the patient. Lipton adds that "using Freud's terminology, it seems clear that as the basis of the unobjectionable transference feelings of the patient he established a relationship with the patient which was *not technical*" (261).

Freud didn't believe that his candid, often personal behavior with his patients was harmful or countertransferential. He believed it was helpful, simply because it derived from natural and spontaneous expressions of his relationships with them. He was exercising candor, just as he, in turn, asked them to do with him. Lipton concludes that many of Freud's critics see the psychoanalytic relationship less in terms of a collaboration than as a treatment approach that is dictated, unilaterally, by the analyst. The aims of the treatment are less important than the analyst's behavior, which is increasingly conceived in terms of neutrality. Analysts today seem more concerned—even obsessed—with avoiding errors, as though this factor alone determined the outcome of treatment: "The meticulous avoidance of [the analyst's] interventions lends to modern technique a prospective or prophylactic approach rather than a retrospective one" (262).

Freud's so-called gratifying behavior with Lanzer could only be perceived as gratifying from the perspective of modern technique, not from Freud's. Although I admire Lipton's attempt to clarify the gradual shift in analytic technique away from spontaneous, personal gestures—a critique I'm in basic agreement with—I'm not so sure that it's necessary to draw such a strict line between the so-called personal and technical aspects of each analyst's behavior. Strictly speaking, analysts don't have a personal relationship with their patients if they are being paid to perform a service. On the other hand, the analyst's person is the instrument of treatment, so how on earth could it be excluded? Lipton's attempt to separate the two becomes problematical because Freud himself argued that the expression of human concern and sympathetic understanding—both of which Lipton would define as personal—is essential for fostering the development of the patient's positive transference, a technical precondition for analyzability. Obviously, Freud believed it was *through* the personal relationship (fostered between analyst and patient) that the *analysis* of that relationship became possible—and necessary. The two weren't "separate but equal," as Lipton implies, but intertwined, each in the other. How could it be otherwise?

Apparently, a remarkable difference in emphasis has emerged between Freud's conception of technique and that of many contemporary analysts. Whereas Freud was primarily concerned with fostering the positive transference (i.e., "rapport"), Freud's critics seem to favor fostering a sense of deprivation instead. This shift can be argued on its own merits, and should be. But it doesn't reflect Freud's intention, so why imply that it does? If we identify the specifically personal and spontaneous aspects of the analyst's behavior with those occasions in which he overtly expresses feelings of concern, interest, and support, then Freud's use of neutrality and abstinence apparently didn't prohibit him from being spontaneous and even affectionate with his patients. The degree to which it is advisable to reveal oneself to patients in treatment should be determined, as Freud told Ferenczi, by tact rather than categorical rules. What about the claim that Freud subsequently abandoned this behavior after his analysis of

Lanzer? Lipton rejects this contention too, citing numerous accounts by Freud's former patients—such as Wortis (1954), Doolittle (H.D. 1956), and Blanton (1971)—who were analyzed by Freud during the last decade of his life. Every one of them demonstrate Freud's unreservedly spontaneous style, by today's standards—the one he adopted in his analysis of Lanzer.

In another study, Haynal (1989) concurs with Lipton that "Freud's activity was never restricted to interpretation but that he also formed a 'personal non technical relationship' with his patients" (7). He refers to several of Freud's former patients—many of whom became psychoanalysts—who remarked on his candid behavior. For example, Jeanne Lampl–de Groot, according to Haynal, "feels she was greatly influenced as an analyst by Freud's 'carefully selected alternation of "strict neutrality" and human relatedness' " (8). Turning to an account by Medard Boss, one of the first "existential analysts," "Boss notes with astonishment, 'During the entire time I was privileged to be in analysis with him, he acted quite differently to what one would have expected . . . from his views on the analyst as a mirror' " (12). Kardiner, another analyst once treated by Freud, was also struck by his ostensibly unconventional behavior: "Kardiner says that Freud sometimes mentioned personal matters to people in analysis with him: family preoccupations, the death of his daughter Sophie, Anna's analysis, her hesitancy to get engaged" (12).

Kardiner also reported that Strachey and Rickman were amazed to hear these accounts of Freud's behavior, because in their analyses with Freud he never said a word! Apparently, Freud's behavior depended on the patient being treated. It may also explain why some analysts are more "classical" than others, depending on how Freud chose to handle their analysis. Haynal concludes that "altogether, his remarks suggest an atmosphere where occasionally the direct expression of the analyst's feelings can be made without undue concern about a 'neutral' analyst" (9). These accounts also suggest that Freud's less than neutral behavior wasn't merely a phase in his development, but was consistent with the way he customarily practiced psychoanalysis. This is confirmed by Racker, who observed that Freud "actively participated in each event of the session, giving full expression to his interest" (1968, 34–35). In fact, Freud was so involved in the act of interpreting his patients' remarks and asking questions that Racker believed his analytic sessions were "a straightforward *dialogue*"

(35). He concludes that "those who link the concept of a 'classical technique' with a predominance of the monologue on the part of the patient and with few and generally short interpretations on the part of the analyst, will have to conclude, as I have said, that in this aspect Freud was not a 'classical' analyst" (35).

In light of the current emphasis on reducing the entirety of psychoanalytic treatment to the analysis of transference phenomena, Haynal concludes that Freud's analytic technique, in practice, was "contrary to the rule that transference should be consistently interpreted" (10). And although Gill was critical of Freud's decided neglect of transference interpretation, he nonetheless agrees that "the effort to subsume the entire relationship under technique has undesirable consequences for the therapy situation. . . . It robs the personal relationship of the spontaneity it must have to be genuine" (1982, 104). He concurs with Lipton that

> a major trend in current practice is to expunge the personal relationship instead of recognizing it as part of the *inevitably existing actuality of the analytic situation.* . . . What has not been perceived is where the real problem lies, that is, *the error of subsuming the entire relationship under technique* and failing to analyze the effects of the actual situation in the transference. (141; emphasis added)

In fact, many analysts today apparently believe the "actual" relationship between analysts and their patients is harmful. The comments by Kanzer, Langs, and Mahony, by which they criticize Freud's treatment of the Rat Man, show how "intrusive" and "dangerous" they believe ordinary expressions of interest and concern are. It's remarkable that these analysts should actually identify with Lanzer's occasional complaints about Freud's "intimate" gestures. After all, Lanzer was diagnosed by Freud as a "moderately severe" obsessional neurotic. One of the more common obsessional symptoms is a fear of intimacy. Lanzer was so guilt-ridden that any gesture of kindness was bound to make him feel uncomfortable. He didn't trust these gestures because he couldn't acknowledge his own desire for them. Does this suggest that patients who fear their own desires should be "protected" from being reminded of them? Apparently, many analysts today who practice what Lipton characterizes as "modern" technique believe human relatedness is dangerous. They feel that their patients shouldn't be "subjected" to it. They imply that the analytic "situation"—a term that alludes to but avoids the word *relationship*—should be a haven from interpersonal relatedness. Lipton adds that "these views are in accord with Grunberger (1966), who states that the analytical situation protects the patient from object relationship and with Applebaum (1972) who states that the unseen and largely silent analyst makes every effort not to be a real object for the analysand" (265).

Is this really how we wish to characterize analytic treatment, as an asylum from ordinary gestures of support, concern, spontaneity? In Lanzer's case, Freud's gestures appeared to be helpful. After all, he was cured of his symptoms in a remarkably brief span of time—eleven months! One has to wonder why "modern" analysts identify with fears of relatedness to such a degree that they condemn any attempts to breach such fears with human kindness. Whatever the merits of this view are, the implications of this trend, if it continues, are dismaying. The so-called neutral analysts—a fiction if there ever was one—don't feel able to be themselves, spontaneous and involved. They witness events but are afraid to participate. Freud's conception of neutrality—which was raised in the context of reminding us that psychoanalysis is rooted in the principle of truthfulness—was intended to caution analysts against the temptation to mistreat their patients in any way. To be neutral meant to be *truthful*. The revision of this concept actually advocates the opposite. It counsels analysts to conceal themselves, to show nothing of themselves, their views, their feelings, even their investment in the outcome. This wasn't what Freud had in mind. It's a sad commentary on what psychoanalysis has become when analysts like Freud, who have the courage to be themselves and take risks, are condemned for the very virtues that the "neutered" analyst lacks.

Freud's analysis of the Rat Man is lacking in many respects—just as every case is. Some analysts have claimed that the Rat Man's recovery was nothing more than a "transference cure." He was never actually cured but got well just to win Freud's approval. Had he lived longer, the story goes, he would have suffered relapse because the transference was never analyzed. In fact, we'll never know if the result was a bonafide cure or a flight into health. It is nevertheless futile to judge Lanzer's cure against subsequent innovations in technique that—had they been suggested to Freud even then—would have been rejected by Freud himself as something that was, in *his* opinion, alien to "psychoanalysis."

When we look to what a published case has to offer, we hope to derive from its material something about ourselves. Does it confirm, or instead challenge, the direction in which we are already inclined? Does it alert us to something we've overlooked? When we look back on Freud's analysis of Lanzer, the most notable aspects of the treatment—by universal agreement—are those gestures that are admittedly personal. We agree with and emulate those gestures or condemn them, depending on our point of view. In the end, that point of view is all we have. It derives from what we are, and *who*.

VI

THE END OF ANALYSIS

What is the relationship between the termination of analysis and its cure? Does the termination of a psychoanalytic treatment presuppose the cessation—the "cure"—of a pathological condition, or does termination determine the cessation of treatment simply because it's time to end it? Psychoanalysis arose out of Freud's efforts to discover a cure for hysterical symptoms. Over a period of time, he gradually developed a method of treatment whose original purpose markedly changed. His treatment of hysterics taught Freud some surprising things about human nature, particularly a variety of so-called pathological conditions that derive from our innate propensity to "forget" painful experiences, especially in childhood. Specifically, we tend to repress those inevitable disappointments in love that every child endures. In other words, Freud discovered that human beings are remarkably prone to self-deception. Many of the hysterical symptoms that patients typically presented to their physicians—principally neurologists and psychiatrists—occasioned a predilection for suppressing their erotic wishes while concealing any knowledge of their efforts at suppression. How was one to diagnose their "illness": the somatic symptom that brought them to treatment, or the underlying *fear*—a psychological phenomenon—that caused the symptom in the first place?

In order to treat a medical condition, that condition has to be diagnosed. Without a condition to treat, there would be nothing to cure. If the physical condition is a ruse that harbors something mental instead, is the mental, in turn, the true illness? Or does the notion of illness merely prolong the original error in diagnosis, a metaphor for the somaticized symptom that couldn't have been "treated" in any case? Due to Freud, we have learned to appreciate how coincidental it was that hysterical symptoms ever came to be diagnosed from a specifically medical perspective. Self-deception and fear of sexual intimacy are hardly medical concerns, properly speaking. But when these incidents of concealment and secrecy give rise to somatic—and even suicidal—symptoms, the physician is bound to get involved. In Freud's day there was nowhere else to turn. Everyone assumed that these symptoms were medical illnesses of some kind or other. The problem was to determine what they were. When neurotics consulted physicians hoping to pour their heart out about their pain of brokenheartedness, they discovered that their doctors weren't really interested in listening to their troubles and—worse—didn't take them very seriously. Physicians, because of their medical training, were already convinced that these problems were organic in nature, caused by a functional disorder of the nervous system.

Today, psychiatrists are more knowledgeable about the acts of suppression that promote somatic symptoms. Today, all of us are more likely to appreciate how frightened we are to even think about our anxieties, and how important it is to talk about them. Today, there's an elaborate infrastructure of psychoanalysts and psychotherapists who earn their living, more or less exclusively, by listening to such patients' complaints. Consequently, such patients are more likely to seek specifically nonmedical forms of treatment for relief from such symptoms. They're less likely to think of their fears as medical in nature, and they're less likely to seek medical practitioners to relieve them. Psychologists, social workers, marriage counselors, and even a remarkable number of lay-practitioners who possess virtually no "mental health" qualifications are now commonly trained to perform a variety of therapeutic interventions, including psychoanalysis, to relieve such symptoms. As psychoanalytic training and treatment evolved, Freud became convinced that medical training was actually irrelevant as a precondition for analytic education and practice. Soon after the publication of his "technical papers," Freud gradually dropped the sobriquet *doctor* and replaced it with the word *analyst*. This was presumably in recognition of the growing number of nonmedical analysts who were accumulating around him. But it was also a sign that Freud no longer perceived psychoanalysis as a specifically medical form of treatment. He devoted an entire book, *The Question of Lay Analysis* (1959), to the argument that the study of liberal arts, history, and the humanities was the best foundation for a vocation in psychoanalysis.

Consequently, the role that diagnosis played in analytic treatment became increasingly metaphorical. Freud couched his views about human suffering in the broadest diagnostic terms: "neurosis," "psychosis," "perversions." He wasn't satisfied with the terms of his day and kept changing them in order to fit the phenomena he was describing: "psychasthenia" became obsessional neuroses; "inversion" became homosexuality; "dementia praecox" became schizophrenia (borrowed from Bleuler); "narcissistic neuroses" became psychosis, and so on. He only vaguely conceived psychoanalysis as a tool of *psychiatry*. He wasn't interested in elaborating anything like the extensive inventory of "mental disorders" *(DSM III)* that is currently fashionable, even amongst psychoanalysts. This is because Freud didn't conceive of psychoanalysis as a treatment for mental disorders, strictly speaking. He saw it as a device that could be used to liberate a relatively few human beings from the consequences of self-deception. And if our propensity for secretiveness happens to coincide with the manifestation of so-called psychiatric symptoms, our efforts to become more honest with ourselves may relieve some of those symptoms too. But again, maybe not. For many people, any effort to expose what they conceal only increases their anxieties and the symptoms they occasion. Indeed, "relief from symptoms" may be gained by *sedating* their anxieties and leaving their secrets intact, secure from exposure. What proves beneficial in the name of psychiatry—or even many forms of psychotherapy—may render the "fundamental rule" impractical, along with the efficacy of psychoanalysis itself. This is because psychoanalysis isn't principally concerned with relief of suffering, as an end in itself. If it were, it couldn't possibly compete with other offers of help such as, for example, psychotropic medication and even so-called supportive therapies. For lack of a better way of saying it, psychoanalysis, because it examines the way we live, is intended to promote a more sane manner of living. Sometimes the sane alternative is the more painful one. Sanity, in and of itself, doesn't relieve suffering, but the unmitigated and deliberate avoidance of suffering inevitably leads to greater—not less—insanity. This is the paradox on which psychoanalysis rests: suffering and psychopathology aren't necessarily the same thing.

This is why diagnosis wasn't a particular concern of Freud's (Ellman 1991, 26), whereas analyzability was. If one isn't careful, the question of analyzability can easily be confused with "treatability" or "curability." In fact, the question of the one supercedes and determines the prognosis of the other. When determining a prospective patient's capacity for following the fundamental rule, the question that arises in the analyst's mind is simply: "Is this person capable of being honest with me?" Unless that person is, it becomes futile to extend one's inquiry to the "treatable" and "curable" criteria. When we examined how Freud treated this issue in practice (see chapter 18), we saw how he used his preliminary queries and diagnostic impressions to determine a patient's capacity for openness, honesty, and candor. Psychotic and severely depressed candidates for treatment were deemed unanalyzable. The fact that we have since discovered that many psychotics are analyzable doesn't alter the principles of Freud's criteria for analyzability. It confirms those criteria because we now realize that some psychotics possess those very character traits that Freud thought they lacked: openness, honesty, and the capacity for a positive transference.

Laing went even further when he suggested that schizophrenia—like neurosis—could be conceived as a form of experience instead of medical or psychiatric "disease" (Laing 1967). The psychiatric community was skeptical, and still is, just as it was when Freud introduced his views about hysteria. In spite of the innovations that Freud and Laing—advocating the psychoanalytic and existential perspectives, respectively—introduced, the tide of opinion has turned against them. Today, "studies" suggest that schizophrenia is a genetic, neurological disorder. In other words, schizophrenia doesn't "mean" anything. It just is. Even newer "studies" suggest that depression, mania, alcoholism, appetite, even "obsessive-compulsive disorder" are also genetically determined, neurological dysfunctions of the brain, waiting for the pill or operation that—any day now—will cure, or control, this "disease." The evidence—scientific to be sure—suggests this is so. How much time have we left before psychoanalysis—existential or otherwise—becomes obsolete, an artifact of a romanticized but discredited past when human beings indulged in that quaint practice of simply talking to one another, and listening to what each has to say?

Increasingly, psychoanalysts are intensely concerned with diagnosis. Many are worried that their medical colleagues—the nonanalytic ones—are leaving them behind. Feeling the need to posture themselves in the vanguard of psychiatry and not its periphery, they're determined to be even more "scientific," even more up to date than their rivals. Newer and more novel pathological categories, conditions, entities, and impressions are discerned at a startling pace. Some of them—like the narcissistic and borderline conditions, are, in turn, adopted by the mainstream psychiatric community. Not to be left behind, even psychologists are hot on their heels, using their "projective devices" for determining this or that disorder even more efficiently—and "objectively"—than their medical colleagues. As a consequence, psychoanalysis has insinuated its way into the mainstream of the medical and mental health community in a fashion that Freud never thought possible—or desirable. This is the same community, after all, that is rooted in the traditional *medical* treatment model of diagnosis-treatment-cure, a model that continues to raise questions about the aims and instruments of psychoanalysis, as Freud conceived it. That doesn't mean that medicine and psychoanalysis are incompatible. Medical doctors have as much right to become psychoanalysts as do teachers, social workers, psychologists, the clergy, or anybody else. But the tradition of "healing the mind" has a history and scope that far outstrips its relationship with medicine (Alexander and Selesnick 1966). Historically, philosophy, education, and religion have been just as concerned with the dynamics of self-deception and its consequent toll on society. In fact, many of Freud's ideas about the nature of human suffering—and its "treatment"—derive from Greek philosophy, not medicine. It's time we reconciled ourselves to this fact.

This is why psychoanalysis is in decline, and why it is slowly dying as a "treatment" modality. It was never suited to be one in the first place. As analysts try to compete with advances in biochemical medicine, which often relieves suffering instantly, and the increasing numbers of "supportive" therapies whose recipients are impressed with their easy consolation, they discover that analysis is relatively ineffectual for that purpose. It simply doesn't cure symptoms the way we would like it to; yet, it puts itself out as the premiere method of doing so. In fact, it is a poor means of obtaining "relief" from suffering. We all know that it usually increases it.

This was the paradox that confronted Freud when he wrote his last technical paper, "Analysis Terminable and Interminable" (1964a), only two years before his death. Whatever meaning the psychoanalytic "cure" is intended to convey, the eradication of suffering is hard to justify. Yet, it is because of suffering that one enters analysis in the first place. Is it merely a failure whose time has passed, or is its aim—however hard to define—somehow more subtle than relief from suffering implies? Freud believed that whatever conception of cure we adopt, it should be relative to the capacities of each patient. Specifically, all analytic patients need to determine for themselves what their goal will be. Is it relief from suffering? Or is it a more sane existence? Do they understand what they aspire to? Are they even capable of pondering this question?

The aims of psychoanalysis raise questions that need to be asked again and again. Its purpose can't be reduced to medical "cures" of everchanging "diagnoses." Still, there is an aim to analysis. Psychoanalysis isn't, whatever its critics may say, aimless. It isn't merely—nor can it be reduced to—a technique in search of a purpose. The questions we raise pertaining to its aims are all the more challenging because they can't credibly rely on conventional notions about "mental health," "remission of symptoms," and the like. If not these, then what are the aims of psychoanalysis, according to Freud?

We touched on this question earlier, toward the end of Freud's "On Beginning the Treatment" (see chapter 18). In fact, the need to determine the *timeliness* of one's termination displaces our conventional notions about the kind of "cure" that informs the termination of a typical medical intervention. If psychoanalysis enjoyed a ready-made cure, its terminations would be axiomatic. We would simply terminate the analysis when the patient was cured. But we know this is never really the case (Freud said as much when he terminated his treatment of the Rat Man; despite the cessation of his symptoms, Freud would have gladly prolonged his analysis if not for the intervention of "mitigating circumstances"). The fact that we still debate this issue is our most constant reminder that the so-called analytic cure has become a necessary, though often confusing, metaphor. Whatever else it implies, a successful termination suggests that one's patients ended treatment on a positive note, more or less optimistically, more honest with themselves than before. How, then, is success determined if not by eliminating "illness"? This is the question Freud attempted to answer in this paper, his final word on the matter.

25

Psychoanalysis, Terminable— or Impossible?

Freud's "Analysis Terminable and Interminable" (1964a) represents his final effort to review the efficacy of analytic treatment and its limitations. Though it is frequently characterized as his last paper (actually next to last; "Constructions in Analysis," 1964b, was published a few months later) on the subject of technique, it is essentially a theoretical effort. Those who turn to this paper seeking practical advice on the art of termination are invariably disappointed. Freud says very little about termination itself. Instead, he seeks to review the aims of psychoanalysis and the obstacles that lie in their path. In choosing this manner of addressing such a pivotal question, this paper is surely one of his most subtle and, consequently, difficult to understand. Freud's command of the subject is even more remarkable when we recall that he was in his eighties when he wrote it, suffering miserably from the cancer that was consuming his body and finally killed him two years later. His powers of perception and communication appear not to have suffered in the slightest, in spite of his condition and advanced age.

It was in this paper that Freud offered his notorious allusion to psychoanalysis as one of those "impossible professions"—along with politics and education. In fact, the degree to which psychoanalysis is at all possible is the principal question that concerned Freud throughout this paper. He acknowledged that analysis is a lengthy affair. Consequently, considerable effort has gone into finding ways of limiting its duration. Many of these efforts, however—such as Rank's attempt to reduce analysis to a simple form of "trauma therapy" (Freud 1964a, 216)—have only succeeded in rendering versions of psychoanalysis that are less effective in the long run. Freud attributed the seemingly needless prolongation of analytic treatment to the patient's own resistances to change, resistances that are frequently confused with the pathological suffering they occasion. If only they could be made to abandon their resistances the duration of treatment might be shortened accordingly. Freud actually offered a device for especially intractable cases, such as he used in his analysis of the Wolf Man. Simply announce a termination date—perhaps one year in the future—and thereby compel patients to accept that they have a limited amount of time in order to resolve their neurosis. Whatever momentary gratification they may enjoy from their relationship with the analyst will become threatened, and the reality of their situation will be brought home to them. Though this stratagem appeared to have succeeded at the time, Freud admits that ultimately it failed. Some years later his former patient suffered a relapse and resumed treatment. The Wolf Man became the most famous of psychoanalysis' "interminable" patients, never having achieved the hoped-for gains from his analyses with Freud and his subsequent therapist, Ruth Mack Brunswick.

Attachment to the person of the analyst is only one type of resistance that may complicate the termination of treatment. Many of these obstacles seem impossible to influence. Freud even asks: "Is there such a thing as a natural end to an analysis—is there any possibility at all of bringing an analysis to such an end" (219)? What does it mean to bring an analysis to an end? What do we expect to have happened because of it? Practically speaking, analysis has ended when the two participants cease meeting. Freud proposes, however, that two conditions should have been met before agreeing to terminate: "First, that the patient shall no longer be suffering from his [her] symptoms and shall have overcome his anxieties and his inhibitions; and secondly, that the analyst shall judge that so much repressed material has been made conscious, so much that was unintelligible has been explained, and so much internal resistance conquered, that there is no need to fear a repetition of the pathological processes concerned" (219).

Freud's characterization of the optimally completed analysis, ambitious though it sounds, includes qualifications. He limits its criteria to the specific symptoms that patients happen to possess at the time of treatment, and the particular anxieties *they know* they are suffering. Further, he limits the amount of unconscious material that should be made conscious—the quota of truths disclosed during analysis—to the specific pathological processes that happen to come up in the treatment. At first glance, this apparently ambitious characterization of a "completed" (note the word *cure* has not been used) analysis sounds somewhat less ambitious when contrasted with Freud's description of a truly ambitious one; one in which "the analyst has had such a far-reaching influence on the patient that no further change could be expected to take place in him [her] if his analysis were continued. It is as though it were possible by means of analysis to attain to a level of absolute psychical normality—a level, moreover, which we could feel confident would be able to remain stable" (219–20).

Do such achievements ever actually occur? Freud believed they do. Because they are rare, however, they can hardly serve as the standard that one may apply to each treatment. In fact, even the more modest standard for termination is difficult to achieve. Why? Freud suggests that in the (relatively) successful treatments, a number of conditions needs to be met; conditions that are determined by the etiology of the neurosis being treated. The etiology of every neurosis rests on three factors: (a) the strength of the instincts; (b) the effects of early trauma; and (c) the relative strength—or "alterations" to—the patient's ego. The implications of Freud's triadic formula run through the entirety of this paper—just as their effects are felt throughout the length of treatment and, in significant ways, determine its outcome.

One important feature of this paper is the way Freud couches the same concerns that he discussed earlier in his analyses of Dora and the Rat Man now in terms of his structural model. The antithesis between the id's instincts and the ego's efforts to comprehend them dominates this new perspective. If children's instincts are too strong (which is to say, if the force of their need to obtain gratification exceeds their grasp) then their ego (their ability to bear frustration) will be overwhelmed. They will erect defenses against their anxieties that may inhibit the development of their personality and compromise their ability to perceive and accommodate reality. On the other hand, children's instincts may not be the problem. Instead, a traumatic event in their environment—in their relationships with their parents, for example—may overwhelm their ability to accommodate the frustrations encountered. Consequently, they will erect defenses to ward off the anxieties brought about by reality. Significantly, the traumatic etiology of neurosis is—in Freud's opinion—infinitely more treatable than the constitutional (i.e., "instinctual") ones.

His reasons aren't hard to fathom. If neurotic patients are dealing with the effects of their environment and the ways they customarily cope with it, psychoanalysis can help them discover the traumatic (e.g., disappointing) events in their history that they have never learned to accept. Their ego (which in this context entails their capacity to accommodate reality) should be capable of investigating the nature of their suffering and learn to value the eventual benefits of this new understanding. But if their neurotic conflicts derive from excessive demands for gratification, all that they are bound to discover as a consequence of being analyzed is that they are excessively demanding. This is a hard pill to swallow, and a truth about themselves that they may be no more prepared to accept now than they were as children. In effect, they still are children, coping with the same problems, and the same complaints. It is this type of etiological history that was bound to further compromise and alter patients' egos when they were children; prompting them to develop a habitual pattern of defensiveness whose purpose was—and still is—to reject those realities that arouse uncomfortable levels of frustration. While the so-called traumatic forms of neurosis are more suited to a successful termination of treatment, those that derive from a predominantly constitutional etiology—and all neuroses, as we know, contain elements of both—are more likely to prove "interminable." This isn't to say, however, that "altered egos"—patients whose perception of reality is excessively compromised due to the prevalence of their defenses against it—are always due to the strength of their "instincts" (i.e., their desire for gratification). There is a predilection in some people to defend themselves against reality irrespective of etiological factors. Perhaps this factor, too, has an "etiology" of its own. It may be a question of personality, or even conditioning. We don't know. But this question prompted Freud to introduce an element of ambiguity into every analysis that I am inclined to call "existential." It is an element that cannot be foretold or easily explained. It seems that some patients are simply more amenable to the effects of analytic treatment. Freud gives us two examples of how this constellation of forces conspires to determine the outcome of treatment and its aftermath.

The first example pertains to Freud's analysis of Ferenczi. The treatment was rather brief yet ended successfully. His patient resolved some previously chronic issues concerning his rivalry with men and he subsequently married and continued a close collegial relationship with Freud. But years later Ferenczi, for no apparent reason, developed feelings of aggression for his former mentor and even accused Freud of not having given him a "thorough" analysis. He charged that he (Freud) failed to analyze his negative transference, which, Ferenczi believed, was only now emerging.

But Freud refused to accept Ferenczi's argument for two reasons. First of all, the negative transference hadn't emerged of its own accord during the treatment, so how was he to "analyze" something that didn't exist? Should he have contrived to force his patient's negative feelings to the surface? And how was he to presume that they existed in the first place? Anyhow, now that they had arisen, why did Ferenczi not analyze them himself? Why blame Freud for not having "unearthed" them sooner? After all, he was now claiming that these feelings were specifically transferential so, by definition, he was proposing that they didn't concern Freud at all but a figure in his childhood.

His second reason for rejecting Ferenczi's argument derives from the insinuation that his former patient's feelings for his analyst during the treatment were *exclusively* transferential. We know that Ferenczi went on to develop a conception of countertransference that was significantly at odds with Freud's; one in which the analyst assumes enormous responsibility for the outcome of treatment. He suggested that Freud's countertransference feelings prevented him from exploring his (Ferenczi's) latent hostility. But Freud rejects this argument—a pivotal one in terms of contemporary analytic practice—by reminding us that every analysis also occasions real feelings that the participants experience for each other, as well as the transferential. His affection for Ferenczi had been genuine, as had been his former patient's for him. It would seem that Ferenczi's belated conviction that his analysis had "failed" to free him of sentiments he was now experiencing was due to his being *predisposed* to doing so rather than the fault of his former analyst, or even of the analysis itself. There was no way of predicting this would happen and, now that it had, there was apparently no reasoning with Ferenczi to see things differently. This is an example of an "alteration in one's ego" that now assumes a life of its own, prompted, perhaps, by latent instinctual urges. We know that this "conviction" became a central feature of Ferenczi's analytic theories. It became an essential feature of his personality as well.

Freud contrasts this example with another, one that would seem to be its opposite, but similar to the first. He treated a woman who had suffered from hysterical symptoms since puberty, making it difficult for her to walk. After nine months of treatment, her symptoms disappeared and this woman, "an excellent and worthy person," resumed her life. But she was subsequently beset with a number of disastrous difficulties over which she had no direct control. Financial losses and family misfortunes prevented her from achieving the happiness she had hoped for. Unmarried, she grew older realizing that her chances at love were slipping away. Years later, she required a hysterectomy and fell desperately in love with her surgeon. She became frustrated and withdrew into neurotic, masochistic phantasies but was unable to resume her analysis. She died a broken woman. Freud had no way of knowing if her subsequent neurosis was somehow related to the original one or independent of it. But he was convinced that had it not been for the innumerable traumas she suffered in the years that followed her analysis, her second neurosis would have never developed.

In the first example, there was no hint of subsequent traumas that might have explained his former patient's (Ferenczi) change in personality. His hostility was due to an inherent feature of his personality rather than the circumstances in his life. He was eventually overwhelmed by latent constitutional factors that his ego was unable to accommodate or understand. In the second case, his former patient had been subjected to one trauma after another that, collectively, were simply more than her ego could be expected to endure.

Freud conjectured that the skeptic, the optimist, and the ambitious person would each derive a different lesson from these two examples. The skeptic will conclude that no matter how successfully an analysis is conducted, nothing can insure against subsequent outbreaks of symptoms. The optimistic and ambitious analysts look forward to the day when psychoanalysis will evolve into a more effective form of treatment that will guard against the kinds of subsequent recurrences that Freud outlined above. Freud questions the optimist's ambition (a sign of therapeutic ambition) and challenges the presumption that neurosis (like medical illness) can be isolated and treated in such a way that will eradicate it. After all, if neuroses—in fact, all forms of psychopathology—are the consequence of self-deception, prompted by our unwillingness to accommodate harsh truths, then how could any form of treatment possibly inoculate us from future tragedies that we're helpless to prevent? If each of us has our limit to what we can bear before "defending" ourselves against pain, how can we determine what those limits are *until* we encounter them? Unlike military training, psychoanalysis doesn't contrive to *create* miserable conditions in order to strengthen our resolve against artificially imposed frustrations. It can only give us the opportunity to examine the life we are already living.

This prompted Strachey to infer that Freud's views about the potential effectiveness of psychoanalysis changed over the years. Strachey suggests that "according to the earlier view the analytic process seems to have been considered as capable of altering the ego in a more *general* sense and one which would persist after the end of the analysis" (Freud 1964a, 214); whereas now Freud seems to be saying that analysis is incapable "of dealing with a conflict that is not 'current' and of . . . converting a 'latent' conflict into a 'current' one" (214). Whereas this is probably true, this maturing of Freud's position doesn't necessarily comprise a "shift" or "alteration" in his views. It seems rather consistent with his thoughts about the nature of analytic truth and our resistances to it. While our capacity to *become* truthful generally bolsters our efforts to *remain* truthful, our resolve to *be* truthful depends on the circumstances—in reality as well as in ourselves—each of us comes to encounter in the course of our lives. Fate plays a decisive role in our capacities as well as our circumstances.

This is the point, perhaps, where the conception and terminology of Freud's recently imposed "structural model" begin to challenge the subtlety of his thinking. In a recent study, Arlow chastises Freud for still referring to the "abandoned" topographical model while working from a frame of reference in which it has been replaced with the structural, so that "the two frames of reference are used side by side, sometimes in a contradictory fashion" (1991, 44). Indeed, discussing his views in terms of a "newer" model of the mind begs the question whether Freud's views have changed or merely the terms that describe them. Freud raises the notion of an antithesis between the individual's instinctual urges and his ego—between the so-called primary and secondary processes—repeatedly throughout this paper. Each time he addresses this issue the question of constitutional (i.e., "congenital") factors in the etiology of neuroses arises. We customarily depict the constitutional factor as that which we're born with, but Freud corrects this common misunderstanding:

> However true it may be that the constitutional factor is of decisive importance from the very beginning, it is nevertheless conceivable that a reinforcement of instinct coming later in life might produce the same effects. If

so, we should have to modify our formula and say 'the strength of the instincts *at the time*' instead of 'the *constitutional* strength of the instincts.' (1964a, 224)

What are the implications of this qualification? For one thing, it replaces the notion of constitutional factors as those that are exclusively "historical" or developmental in nature with one that is specifically dynamic, even ontological. All of us struggle with our instincts—our emotions, our passion, our fears, our will to live, our resolve—*at all times,* at each moment of our lives. The outcome of our conflicts and the struggles they occasion aren't predetermined for us. We come to favor certain affects over others. The strength of those instincts—our desire—works for us and against us, depending on the situation. The structural model was intended to show how a "strengthened ego" is capable of surmounting the demands of passions whose satisfaction has become impossible. This "newer" understanding was supposed to help us conceptualize the ambiguous nature of an ego whose strength lies in its ability to accept reality, and its weakness in the inclination to deny it. When we say that the aim of analysis is to "strengthen the ego," we're talking about a person's willingness to face the truth about the (unrealizable) aims his instincts compel him to placate. That's because the neurotic's weakened ego is incapable of listening to reason. He's unable to reflect on what's causing his frustrations or understand the interpretations being offered. Freud even suggested that this "quantitative" factor in psychoanalysis— the brute force of our quest for gratification—was being neglected by his followers. This (sometimes immovable) force often explains the insurmountable obstacles to a successful termination. It may compromise one's capacity for accepting a disappointing reality and even to maintain an honest relationship (an "analytic attitude") with one's analyst. This form of analytic "failure," however, isn't a failure of technique or even of analysis. It is simply the arbitrary limit of a given individual's capacity to accept the anguishing nature of his or her existence.

Why are analysts nowadays more likely to attribute analytic failures to erroneous technique than to the limitations of the patient being analyzed? Why, in turn, are Freud's remarks and his rather sober tone in this paper commonly rejected as "pessimistic"? Has psychoanalysis really advanced that much? Or are we still struggling with the same questions, and the same limitations? The call for more effective—and ambitious—efforts to succeed with analytic patients where others have failed isn't new. Freud questioned these sentiments and argued against them when he wrote this paper. In a tone that is evocative of the technical papers he wrote between 1911 and 1915, Freud still pleads against the therapeutic ambition he believed is so detrimental to the efficacy of analytic treatment. The call to "try harder," to interpret more cleverly, to analyze resistances more astutely, and even to prolong the duration of analysis more interminably are all rejected by Freud because, "however much our therapeutic ambition may be tempted to undertake such tasks, experience flatly rejects the notion" (231). Much later, Winnicott concurred that the overzealous analysis of resistances, although often technically correct, was generally ineffectual because "the patient's False Self can collaborate indefinitely with the analyst in the analysis of defenses, being so to speak on the analyst's side in the game" (1960, 152). This is why efforts to force latent issues to the surface only succeed in turning one's patients against the analysis. Besides, why arouse a crisis in the treatment when we know that analysis is not at its best when confronted with acute—contrived or otherwise—expressions of erotism, fear, or hostility? Efforts to lance a boil that hasn't come to the surface only succeed in releasing blood—and creating a newer "injury" for which analysts themselves are responsible.

If we are helpless to provoke or in any way manipulate what we are convinced (perhaps erroneously) are *latent* issues that simply haven't surfaced, then where should our efforts be inclined? We should reconcile ourselves to the surface—what patients actually *experience* in the course of their analysis. Perhaps, for this reason, Freud spends a lot of time exploring that aspect of experience we do have some influence over, the one concerning an "alteration in one's ego." Freud's increased reliance on the structural model inevitably forces us to find some thread that links the old model with the new. Remember how the "alteration of the ego" comprises one of the three etiological factors that accounts for neurotic conflict. Every onset of neurosis is due to either (a) the strength of instincts having overwhelmed one's ego; (b) the factors in one's environment; or (c) the ego itself having been "weakened" so early in its development that it couldn't withstand the constitutional or traumatic forces that, under normal circumstances, it would have. Consequently, the aim of analysis is to (a) establish a rapport with patients' egos in order to analyze the crippling effects of their excessive instincts and/or traumatic injuries, and (b) to strengthen patients' egos in order to further their collaboration with their analyst's efforts to understand them. Still, we mustn't ignore that one's ego, due to its history of having combated these congenital and traumatic forces (unsuccessfully), has probably been "altered" and is thus compromised in its development.

What, exactly, does the notion of a "weakened" ego depict? What does it mean to "strengthen" one's ego? What part do "defenses" play: do they strengthen or weaken? Finally, how is Freud's preoccupation with the nature of truth addressed in this newer, more "structural" terminology? Does it vanish altogether in favor of adaptational concerns? Or does it persist, but in metapsychological clothing? A weakened, or altered, ego is the consequence of a time when children, unable to accept their frustration, opt to repress the wish that caused their frustration in the first place. Due to this act of repression, they "accommodate" reality but don't, strictly speaking, *accept* it because, in order to live with what they can't have, they have to pretend it no longer matters to them. In turn, the circumstances that elicited their repression need to be altered too, in order not to notice that something was repressed (1964a, 236–37). These alterations—actually, obfuscations—of the children's perception of reality compromise their capacity to perceive the real situation and accept it. This is because, in order to comply with something—even when we haven't a choice—we must see it for what it is. The tendency to compromise one's perception of a frustrating reality is how Freud conceives an "alteration of the ego."

Thus the ego is inherently ambiguous and serves a complex purpose. It has to perceive reality in order to understand the context that may or may not complement its aims. But if the reality it perceives is unbearable, the ego is able to lie to itself while concealing the desires that were frustrated. This compromises the ego even more. It becomes paralyzed. It can neither service its desires or abandon them. It resorts to phantasy instead. In its weakened state, it becomes defensive. It becomes even less able to tolerate reality. (Freud believed the neurotic is more prone to repressing the wishes that are in conflict with reality, whereas the psychotic is more liable to distort reality itself. All neuroses and psychoses, of course, are a combination of the two.) Novel as it first appeared, Freud's "structural" characterization of the ego wasn't entirely new. It conforms in significant ways to the picture of mental functioning he proposed earlier in "Formulations on the Two Principles of Mental Functioning," published in 1911. We already saw (chapter 3) how Freud depicted the ego in that paper and later still, in *The Ego and the Id* (1961f), as not completely in "command" of itself. The ego, whether we like it or not, is in the service of forces it can never resolve. It's nothing more than a "submissive slave" who, now, tries to serve its desires and, later, the realities they oppose. The ego is sometimes less concerned with determining the truth than with occupying a position somewhere "midway between the id and reality" (1961d, 56), where it serves both masters, equally. Yet, by trying to please everybody, "it only too often yields to the temptation to become sycophantic, opportunistic and lying, like a politician who sees the truth but wants to keep his place in popular favor" (56).

If this inherent ambivalence characterizes the fundamental nature of the ego, which feels compelled to serve truths but just as easily conceals them, then what are analysts supposed to do when they encounter these tendencies in their patients' neuroses? They need to reintroduce their patients' egos to the truths they have been hiding, and help them to recognize the distortions that subvert this process. Analysts can only hope to accomplish their task by helping their patients to, (a) see what the truth is and (b) discover the reasons they have chosen to distort it (Freud 1964a, 237–39). Patients' resistances to this process are conceived in terms of their incapacity to *tell* the truth, which corresponds to the initial "alteration of ego" when they were unable (as children) to *accept* the truth. A "weakened ego" is only weakened in proportion to one's *fear* of the truth, whereas a "strengthened ego" has no need to erect defenses *against* the truth. Eventually, however, one has to acknowledge how unwieldy Freud's structural model becomes in actual practice. The patient's ego—the *person* with whom we are engaged in this incredible struggle—is also the desiring subject whom the ego is trying to serve. We could never come to terms with our truths in the first place if our egos weren't capable of being at one with our "instincts." In fact, the structural model's failure to fully explain the nature of *unresolvable* resistances prevented Freud from finally equating "resistance" with "defense." Why do some analyses succeed and others fail? Can this quandry be explained by defense alone? Freud thought not. If the aim of analysis is to be less secretive by becoming more truthful, then the resistance we employ against this effort is inevitably intended to "protect" ourselves from realizing that goal. If we escape the treatment with our conflicts intact, we will likely face the same impasses later; perhaps long after the analysis is over. When he attributed a portion of one's resistance to the ego specifically, Freud was pointing to that aspect of ourselves that is prone to lying. We defy reality as long as we get away with it. The ego's capacity to discover truths is only equalled by its ability to distort them, through the "defenses" that serve to protect us from a reality with which we are intimately acquainted.

But there's another form of resistance that doesn't entirely conform to the one I've just described. In fact, it crops up in those treatments that are frequently the most interminable. Referring to them as "id resistances," Freud hoped to draw our attention to those patients who seem innately drawn to their suffering, who are so protective of their impulses and so willing to serve them that the truth about the conflicts they're embroiled in are of secondary importance to them. In his paper on "working-through" (see chapter 20), Freud attributed the deepest layers of resistance to the strength of one's instinctual urges, to one's *need for pleasure.* It's as though some patients are so committed to repeating their infantile dramas that all the frustration in the world won't prompt them to change, or even to question, their behavior. The resistance to change is so deeply entrenched they're resigned to it. Some analysts mistakenly depict these resistances as ego defenses. Freud, however, reminds us that we should "not overlook the fact that id and ego are originally one" (240). In other words, the more we become acquainted with our patients' resistances we begin to realize that we're witnessing a resistance to the movement and revelation of their existence, no matter how much their ignorance costs them. The so-called id-resistance doesn't refer to repression of instinct so much as a wilfulness at the depths of one's being, seemingly employed to act against one's own interests.

Some resistances are derived from innate, deep-seated aims instead of the circumstances (in one's environment) that occasion traumatic injury. Many patients find change difficult because their libido (desire) is "adhesive" and resistant to any change whatsoever. Others change—displace their libido—rather easily, but so easily there's no stability to their lives. Positive cathexes evaporate as easily as problematic ones. None of these forms of resistance are adequately explained by the term *defense mechanism.* They seem to have a life of their own. These considerations prompted Freud to hypothesize the existence of a "negative therapeutic reaction," which he originally outlined in *The Ego and the Id* (1961d, 49) and, later, in "The Economic Problem of Masochism" (1961c). In fact, Freud's skepticism about the possibility of change with "interminable" patients can be laid at the doorstep of this descriptive term. In *The Ego and the Id,* Freud describes such patients thus:

> There are certain people who behave in a quite peculiar fashion during the work of analysis. . . . They show signs of discontent and their condition invariably becomes worse. One begins by regarding this as defiance . . . but later one comes to take a deeper and juster view. . . . Every partial solution that ought to result . . . in an improvement . . . produces in them for the time being an exacerbation of their illness; they get worse during the treatment instead of getting better. (1961f, 49)

Paradoxically, such patients appear to get worse, not because of the treatment itself but because they're attached to their own suffering. Freud was at a loss to explain why this is so, but his view that such patients exist—and that lack of progress was ultimately their responsibility, not the treatment's—is consistent with a conception of the human condition that is more existential than "medical." This partly accounts for the argument between Freud's detractors, who characterize his clinical views as primitive or outdated, and Freud himself, who accuses his critics of falling prey to "therapeutic ambition." Why should so many patients stay chained to their suffering when a means is available to be shed of it? Freud turned to his theories on guilt and moral masochism as a posssible explanation. In "The Economic Problem of Masochism," Freud suggested that

> the satisfaction of this unconscious sense of guilt is perhaps the most powerful bastion of the subject's (usually composite) gain from illness—in the sum of forces which struggle against his [her] recovery and refuse to surrender his state of illness. *The suffering entailed by neuroses is precisely the factor that makes them valuable to the masochistic trend.* (1961c, 166; emphasis added)

Freud became increasingly dubious, however, about the proposition that masochism and unconscious guilt could be justified in terms of *pleasurable* gain. His hypothesis of a "death drive," which he returns to in this paper, suggests a parallel drive, in addition to erotism that competes with pleasure for relief from anxiety. One of the features of Freud's hypothesis—wedded, to some extent, to a biological foundation—is its reliance on the *anticipation* of a gain that is, in itself, pleasurable. Some of the most intractable forms of phantasy, for example, which arise in the erotic transference, include the anticipation of the analyst's capitulation.

Some patients receive so much gratification from their wishful phantasies that the analyst is unable to defeat their resistance to analyzing them. Guilt may also offer a surreptitious form of satisfaction that is derived from self-punishment. It may be sufficiently powerful to undermine the potential gains of the treatment. The notion of "self-punishment," moreover, doesn't necessarily mean these alternative gains are entirely devoid of pleasure. Perhaps Freud's hypothesis of a "death drive" simply depicts an unconventional form of pleasure, wedded to a release of aggression, directed against life itself. What sweeter victory of narcissistic omnipotence than one that might finally conquer life's exasperating toll of defeat and capitulation? The notion of a "negative therapeutic reaction" might explain the ostensibly incomprehensible behavior of those patients who seem to derive more comfort from resisting the treatment than submitting to it.

Freud's conception of a "death drive" has always been controversial. It stands out amongst his later theories as having been almost universally rejected. The idea that each of us contains an innate impulse toward self-destructiveness is antithetical to the sensibilities of those analysts—the vast majority of them—who prefer to see human nature in "evolutionary" terms; in terms that suggest we are constitutionally driven to preserve the perpetuation of our existence. But the commonplace rejection of the death "instinct" can also be attributed to the increasing loss of favor with Freud's instinctual theory, generally. In Britain, virtually all of the object relations theorists have either rejected Freud's drive model outright (Fairbairn 1952; Guntrip 1968) or altered it so drastically that its original impetus barely survives (Winnicott 1960). Even Melanie Klein, alone in her adoption of Freud's death drive model, came to favor the language of "object relations" and "primitive defenses" in her late work (1957). In the United States, those analysts who defend Freud's drive model, following Hartmann (1958), have replaced Freud's notion of a primary "self-destructive" instinct with an "aggressive" one directed at an object outside of oneself. The idea that humans engage in self-destructive behavior, simply for the sake of their destruction, is summarily rejected. Instead, they retain a version of Freud's earlier theory in which he attributed masochistic behavior to a secondary aim, which was principally directed against an other. Many aspects of spiteful and suicidal behavior can be attributed to a form of aggression that is turned inward as a means of attacking an object (external).

Freud eventually became convinced, however, that the pleasure principle couldn't explain all forms of self-destructiveness. One example of what he was driving at is the "negative therapeutic reaction." How could psychopathology—presumably a form of suffering—be rooted in the same pursuit of pleasure that serves as the model for psychic health? If the concept of pathology is going to make any sense, shouldn't it be rooted in *suffering* itself? Prior to introducing the death drive Freud had attributed "moral masochism" to the effects of unconscious guilt. Self-punishment appeases the guilt we feel for hating the person we love. A principal feature of the Rat Man's obsessional neurosis was his guilt for hating his father. Once the source of his guilt was acknowledged, it disappeared. This explanation, however, eventually lost favor on *theoretical* grounds. The persistence of resistances to treatment persuaded Freud that a revision in his drive theory was inevitable. Others began to question even the validity of the drive model (Fairbairn 1952). Freud acknowledged that self-destructiveness couldn't always be explained by the term *gain from illness*. Yet, something appeared to drive some patients to prolong their suffering inexorably, something that simply can't be reduced to their "defenses" against anxiety.

Alongside our innate lust for life and its consequent pursuit of gratification, Freud conjectured a parallel drive that strives to annihilate suffering entirely. This idea was vaguely hinted at earlier in Freud's conception of a pleasure principle whose goal is to satisfy desire. Theoretically, the *satisfaction* of a desire would completely eliminate it. In practice, this only happens partially and temporarily. Because of this paradox, Freud—reluctantly—revised the pleasure model. Now "pleasure" is no longer juxtaposed with "reality." Instead, life (Eros), which now includes the sexual function, is juxtaposed with death (Thanatos), whose aim is *avoiding* strife. The consequences of this reformulation are remarkable. For one thing, Freud's conception of sexuality—long criticized by other schools of analysis for being too narrow—becomes subsumed under the "life drive," which modifies the nature of love. Sexuality now serves love instead of the other way around. Freud's conception of pleasure is also altered. It is no longer preoccupied with eliminating the frustrations caused by desiring, but with accommodating them instead. Healthy, pleasure-seeking and life-affirming individuals, *bear* frustrations in the service of their aims. They no longer seek to vanquish them altogether. In fact, the optimal state of pleasure—of life—include frustration and hardship. There's no better example of this than the higher forms of love that involve the pleasure of sacrifice and the capacity to bear suffering in deference to the object of one's love. This is the kind of love—epitomized by Christian *agape*—that Freud characterized as "genuine" in his paper on transference-love (see chapter 5). The need to eradicate suffering once and for all by deadening one's experience of it is now attributed to the "death" drive. Hence it becomes a factor not only in pathological forms of suffering, specifically, but also plays a part in our everyday preoccupation with avoiding the kind of hardships that are inherent in life itself.

On closer examination, is the death drive actually a drive toward *death?* Is it an "instinct" in the sense that we usually understand this term? The answer to both of these questions is "no." The common tendency to take Freud's terms too literally probably accounts for some of the opposition he encountered with this revision of the drive theory. In the first place, Freud didn't use the term *instinct* in the sense of animal instinct. He even referred to instincts in the *New Introductory Lectures on Psychoanalysis* as "our mythology" (1964c, 95). In a recent review of Freud's instinct theory, Andre Green (1991, 124–41) suggests that Freud's conception of drive is actually *metaphysical,* because it isn't specifically rooted in conventional notions of biology (136). Freud's so-called drive model, which he tried to justify with biological theories of organicity, serves to account for *life's aims* in terms that are predominantly ontological. Because Freud doesn't couch these questions in spiritual or even sociological terminology, it leaves him open to the charge of advocating an exclusively biological model that neglects humanistic and intersubjective considerations. Nothing could be further from the truth. In fact, his argument in favor of a "death drive" is essentially an existential theory. If we don't give Freud the room to explore its relationship to biology, it would remain a purely psychological conception—but a psychology that is cut off from its roots, without a body.

This is why the word *death* in Freud's newer, more philosophical formulation shouldn't be taken so literally. When Freud was told by one of his followers that his notion of Thanatos was remarkably similar to the Buddhist conception of Nirvana—the elimination of all strife by overcoming desire—he promptly nicknamed his death instinct the "Nirvana complex." This is because the aim of the "death drive" isn't literally death. Its goal is simply to eradicate suffering, an aim that, were it achieved, would eliminate life itself—figuratively speaking. Ironically, when this aim is employed by a neurotic conflict, it only substitutes one form of suffering for another. Short of actual death, the "death drive"—once it's gained ascendence—stifles our capacity to enjoy life because we're so obsessed with evading it. This is what Freud meant by the "negative therapeutic reaction," a reaction against a truth that, once discerned, elicits unacceptable levels of anxiety. We suffer *because* we desire. We either evade it or accept it as a fact. Analytic treatment, if it's at all successful, actually increases the suffering we associate with pleasure. This is paradoxical because, by trying to escape suffering, we become even more alienated from ourselves. Analysis, which heightens our experience of suffering, may feel intrusive and become a new source of danger.

26

The End of Analysis

Is the near-universal rejection of Freud's conception of a "death drive" due to its inherent biologism, or because of the profoundly existential dimension to the questions it compels us to ponder? This remarkable paper—wide-ranging in its scope and free-wheeling in its excesses—is essentially a reappraisal of his views about the nature of suffering. Freud emphasized the limits imposed on one's efforts to even understand what suffering is about, much less relieve it. If the aim of analytic treatment is the relief of suffering, how does one reconcile this aim with the notion of a death drive whose purpose—pathogenic to be sure—is *eliminating* suffering by any means?

Since the beginning of Western thought, philosophers, physicians, and mystics have been concerned with the nature of suffering. From earliest times we have insisted on understanding what suffering is about and finding ways of easing it, accommodating it, accepting it. Freud, though trained as a physician, was never willing to accept the specifically medical approach to suffering, that it should be relieved by any means possible, whatever the cost. He knew, from personal experience, that life entails suffering. The patients he treated suffered miserably. Yet, they seemed peculiarly intolerant of it. Because their desires caused them frustration, they would suppress those desires that they attributed to suffering. How could psychoanalysis help them? Whatever one might have hoped it could do, it can't be expected to relieve the kinds of suffering that life requires in pursuit of life's aims. In other words, life subjects us to suffering. Life, in turn, eases its burden with pleasure. In fact, we're only capable of pleasure in the first place because we suffer. In turn, we suffer because we value pleasure so highly we can't live without it. How can we come to terms with this equation, which entails frustration by its nature?

Neurotics, by definition, find this equation difficult—if not impossible—to endure. They feel, to relative degrees, that life is cheating them. They resent suffering and want to rise above it. To the degree they are successful they miss the point of life entirely. They're so preoccupied with controlling their suffering they forget what life is about. This was the type of person Freud wanted to help, the one for whom psychoanalysis might be used for coming to terms with life, by living it without fear. In *Beyond the Pleasure Principle* (1955a), where Freud introduced the death drive, he argued that "strictly speaking it is incorrect to talk of the dominance of the pleasure principle over the course of mental processes. If such a dominance existed, the immense majority of our mental processes would have to be accompanied by pleasure or to lead to pleasure, whereas universal experience completely contradicts any such conclusion" (9). In other words, our existence is primarily concerned with suffering. Life *is* suffering. This is the context in which the "life" drive (actually, *love* drive) and "death" drive are juxtaposed. Because we suffer, life occasions a motive force to attain the good—pleasure—and to live one's life in the service of goodness, to feel good, give it and receive all the good we can get. We're able to feel good only because we suffer, and we suffer when the good is threatened or taken away. The anticipation of losing what's good —the experience of danger—is a major source of suffering, which Freud called "perceptual unpleasure" (11). Because the "life drive"— Eros—doesn't relieve suffering but causes it, our only recourse to relieve the suffering life occasions is to deaden our experience of those pleasures we associate with living.

One of the most remarkable implications of Freud's conception of the "death drive" is the effect it has on our understanding of anxiety. The trend in analytic theory since Freud has been to attribute anxiety to (a) castration and its relation to repression, or (b) the threat of loss, giving rise to a host of ever more complicated —and archaic—defense mechanisms. On the other hand, the death drive imposes a new conception of danger: life itself. Because life causes anxiety, the ego is forced to either accommodate the anxiety that life occasions or protect itself against it. But because we are fundamentally divided between life and death, strife and relief, participation and withdrawal, the relative importance of our defenses against the anxieties life imposes receded in Freud's thinking. In this new model one's ambivalence about pursuing what is pleasurable (what is good) is determined by instinctual (actually, ontological) motives, not mental mechanisms, per se. This was why Freud's death drive model found little cheer amongst those analysts who were drawn to the inherently psychological language of the structural model, introduced in 1923, three years after *Beyond the Pleasure Principle*. The two revisions— the death drive in 1920 and the structural model in 1923—don't quite fit. One emphasizes drives on the level of ontology; the other emphasizes defenses on the level of psychological mechanism. Freud never attempted to fit the two models together, perhaps because they're incompatible. This is probably why analysts who welcomed the structural model and the analysis of defense it fostered rejected the death drive so readily. If psychoanalysis, following Freud, shifted its emphasis from a "psychology of mental operations" and toward an *ontology of suffering*, it would become more philosophical and less scientific, less indebted to medical and psychological sciences and more conversant with ethics and epistemology, even metaphysics. Recent preoccupations with linguistics—though instructive—miss this point.

When Freud returned to the death drive in "Analysis Terminable and Interminable"—written seventeen years after he introduced the concept—he knew he was virtually alone in this new way of conceptualizing the nature of suffering. Though he adopted the sobriquet "Nirvana complex" from Buddhism as a metaphor for his conception of Thanatos, it was a Greek philosopher (a pre-Socratic) to whom he turned to justify this controversial theory. Like Freud, Empedocles believed that life is governed by two basic forces, love and strife, which Freud equated with Eros and destructiveness (1964a, 245–46). Freud wasn't acquainted with Empedocles when he conceived the death drive, so he didn't actually inspire Freud's theory. It's telling, nevertheless, that Freud turned to a *philosopher* to defend his views against his critics in the analytic mainstream. And not just any philosopher, but a Greek. We needn't look that hard, however, for another philosopher who Freud was acquainted with at the time he conceived the death drive; a philosopher who—through Brentano—had a profound impact on his thinking as a whole: Aristotle.

One of the principal themes that preoccupied Freud in his formulation of the death drive was the nature of suffering and its relationship to the good: pleasure. In the opening sentence to the *Nicomachean Ethics*—a book with which Freud was intimately familiar—Aristotle proclaimed that "every art and every inquiry, and similarly every action and choice, is thought to aim at some good; and for this reason the good has rightly been declared to be that at which all things aim" (1985, 1729).

And what is the "good" in Aristotle? The good was equated with the pursuit of happiness. Aristotle observed that, for most people, pleasure was the purpose of life and, consequently, the highest good. But Aristotle believed there was a higher good still: virtue. He believed this not because it served utilitarian aims—such as relief from suffering—but because virtue is its own reward. The virtuous person is happy—at least with himself—whereas the person who pursues only pleasures is always in danger of losing them. The highest virtue of all was honesty—the epitome of Freud's fundamental rule of psychoanalysis.

Even a casual reading of the *Nicomachean Ethics* shows the enormous debt Freud owed to Aristotle's thinking about the nature of life. In his earlier conception of the pleasure principle, Freud translated the implications of Aristotle's ethics into one fundamental, motivating, force in life: the pursuit of pleasure. In turn, this motive force complemented a specifically thoughtful side to the self—the ego—which is principally preoccupied with concerns about the consequence of one's behavior. Basically, the ego was ostensibly concerned with virtue, which was often opposed to pleasurable aims. With his introduction of the death drive, Freud finally integrated Aristotle's ethics into his (Freud's) drive model so that the pursuit of the good now includes virtue. They're no longer opposed. While Aristotle's and Freud's formulations aren't entirely interchangeable—after all, Aristotle lacked a conception of the unconscious—Aristotle's views about the limits of pleasure approximate an uncanny resemblance to Freud's conception of Thanatos. In turn, the cultivation of virtue is consistent with Freud's conception of Eros when it serves the highest aim of all: the love of truth.

This is why honesty is so vital to psychoanalysis. A capacity for honesty—in fact, a *love* for honesty and truth—is essential for anyone who aspires to change his or her manner of being. Without it, the intrigues that occasion pathogenic conflict only increase, prompted further by the paranoid fear of being found out. Freud's conception of Eros finally offered a theory of the personality that justified his technique, the basis of which is *fidelity to revelation*. The fundamental aim in life—in the face of interminable suffering—is to feel good by *being* good; by endeavoring to be truthful and accepting realities. Psychoanalysis may indeed relieve suffering, but only in Zen-like fashion: not by trying to suffer less, but by submitting to what life is about. This partially explains Freud's somewhat cautious tone in "Analysis Terminable and Interminable." The skill of analysts is important, but only insofar as they understand the nature of their role and are capable of serving it. The rest is up to their patients and the aims *they* feel compelled to serve.

And what if those aims endeavor to serve the "negative therapeutic reaction," whose purpose, after all, is "death"? First, it's important to remember that neurotic conflict isn't actually caused by the death drive. The neurosis itself is independent of it. Yet, neurotic conflict compels us to avoid the anxieties we experience when disappointed by reality. We perceive reality—"life"—as dangerous and withdraw into phantasy. The neurosis is comprised of a conflict between phantasy and reality. We can't accept reality for what it is. What, then, epitomizes the realities we're unable to accept? Basically, it comes down to feeling unloved. Consequently, we deny that we need the love we feel without and twist reality accordingly. But this is untenable, because we still desire what we insist we don't. In fact, the *persistence* of desire is the basis of neurotic conflict. Though we employ repression in order to ease suffering, it's because we can't help but desire that we eventually need help. When the knot that we're in is, in turn, analyzed, the analyst meets our resistance. Most of these resistances are employed against knowing and telling; knowing more about our experience and admitting what we already know about it. But there's another kind of resistance that comes from our nature, that is opposed to the life that we're living. This resistance isn't actually a product of neurotic conflict. Like transference, it is ready to hand and becomes abducted by the neurosis when it needs to insure its survival. When the weight of frustration is unbearable, the *relief* from suffering may become a resistance to the treatment, even competing with it. The death drive, always at the ready in times of hardship, becomes an agent provocateur, offering asylum from one's suffering by deadening the lust for life itself (Thompson 1985).

Toward the end of his life Freud emphasized those resistances he believed emanated from drives—from desire. Unlike so many analysts today, he gradually distanced himself from a preoccupation with—and technically, an analysis of—*defense*. He doubted that defense mechanisms could explain the prevalence of moral masochism, unconscious guilt, and the negative therapeutic reactions manifested by some of the patients he treated. He suspected that many failed analyses could be attributed to a deep-seated wish to circumvent the pain of living, even at the cost of living any kind of life at all. In effect, we withdraw from life itself. We're so sick of suffering we'll do anything to escape it. The treatment, which aims to examine one's suffering, becomes an instrument of the suffering we seek to disavow. Since our intolerance of suffering can't actually be "diagnosed," it can't be *treated*. This seemingly radical assessment, however, wasn't especially new to Freud's way of thinking. As early as 1905 (Freud 1953c) he believed that "poor character" shouldn't be confused with psychopathology. Some people are simply "good for nothing." They haven't the moral fiber to bear suffering. Just because we suffer doesn't mean we can always be "diagnosed" and "treated." Nor does the successful treatment of a neurotic conflict necessarily improve one's character, though it sometimes helps. The disposition toward self-concealment doesn't always foster the kind of *moral* conflicts that psychoanalysis was intended to resolve. If we deceive, but do not experience any conflict because of it, all the analysis in the world can't impose a solution on something that we can't acknowledge is amiss. Like Aristotle, Freud believed that character has to be cultivated and developed. One doesn't build character by devising ways of relieving suffering, but as a consequence of coming to terms with it. This makes the goal of analysis, at the very least, ambiguous. That's because the kind of suffering analysis is intended to relieve isn't *pain,* specifically. It can only help us surmount the alienation we feel when we live in *anticipation of disappointment.* Our ability to overcome this fear, by learning to accommodate it, relieves our alienation—but not *suffering* itself. This—perhaps unsettling—dimension to the aims and capacities of analysis was also exploited by Winnicott. He linked the fear of suffering and our wish to abolish it to omnipotence, whose demands merely distance us even further from actual living:

> If we are successful we enable the patient *to abandon invulnerability and to become a sufferer.* If we succeed life becomes precarious to one who was beginning to know a kind of stability and a freedom from pain, even if this meant non-participation in life and perhaps mental defect. (1989, 199; emphasis in original)

In other words, life without suffering is an illusion. Neurotics, to the degree they can't tolerate the anguish that life imposes, hope to circumvent it. That's because their capacity for anguish simply isn't equal to their reach.

Why does life elicit more anguish in some than in others? This was one of the questions Freud pondered after his analysis of Dora. Most analysts today attribute the abrupt termination of her treatment to Freud's handling of the transference. Freud himself acknowledged this oversight, but never attributed this to the failure of her analysis. Why? Though he didn't know it then, Dora's unexpected decision to stop the treatment when she did is a perfect example of a "negative therapeutic reaction." Though the work was progressing, Dora wasn't. The way that she terminated—an act of vengeance against Freud's influence—was symptomatic of her aggression against her father and Mr. K. But that doesn't explain why she terminated when she did. If all she wanted was to punish Freud, why leave? There were other, perhaps more effective ways of achieving that goal. Nor was her sudden departure a consequence of erotic transference. There was little, if any, evidence she was attracted to Freud, nor did she appear to feel rejected by him. She abandoned the treatment because *it threatened to make her well*. It manifested in her a "negative therapeutic reaction." Dora's symptoms were treasures she wasn't about to relinquish—as Felix Deutsche (1985), years later, confirmed. She was so masochistically attached to them that nothing—not even pleasure—could compete with the feeling of triumph, omnipotent to be sure, they provided. Whether we follow Freud in his speculations about a propensity toward self-destructiveness or reject it—and we know most analysts have chosen the latter—the efficacy of the negative therapeutic reaction as a concept still retains its value. In fact, the term is commonly used even by those analysts who dismiss the notion of a death drive. The term is now commonly used to characterize a reaction against the treatment whenever one had anticipated progress. Since this reaction is elicited by the analysis itself, it is construed as an act *against the treatment*. As a technical term, it simply alerts us to those reactions we sometimes elicit from our patients precisely because the treatment is proceeding satisfactorily.

Perhaps this was why Freud, by today's standards, didn't believe in lengthy analyses. The Wolf Man, whose analysis and reanalysis lasted some five and a half years, was an exception to the rule. In fact, the prolongation of his analysis—which, unfortunately, we can't pursue more thoroughly—proved futile. Freud believed that even one year was a long time to stay in treatment. Ten years—not uncommon nowadays—was unthinkable. Perhaps we avoid termination by allowing analyses to go on as long as they do, hoping for some sign of "recovery." In his later years, Freud frequently set a limit to the duration of a treatment at the beginning of the analysis, typically six months or a year. Though this was more usual in his "didactic" analyses, this practice was in stark contrast with the custom today, when even training analyses are often interminable.

The ambiguous tone of Freud's comments about termination is especially puzzling to those who still conceptualize analysis as a medical treatment for psychiatric illness. Many believe that Freud didn't allow the vast majority of his patients sufficient time to achieve a more lasting benefit from their treatment. Was Freud constitutionally incapable of conducting lengthy analyses? Was he too impatient to tolerate the seemingly endless detours that most analytic treatments require? In fact, Freud believed that the prolongation of analysis is frequently a consequence of countertransference, when it violates the rule against *therapeutic ambition*. Therapeutic ambition, a form of countertransference, is difficult to recognize. When we commit it, it's usually because we only want to help. On a narcissistic note, we may simply be too eager to "cure" every patient we treat. Sometimes, using Freud's analogy, surgeons need to sew up the wounds and let go, knowing they've done all they can. This was one of the reasons Freud believed all therapists should submit to analysis themselves, to help them to endure and understand the unique pressures of analytic practice. He never thought, however, that it should be as thorough as the analysis to which one's patients are typically subjected. His reasoning was simple. Analysts shouldn't be sick (i.e., uncommonly conflicted) in the first place, so why should they require a lengthy treatment? Instead, Freud emphasized character, the personality traits that analysts happen to possess when entering this profession. Which character traits did Freud value the most? What qualifications did he believe each analyst should possess?

> He must possess some kind of superiority, so that in certain analytic situations he can act as a model for his patient and in others as a teacher. And finally he must not forget that the analytic relationship is based on a love of truth—that is, on a recognition of reality—and that it precludes any kind of sham or deceit. (1964a, 248)

All the analysis in the world won't make people more honest than they were capable of being at the beginning of treatment. This is just as true for future analysts as it is for the patients they analyze. If anything, the lengthier one's training analysis, the more likely it will serve as a standard for that analyst's future patients; and the more "interminable" those analyses will be, in turn. Given the nature of analysis—its limitations, the unpredictable nature of life, and the possibility for future outbreak of neurotic conflict—Freud advocated periodic "reanalyses" as a resource when one's personal life (or one's patients) become overwhelming. Freud expected this would happen and was loathe to attribute its efficacy to a failed, or "incomplete," analysis. Generally, this advice has been ignored.

What, then, are we "treating" if so much of our suffering and the ambivalence we succumb to because of it can't be attributed to psychopathology, specifically? Psychopathology is rooted in a peculiar form of conflict, not in suffering itself. Yet, we shouldn't confuse this form of conflict with our intrinsic ambivalence about good and evil, life and death, love and hate. Melanie Klein, who adopted and even championed Freud's "death drive," misunderstood this. Unlike Freud, who believed our innate ambivalence is axiomatic, Klein based her entire conception of psychopathology on the conflict between these primal forces (Klein 1937). Consequently, there is no clear distinction in her theories between pathology and health, between sanity and madness. Though neurotic conflict, in a manner of speaking, is "internalized," it is a consequence of our conflict *with reality,* the nature of which isn't that easy to determine. In fact, psychopathology is a *flight* from suffering. That's why it can't be reduced, strictly speaking, to pain alone. Unlike psychiatry, whose goal is the unadulterated relief of suffering, psychoanalysis is a medium through which we strive to repair our relationship with reality. Hence, our experience—or nonexperience—of reality assumes precedence over our intolerance of suffering.

What, then, is reality, basically? This is a big question. It's like asking, "What is the meaning of life?" It is such a huge question that some people think it's inappropriate to ask it. Freud didn't *ask* this question, but his conception of psychopathology presupposes a definite view of its nature. He assumed that all of us are fundamentally concerned with reality. He painstakingly explored the variety of ways that he and his patients came up against it in their lives. Sometimes, he spoke of reality as "necessity": that which must be accepted. Reality is what we have to reckon with. It's what we can't, with any honesty, deny. This dimension of reality—its irrefutability—gives rise to the harshness that we sometimes associate with it, because it's something we can't manipulate or control. We never really "understand" reality. We come to know it through our *encounter* with it. That doesn't mean, however, that reality is necessarily harsh. Freud realized how seductive the world of phantasy—of *pretense*—can be when reality becomes so frightening that we do what we must to avoid it. Yet, he never reduced reality to necessity. It also has the power to *compel*. If it didn't, we'd probably have very little to do with it. This dimension of reality—its attraction—explains how psychoanalysis comes into its own. It draws us in and helps us experience things as they are. Reality isn't simply "external"; it invites me to *belong* to what's separate and to make it a dimension of my life.

Freud believed that subsequent to termination we may need, from time to time, to resume analysis again. This is because he never envisioned termination as a *cessation*. And even if analysis is never formally resumed, termination never entails a categorical "end" to one's experience of it. Every analysis lives on, if only in our minds. Some analysts depict termination as a transformation from a psychoanalysis to self-analysis. But this can be misleading because it implies that one has effectively "graduated" from the relationship with one's analyst to one of independence. Although this idea has a certain appeal, it confuses the termination of psychoanalysis with the completion of an education. Nor does it characterize Freud's conception of it which, if anything, was the opposite. When analysis is over we continue to think about what happened in the course of it. We try to understand and make use of the things that eluded us at the time. We mine the material and conversations for the sense we might make of it, long after the analysis has ended. We may eventually opt to resume analysis, or not. But like a child who's left home, we take with us what was essential. We take care to protect what we kept from danger. We keep it alive. We couldn't leave it behind if we tried, because it's fostered our way of thinking, our manner of being in the world. Because it's given us our history—in fact, it's opened that history up—it shows the way to the future. Some have attributed this aspect of analysis—its permanence—to the internalization or introjection of the analyst into the patient's unconscious. I'm not expecially drawn to this way of seeing it. It sounds excessively "psychological." Freud implied that the survival of the analyst's influence can be attributed to the depth of love one happens to feel for the analyst. Perhaps this only happens when we manage to leave the treatment without rancor.

Freud knew that the potentially therapeutic effects of a psychoanalysis aren't axiomatic. Termination guarantees nothing. In the end, we choose whatever importance we permit analysis to have. The risk every analysis entails and the impossibility of foretelling its impact epitomize its inherently existential nature. Its "end" is simply a new beginning. This was demonstrated in a remarkable exchange that the Wolf Man had with Freud while he was still in analysis with him. It concerned the potential effects of termination (Obholzer 1982). The Wolf Man asked if he would be restored to psychic health once the dynamics of his childhood history became known. Freud replied that the answer to his question wasn't that simple:

> Freud said that when one has gone through psychoanalysis, one *can* become well. But one must also *want* to become well. It's like a ticket one buys. The ticket gives one the possibility to travel. But I am not obliged to travel. It depends on me, on my decision. (43; emphasis added)

The Wolf Man realized that this characterization of termination effectively refuted the common assumption that Freud believed in determinism. If our unconscious motives are said to determine our conscious decisions, what determines our *unconscious*? The line between the two isn't so easy to define. Surely, each determines the other. Our conscious choices help determine what becomes unconscious as well. The termination of analysis confronts each of us with a choice. Will we, in effect, use the "ticket" it gives us, or will we neglect it or, worse, lose it without a trace? We may use it initially but neglect it as time goes by. Fate, too, plays a hand. We may find that the future occasions fresh challenges that simply overwhelm our previously effective efforts. If that happens, we'll have to decide what to do about those unforeseen consequences, whether to seek help or persist in our folly. Whatever we choose, whether that choice inhibits or transforms, we will have to wait and see.

References

Alexander, F., and S. Selesnick. 1966. *The history of psychiatry.* New York: Harper and Row.

American Psychiatric Association. 1987. *Diagnostic and statistical manual of mental disorders* (3d rev. ed.). Washington, D.C.: American Psychiatric Association.

Applebaum, A. 1972. A critical re-examination of the concept "motivation for change" in psycho-analytic treatment. *International Journal of Psycho-analysis* 53: 51–59.

Aristotle. 1985. *The complete works of Aristotle,* 2 vols. Ed. J. Barnes. Bollingen Series. Princeton: Princeton University Press.

Arlow, J. 1991. A new look at Freud's "Analysis terminable and interminable." In *On Freud's "Analysis terminable and interminable,"* ed. J. Sandler, 43–55. New Haven: Yale University Press, 1991.

Binswanger, L. 1963. *Being in the world.* Trans. Jacob Needleman. New York: Basic Books.

Blanton, S. 1971. *Diary of my analysis with Sigmund Freud.* New York: Hawthorne Books.

Boss, M. 1963. *Psychoanalysis and daseinsanalysis.* Trans. Ludwig Lefebre. New York: Basic Books.

Brenner, C. 1979. Working alliance, therapeutic alliance, and transference. *Journal of the American Psychoanalytic Association* 27: 137–58.

Burston, D. 1991. *The legacy of Erich Fromm.* Cambridge: Harvard University Press.

Deutsch, E. 1985. A footnote to "Freud's fragment of an analysis of a case of hysteria." *In Dora's case: Freud-hysteria-feminism,* ed. C. Bernheimer and C. Kahane, 35–43. New York: Columbia Univ. Press.

Edelson, M. 1988. *Psychoanalysis: A theory in crisis.* Chicago: University of Chicago Press.

Ellman, S. 1991. *Freud's technique papers: A contemporary perspective.* New York: Aronson.

Erikson, E. 1985. Reality and actuality: An address. *In Dora's case: Freud-hysteria-feminism,* ed. C. Bernheimer and C. Kahane. New York: Columbia Univ. Press.

Ey, H. 1978. *Consciousness: A phenomenological study of being conscious and becoming conscious.* Trans. J. Flodstrom. Bloomington: Indiana University Press.

Fairbairn, W. R. D. 1952. *Psychoanalytic studies of the personality.* London: Routledge and Kegan Paul.

Farias, V. 1989. *Heidegger and Nazism.* Trans. P. Burrell and G. Ricci. Philadelphia: Temple University Press.

Federn, P. 1952. *Ego-psychology and the psychoses.* New York: Basic Books.

Ferenczi, S. 1980. *Further contributions to the theory and technique of psychoanalysis.* Trans. Jane Suttie. New York: Brunner-Mazel.

Frankl, V. 1968. *Psychotherapy and existentialism: Selected papers on logotherapy.* New York: Clarion Books.

Freud, S. 1953–73. *The standard edition of the complete psychological works of Sigmund Freud.* 24 vols. Ed. and trans. J. Strachey. London: Hogarth Press. (Referred to in subsequent references as *S.E.*)

————. 1953a. *Fragment of an analysis of a case of hysteria. S.E.* 7: 1–122.

————. 1953b. Freud's psychoanalytic procedure. *S.E.* 7: 249–54.

————. 1953c. On psychotherapy. *S.E.* 7: 257–68.

————. 1955a. *Beyond the pleasure principle. S.E.* 18: 3–64.

————. 1955b. *Group psychology and the analysis of the ego. S.E.* 18: 67–143.

————. 1955c. *The interpretation of dreams. S.E.* 4–5: 3–463.

————. 1955d. The neuro-psychoses of defense. *S.E.* 3: 45–68.

————. 1955e. *Notes upon a case of obsessional neurosis. S.E.* 7: 153–320.

————. 1957a. The future prospects of psychoanalytic therapy. *S.E.* 11: 139–51.

————. 1957b. On the history of the psychoanalytic movement. *S.E.* 14: 7–66.

————. 1957c. On narcissism: An introduction. *S.E.* 14: 67–102.

————. 1957d. On the universal tendency to debasement in the sphere of love. *S.E.* 11: 177–90.

————. 1957e. The unconscious. *S.E.* 14: 159–215.

————. 1957f. "Wild" psychoanalysis. *S.E.* 11: 219–27.

————. 1958a. The dynamics of transference. *S.E.* 12: 97–108.

————. 1958b. Formulations on the two principles of mental functioning. *S.E.* 12: 215–26.

————. 1958c. The handling of dream-interpretation in psycho-analysis. *S.E.* 12: 89–96.

————. 1958d. Observations on transference-love (Further recommendations on the technique of psycho-analysis III). *S.E.* 12: 157–71.

————. 1958e. On beginning the treatment (Further recommendations on the technique of psycho-analysis I). *S.E.* 12: 121–44.

————. 1958f. *Psychoanalytic notes on an autobiographical account of a case of paranoia (dementia paranoides). S.E.* 12: 3–82.

————. 1958g. Recommendations to physicians practising psycho-analysis. *S.E.* 12: 109–20.

————. 1958h. Remembering, repeating and working-through (Further recommendations on the technique of psycho-analysis II). *S.E.* 12: 145–56.

———. 1958i. *Totem and taboo. S.E.* 13: 1–161.

———. 1959a. *Inhibitions, symptoms and anxiety. S.E.* 20: 77–174.

———. 1959b. *The question of lay analysis. S.E.* 20: 179–258.

———. 1960. *The psychopathology of everyday life. S.E.* 6: 1–279.

———. 1961a. *Civilization and its discontents. S.E.* 21: 59–145.

———. 1961b. The dissolution of the oedipus complex. *S.E.* 19: 172–79.

———. 1961c. The economic problem of masochism. *S.E.* 19: 157–70.

———. 1961d. *The ego and the id. S.E.* 19: 3–66.

———. 1961e. The infantile genital organization. *S.E.* 19: 140–45.

———. 1961f. The loss of reality in neurosis and psychosis. *S.E.* 19: 182–87.

———. 1961g. Neurosis and psychosis. *S.E.* 19: 148–53.

———. 1962. On the psychical mechanism of hysterical phenomena: A lecture. *S.E.* 3: 25–39.

———. 1963. *Introductory lectures on psychoanalysis. S.E.* 16: 67–143.

———. 1964a. Analysis terminable and interminable. *S.E.* 23: 209–53.

———. 1964b. Constructions in analysis. *S.E.* 23: 255–69.

———. 1964c. *New introductory lectures on psychoanalysis. S.E.* 22: 3–182.

———. 1966a. Case of a successful treatment by hypnotism. *S.E.,* 1: 115–28.

———. 1966b. Project for a scientific psychology. *S.E.* 1: 283–398.

Freud, S., and J. Breuer. 1955. *Studies in hysteria. S.E.* 2: 1–306.

Gay, P. 1988. *Freud: A life for our time.* New York: Basic Books.

Gill, M. 1982. *Analysis of transference, Vol. 1: Theory and technique.* New York: International Universities Press.

Gray, P. 1982. "Developmental lag" in the evolution of technique for psychoanalysis of neurotic conflict. *Journal of the American Psychoanalytic Association* 30: 621–55.

———. 1986. On helping analysands observe intrapsychic activity. In *Psychoanalysis: The science of mental conflict-essays in honor of Charles Brenner.* Ed. A. Richard and M. Willick, 245–62. Hillsdale, N. J.: Analytic Press.

Green, A. 1991. Instinct in the late works of Freud. In *On Freud's "Analysis terminable and interminable,"* ed. Joseph Sandler, 124–41. New Haven: Yale University Press

Grunberger, B. 1966. Some reflections on the Rat Man. *International Journal of Psycho-analysis* 47: 160–68.

Guntrip, H. 1968. *Schizoid phenomena, object-relations and the self.* London: Hogarth Press.

Hamilton, E., and H. Cairns, ed. 1961. *The collected dialogues of Plato.* Bollingen Series. Princeton: Princeton University Press.

Hartmann, H. 1958. *Ego psychology and the problem of adaptation.* New York: International Universities Press.

Haynal, A. 1989. *Controversies in psychoanalytic method.* New York: New York University Press.

H.D. [Doolittle, H.] 1956. *Tribute to Freud.* New York: Pantheon Books.

Heidegger, M. 1962. *Being and time.* Trans. J. Macquarrie and E. Robinson. New York: Harper and Row.

Heidegger, M. 1967. *What is a thing?* Trans. W. B. Barton and V. Deutsch. Chicago: Henry Regnery.

Heidegger, M. 1971. *On the way to language.* Trans. Peter Hertz. New York: Harper and Row.

———. 1977a. *Basic writings.* Ed. D. F. Krell. New York: Harper and Row.

———. 1977b. *The question concerning technology and other essays.* Trans. W. Lovitt). New York: Harper and Row.

Hesnard, A. 1960. *L'ouevre de Freud et son importance pour le monde moderne.* Paris: Payot.

Horney, K. 1987. *Final lectures.* New York: W.W. Norton.

Jones, E. 1955. *The life and work of Sigmund Freud.* 3 vols. New York: Basic Books.

Kanzer, M. 1980. The transference neurosis of the Rat Man. In *Freud and his patients,* ed. M. Kanzer and J. Glenn. New York: Aronson, 1980.

Kanzer, M., and J. Glenn, ed. 1980. *Freud and his patients.* New York: Aronson.

Klein, M. 1937. Love, guilt and reparation. In *Love guilt and reparation and other works.* London: Hogarth Press, 1981.

———. 1957. Envy and gratitude. In *Envy and gratitude and other works.* London: Hogarth Press, 1975.

Kris, E. 1951. Ego psychology and interpretation in psychoanalytic therapy. *Psychoanalytic Quarterly* 20: 15–30.

Lacan, J. 1977. *Ecrits—a selection.* Trans. Alan Sheridan. New York: W.W. Norton.

Laing, R. D. 1960. *The divided self.* New York: Pantheon.

———. 1961. *Self and others.* New York: Pantheon.

———. 1967. *The politics of experience.* New York: Pantheon Books.

———. 1977. Personal communication. April 1.

Laing, R. D., and D. Cooper. 1964. *Reason and violence.* New York: Pantheon.

Laing, R. D., and A. Esterson. 1964. *Sanity, madness, and the family.* London: Tavistock.

Langs, R. 1980. The misalliance dimension in the case of the Rat Man. In *Freud and his patients,* ed. M. Kanzer and J. Glenn. New York: Aronson.

Laplanche, J., and J.-B. Pontalis. 1973. *The language of psychoanalysis.* Trans. D. Nicholson-Smith. London: Hogarth Press.

Leavy, S. 1980. *The psychoanalytic dialogue.* New Haven: Yale University Press.

———. 1988. *In the image of god.* New Haven: Yale University Press.

———. 1989. Time and world in the thought of Hans Loewald. In *Psychoanalytic study of the child,* vol. 44. New Haven: Yale University Press.

———. 1990. Reality in religion and psychoanalysis. In *Psychoanalysis and religion,* ed. J. Smith and S. Handelman, 43–59. Baltimore: Johns Hopkins University Press.

Lefebre, L. 1957. The psychology of Karl Jaspers. In *The philosophy of Karl Jaspers,* ed. Paul Schilpp, 467–97. LaSalle, IL: Open Court.

Lipton, S. 1977. The advantages of Freud's technique as shown in his analysis of the Rat Man. *International Journal of Psycho-analysis* 58: 255–73.

Loewald, H. W. 1980. *Papers on psychoanalysis*. New Haven: Yale University Press.

Mahony, P. 1986. *Freud and the Rat Man*. New Haven: Yale University Press.

Marcuse, H. 1955. *Eros and civilization*. New York: Beacon Press.

May, R., ed. 1958. *Existence*. New York: Basic Books.

McCulloch, W. 1965. *Embodiments of mind*. Cambridge: M.I.T. Press.

Montaigne, M. 1925. *The essays of Montaigne*. 4 vols. Trans. George B. Ives. Cambridge: Harvard University Press.

Obholzer, K. 1982. *The Wolf-Man: Conversations with Freud's patient-sixty years later*. Trans. Michael Shaw. New York: Continuum.

Racker, H. 1968. *Transference and countertransference*. New York: International Universities Press.

Rockmore, T., and J. Margolis, ed. 1992. *The Heidegger case: On philosophy and politics*. Philadelphia: Temple University Press.

Rycroft, C., ed. 1966. *Psychoanalysis observed*. London: Constable.

———. 1968. *Imagination and reality*. New York: International Universities Press.

———. 1985. *Psychoanalysis and beyond*. Chicago: University of Chicago Press.

Sartre, J.-P. 1953. *Existential psychoanalysis*. Trans. Hazel E. Barnes. New York: Philosophical Library.

Schilder, P. 1935. *The image and appearance of the human body*. New York: International Universities Press.

Schneiderman, S. 1983. *Jacques Lacan: The death of an intellectual hero*. Cambridge: Harvard University Press.

Spiegelberg, H. 1972. *Phenomenology in psychology and psychiatry*. Evanston: Northwestern University Press.

Strauss, E. 1966. *Phenomenological psychology: Selected papers*. Trans. Erling Eng. New York: Basic Books.

Thompson, M. G. 1985. *The death of desire: A study in psychopathology*. New York: New York University Press.

Van Dusen, W. 1959. Adler and existential analysis. *Journal of Individual Psychology* 15: 100–11.

Vitz, P. 1988. *Sigmund Freud's christian unconscious*. New York: Guilford Press.

Will, O. A. Jr. 1992. Personal communication. May 1.

Winnicott, D. W. 1965. *The family and individual development*. London: Tavistock.

———. 1976. Ego distortion in terms of true and false self. In *The maturational processes and the facilitating environment*. London: Hogarth Press.

———. 1989. *Psychoanalytic explorations*. Ed. C. Winnicott, R. Shephard, and M. David. Cambridge: Harvard University Press.

Wolin, R., ed. 1991. *The Heidegger controversy: A critical reader*. New York: Columbia University Press.

Wortis, J. 1954. *Fragments of an analysis with Freud*. New York: Simon and Schuster.

Zimmerman, M. 1981. *The eclipse of the self*. Athens: Ohio University Press.

Index

Abstinence, 172–73
Adler, Alfred, 55, 137
"Adolescence and the Doldrums" (Winnicott), 124
Affective ideas, 11
Agape, 262, 187–88n. *See also* Love
Aletheia, 62. *See also* Truth
Altered ego, 250–51, 255–56
Ambivalence: of ego, 256–57; guilt vs., 228; negative transference epitomized by, 183–84; of obsessional compulsions, 219–20
"Analysis Terminable and Interminable" (Freud), 162, 203, 245, 247, 266, 268
Analysts: advised to withhold sympathy, 150–51; aggression toward, 183–84; concern with remembering, 192–204; confidentiality between patient and, 213; continuing influence of, 273–74; countertransference of, xxii, 43–44, 122–23; criticism of Freud's behavior as, 230–40; Freud's recommendations to, 64, 135, 145–54, 242, 271–72; patient's transference-love for, 37–40, 176–80; remaining alert to patients, 64; resistance to, 42–43, 181–82; technique and personality of, 136–39, 207–8; use of abstinence by, 173. *See also* Neutrality; Psychoanalysis
Analytic attitude, 67, 254
Analytic patients. *See* Patients
Analytic schools, xxii
Analyzability, 156–57, 243–44
Anna O., 168
Anxiety: death drive and, 265–66; ego as

reservoir of, 26; Freud's beliefs regarding, 14–18; neurotic vs. realistic, 15; in terms of structural model, 229
Anzieu, Didier, xix
Applebaum, A., 239
Aristotle: correspondence theory of, 59; ethical studies of, 3; influence on Freud, 4, 266–67; scientific approach challenged, 70–72
Arlow, J., 253

Bacon, Francis, 74
Bad faith, 67
Behavior: concerned with consequence of, 267; obsessions and compulsive, 223; self-destructive, 260–61, 270; as type of remembering, 193
Behaviorism school, 2
Being and Time (Sein und Zeit) (Heidegger), 52, 57
Beliefs, 76
Berkeley, George, 3
Beyond the Pleasure Principle (Freud), 22, 133, 265–66
Bilmes, Murray, xxv
Binswanger, Ludwig, 55
Blanton, S., 237
Bleuler, Eugen, 182
Borderline conditions, 157–58, 206, 245
Börne, Ludwig, 168
Boss, Medard, 237
Brentano, Franz, 51–52, 266
Breuer, Josef, 168
Brunswick, Ruth Mack, 248

281

"Case of Successful Treatment by Hypnotism" (Freud), 10
Castration complex, 15–20, 34–35
Causality, 79–82
Certitude, 75, 86, 88
Character, 269
Character disorders, 157
Childhood: adaptive behavior during, 23; defenses erected during, 249–50; development of ego in, 23; expectations during, 25–26; ideal ego of, 45–46; neurosis/psychosis origins during, 28, 32; obsessional neurosis originating in, 214–15; repression, 256; scopophilic urge during, 68; truth of experience during, 124
Civilization and Its Discontents (Freud), 17
Classical pathologies, 206–8. *See also* Hysterical neurosis; Obsessional neurosis
Classical psychoanalysis, 138, 230–40. *See also* Psychoanalysis
Concealment: as basis of psychopathology, 129; of truth, 64–65; uncovering mystery of, 66–68; vs. repression, 65–66. *See also* Truth
Confidentiality, 213
Conscious, 23. *See also* Unconscious
Cooper, David, 56
Correspondence theory, 62
Countertransference: of Freud for Ferenczi, 251; Freud's failure to acknowledge, xxii, 122–23, 127; neutrality to control, 233; therapeutic ambition as source of, 149–50, 153–54, 271. *See also* Transference-love
Counter-will, 9–10, 21, 65

Das Ich, 14
Death drive theory, xxii, 259–60, 262–63. *See also* Anxiety; Existential philosophy
Death of Desire, The (Thompson), xviii, 14
Defense mechanisms, 258, 268–69
Delusions: denied reality patched with, 33; experience of psychotic, 34–36; as key to psychosis, 32. *See also* Psychosis
Dementia praecox, 243
Denial, 33–36
Descartes, René, 3, 75–76, 86
Deutsch, Felix, 126, 270

Developmental lines, 125
Differential diagnosis, 163
Diotima, 188–89
Disclosure: of confidential secrets, 99–100; through language, 62–64
"Dissolution of the Oedipus Complex, The" (Freud), 29
Doolittle, Hilda (H.D.), 237
Dora (Ida Bauer) case: Deutsch's account of, 126–27; dream interpretation during, 110–13, 143; negative therapeutic reaction in, 270; paradox of neurosis and, 97–100; patient deception during, 157; professional criticisms of, 122–32; summary of, 101–9; techniques used in, 93–96, 133–34; termination of, 115–21
Dream interpretation: during Dora (Ida Bauer) case, 110–13; Freud's approach to, 135, 141–44. *See also* Unconscious
Dreams and Hysteria (Freud), 97, 110
Drive. *See* Instinct
Drive model, 262, 267
Durcharbeitung (Freud), 192
"Dynamics of Transference, The" (Freud), 135–36, 175–91, 225

"Economic Problem of Masochism, The" (Freud), 258–59
Edelson, Marshall, 7–8, 13
Educative ambition, 153, 171
Ego: agency preceding formation of, 26; aims of analysis regarding, 255–56; altered, 250–51, 255–56; ambivalence of, 256–57; assault on, 17; development of, 13–14, 23–24; psychosis and, 30; relationship between reality and, 12; resistance governed by, 203; as seat of anxiety, 15; strengthening, 254; and transference neuroses, 27–28. *See also* Id; Superego
"Ego and Reality" (Loewald), 12
Ego and the Id, The (Freud), 17, 27, 256, 258–59
Ellis, Havelock, 160
Ellman, S., 143, 150
Empedocles, 266
Episteme, 82–83
Erikson, Erik, 124–25
Eros, 261, 266–67

Erotic (positive) transference, 185
Erotism, 47, 184. *See also* Love; Transference-love
Errare, 68
Evenly suspended attention, 146–47
Excavation, 67
Excitations, 11
Existential philosophy: criticism of academic philosophy by, 51–52; death drive argument as, xxii, 262; existence according to, 3; Freud's clinical behavior as, xxii; influence of, 55–56; view of reality, 19–20
Experience: benefits of, 195–96, 198–99; of castration anxiety, 20; childhood phantasy, 16; Descartes's rejection of sensual, 75; expectations of love based on, 177–78; free association leading to, 168–69; Freud's discussion of reality, 6; guilt as saving, 66; patient's analysis, 255; of phantasy, 8; propensity to forget painful, 241; psychoanalysis used to explore, 54; of psychotic reality, 6, 34–36; schizophrenia as form of, 244; significance between temporality and, 202–3; of suffering, 261–63; truth from, 63, 77, 124, 131–32; of unconditional acceptance, 225–26; working-through, 199–200
External reality: anxiety caused by, 19–20; conflict between ego and, 17, 27–28; as hostile, 12; psychical reality vs., 9
Ey, Henri, 56

False Self, 255
Fear. *See* Anxiety
Federn, Paul, 55
Feminine neurosis. *See* Hysterical neurosis
Ferenczi, Sandor, 138–39, 153, 208, 250–52
First Law of Motion (Newton), 71–73
Fliess, Wilhelm, 29
Forces, 11
Forgotten feelings, 193
"Formulations on the Two Principles of Mental Functioning" (Freud), 21, 256
Fragment of an Analysis of a Case of Hysteria (Freud), 97
Frankl, Viktor, 56

Free association: cure based on, 68; enhanced by frequent treatment, 162; supine position to enhance, 165–66; to release the unconscious, 82, 166–70
Freud, Sigmund: analytic behavior of, xxiii, 209, 231–40; analytic rules of, xxiii–xxiv; on anxiety, 13–14; compares neurotic and psychotic reality, 27–36; conception of reality, 2–3, 6, 17–20, 53–54; conception of repression, 64–68; death drive theory of, xxii, 259–60, 262–63; dismissal of philosophy by, 1, 51; on ego development, 23–24; failure to acknowledge countertransference, xxii, 122–23, 127; influenced by Aristotle, 4, 266–67; influence of, 55–56; lifetime search for truth by, 52–53, 78; on love/transference-love, 37–49; professional aims of, 1–5; proposals regarding resistance, 203–4; on psychical reality, 7–11; on psychoanalysis, 88–90, 243–44, 247–63; theory of the unconscious by, 21–22; treatment of Dora (Ida Bauer) by, 93–132; treatment of Ferenczi by, 250–52; treatment of Rat Man (Ernst Lanzer) by, 209–40; unique development of, xvii–xviii; use of psychology by, 74; on wishful vs. realistic thinking, 25–26. *See also* Technical papers (Freud)
"Freud's Psychoanalytic Procedure" (Lowenfeld), 134
Fromm, Erich, 55
Fromm-Reichmann, Frieda, 161
Frustration, 179–81
"Fundamental rule," 128, 167, 182, 243
"Future Prospects of Psychoanalytic Therapy, The" (Freud), 134

Gain from illness, 261
Galileo, 72
Gans, Steven, xxv
Gay, Peter: on dichotomy of Freud's technique, 152–53; on Freud's account of Dora case, 97, 122–23, 125, 127; on the Rat Man treatment, 210
"General Account of Psychoanalytic Technique" (Freud), 134
Genuine love, 43–45, 48, 262

Gill, M., 238
God: proving existence of, 3; truth and, 59
Gray, P., 198, 200, 203
Green, Andre, 262
Grunberger, B., 239
Guilt: moral masochism due to, 261; obses-
sive, 214; saving experience of, 66;
sources of, 183n., 217, 228–29; vs. am-
bivalence, 228

Hallucination. *See* Delusions
"Handling of Dream-Interpretation in Psycho-analysis, The" (Freud), 135, 141–44
Hartmann, H., 260
Haynal, A., 237–38
H.D. (Hilda Doolittle), 237
Heaton, John, xxv
Heidegger, Martin: on art of psychoanaly-
sis, 137; on causality, 79–81; conception
of truth, xxiv, 57–65; conception of un-
truth, 64–68; criticism of academic philosophy by, 51; describes experience,
198; extension of philosophy of, xix–xx;
influence of, 55–56; influence of Montaigne on, 169; philosophy of existence
of, xviii, 52; on scientific approach, 70;
on technology, 78–79, 84–85
Hesnard, Angelo, 55
Heuscher, Julius, xxv
Historical truth, 125
Homosexuality, 243
Horney, Karen, 165
Husserl, Edmund, 51–52, 269
Hysterical neurosis: dream interpretation
for, 97; elicited sympathy as symptom of,
150–51; as expression of wishes, 130;
genesis of, 7. *See also* Dora (Ida Bauer)
case; Neurosis

Id: as capable of thought, 26; ego development from, 13–14; ego's conflict with,
17, 27–28; psychosis and strength of,
30; repetition governed by, 203; as
source of passion, 15. *See also* Ego; Superego
Idealization, 46–48
Id-resistance, 258–59
"Infantile Genital Organization, The"
(Freud), 32

Infantile prototypes, 41–42
Infants. *See* Childhood
Inhibitions, Symptoms and Anxiety (Freud),
192, 203
Instinct, 11, 12
Intentionality, 9
Intentions, 111n. *See also* Wishes
International Psychoanalytical Association,
xix
Interpretation of Dreams, The (Freud), 97,
110, 133, 143, 170
Introductory Lectures on Psychoanalysis
(Freud), 8, 170
Inversion, 243

Janet, Pierre, 205
Jaspers, Karl, xviii
Jones, E., 134–35, 138, 209
Jung, Carl, 134, 137, 210

Kant, I., 13, 51
Kanzer, M., 231, 232, 238
Kardiner, Abram, 237
Kierkegaard, Søren, 52, 169
Klein, Melanie, 19, 260, 272
Kraus, Karl, xx
Kris, E., 231–32, 235

Lacan, Jacques, xviii, xix, 55, 165, 208
Laing, R. D., 55, 124, 165–66, 234, 244
Lampl–de Groot, Jeanne, 237
Langs, R., 231–33, 238
Language: concealment through, 64; expe-
rience expressed through, 198–99; of
psychoanalysis, 24–25, 91; representa-
tional theory of, 60–61; as thoughts,
61–62; truth disclosed through, 62–64
Lanzer, Ernst. *See* "Rat Man" (Ernst
Lanzer) case
Laplanche, J., 171–72, 205
Leavy, Stanley A.: on counter will, 65; in-
fluenced by Heidegger, 55; on time and
Freud's concepts, 202; on the uncon-
scious subject, xxv, 10
Lefebre, Ludwig, 56
Lies, 65–66. *See also* Truth
Lipton, S., 234–35, 237–38

Literal (external) reality. *See* Psychical reality

Loewald, Hans: on bias of analytic culture, 209; on distorted reality, 14; on Freud's conception of reality, 12, 17–18; influenced by Heidegger, xv–xvi, 55; on need for father, 17; on philosophical dimension of Freud, 201–2

"Loss of Reality in Neurosis and Psychosis, The" (Freud), 28

Love: derived from infantile prototypes, 41–42; historical views on, 187–89; ideal ego as target of, 45–46; idealization and, 46–47; pathological, 128–29, 186–87; realistic vs. genuine, 43–45, 48–49, 262; of truth, 267; universal need for, 177–78, 185–86. *See also* Transference-love

Lowenfeld, L., 134

Mahony, P., 232–33, 238

Marcel, Gabriel, 51

Marcuse, Herbert, 9

May, Rollo, 55

McCulloch, Warren, 91

"Mechanism of Hysterical Phenomena, The" (Freud), 10

Medical treatment model, 245

Memories, 192–94

Menrath, Walter, xxv

Merleau-Ponty, Maurice, 51

Metaphysics, 3

"Misalliance Dimension in the Case of the Rat Man, The" (Langs), 231

Montaigne, Michel de: affiliation with Freud, xix, 168–69, 196; on experience, 198; on obsessional character, 205–6

Moral masochism, 261

Mother-infant relationship, 23

Motive, 11

Mystification, 234

Narcissistic neuroses, 243

Narcissistic pathologies, 157, 206–8, 245

Nature of knowing, 3–4

Negative therapeutic reaction, 258, 261, 268, 270

Negative transference: positive vs., 183–85; of Rat Man with Freud, 221–22, 225–26

"Neuro-Psychoses of Defense, The" (Freud), 205

Neurosis: castration fear as, 16; compared to psychosis, 28–29, 31–34; conditions for etiology of, 249; disclosure of secrets of, 99–100, 130; dream interpretation during treatment of, 141–44; as escape from suffering, 269–70; existential inclinations and, 119; formation of, 29–31, 268; genesis of hysterical, 7; interpretation of reality and, 12–15; obsessional, 205–11; phantasy preference within, 116, 131; phobias as first childhood, 15; post-treatment trauma and, 251–52; repression during, 68; transference, 184, 196–97; transference-love and, 46–48, 179–81; within structural model, 27–28

"Neurosis and Psychosis" (Freud), 27, 28

Neurotic anxiety, 15

Neutrality: Freud's conception of, 171–74, 239; Freud's violation of, 231, 237; regarding erotic transference, 233–34; rigid interpretation of, 235

New Introductory Lectures on Psychoanalysis (Freud), 262

Newton, Sir Isaac, 70–73, 75

Nicomachean Ethics (Aristotle), 266–67

Nietzsche, Friedrich, 51–52, 169

Nirvana complex, 262, 266

Notes Upon a Case of Obsessional Neurosis (Freud), 213

Oakley, Chris, xxv

"Observations on Transference-Love" (Freud), 37, 136, 171, 175–91, 233

Obsessional neurosis: character of, 205–6; compulsive behavior and, 223; deception as feature of, 226–27; difficulty of, 213; fear of intimacy symptom of, 238. *See also* "Rat Man" (Ernst Lanzer) case

Obsessional type, 207–9

Oedipus complex, 16–18, 29–30

Of Experience (Montaigne), 169, 205

"On Beginning the Treatment" (Freud), 135, 191, 225, 246

"On Narcissism" (Freud), 45

"On Psychotherapy" (Freud), 134, 155–74

"On the Essence of Truth" (Heidegger), 57
"On the History of the Psychoanalytic
  Movement" (Freud), 7
On the Way to Language (Heidegger), 198
Openness rule, 152–53
Ornston, Darius, xix

"Papers on Technique" (Freud), 133
Pathological love, 128–29, 186–87
Patients: aggression toward analysts by,
  183–84; analyst's openness with, 152–
  53; analysts returning love to, 43–44; analysts use of abstinence with, 173; borderline, 157–58; confidentiality between analyst and, 213; determining analyzability
  of, 156–57, 243–44; differential diagnosis of, 163; disclosure of confidences
  from, 99–100; dream interpretation as
  beneficial to, 143–44; erotic yearnings
  of, 37–40; learning from experience,
  195–96; negative therapeutic reaction of,
  258–59; preconceived ideas of, 154; protected from relatedness, 238–39; recognizing transference in, 176–79; remaining alert to, 64; remembering by,
  192–204; role of, 154; stratagem to overcome resistance in, 199–200, 248; supine position of, 165–67; sympathy with-
  held from, 150–51. *See also* Neutrality;
  Psychoanalysis
Phantasies: childhood experience of, 16;
  disguised as memories, 193; escaping reality through, 53–54, 116, 131–32; experience of, 8; gratification from, 259–
  60; of love, 178–80; love of idealized,
  46; psychical reality in terms of, 9; reality
  status of, 2. *See also* Psychical reality
Phenomena, 11
Philosophy: concern with beliefs by, 76;
  Freud's condemnation of, 51; quest for
  truth through, 52–53. *See also* Existential
  philosophy
Philosophy of existence, xviii, 52
Phobias, 15
Plato, 4
Pleasure principle, 43–44, 258, 261
Pontalis, J.-B., 171–72, 205
Positive transference, 183–85
"Prefatory Remarks" (Freud), 98

Primary thought process, 21–24, 253
"Problem of Defense and the Neurotic Interpretation of Reality, The" (Loewald),
  12
"Project for a Scientific Psychology"
  (Freud), 7
Psychasthenia, 205, 243
Psychical reality, 2, 7–9
Psychoanalysis: aims of, 1–2, 76–77, 245–
  46; for analysts, 151–52; beginning treatment of, 155–74; classical, 138, 230–40;
  cure and termination of, 241–46; decline
  of, 245–46; development of analytic
  schools of, xxii; diagnostic criteria for,
  207; disclosure of secrets within, 99–
  100; of Dora (Ida Bauer), 93–121;
  dream interpretation during, 141–44;
  duration and depth of, 162–63, 270–71;
  of Ferenczi, 250–52; free association during, 68, 167–70; Freud on, xxv, 88–90,
  133–39, 243–44, 247–63; Freud's violation of rules of, 231–40; "fundamental
  rule" of, 128, 167, 182, 243; modern
  trends in, 89–92; nature of, xxiii–xxiv, 5;
  psychology as foundation of, 74; psychosis according to, 35–36; quest for doctrine purity, xix; recommended posture
  during, 165–67; revelation of repressed
  wishes during, 130; semantics of, 24–25;
  subjectivity problem in, 65; successful termination of, 197, 273–74; suffering relieved by, 267–68; taking notes during,
  146–48; technique vs. theoretical in,
  175; technology of, 83–84; time and
  money issues of, 160–65; truth and, 88–
  92; used to explore experience, 54; working-through, 192–204. *See also* Analysts;
  Patients
"Psychoanalysis as an Art and the Fantasy
  Character of the Psychoanalytic Situation" (Loewald), 201
Psychologism, 4
Psychology: as ethical science, 170–71; as
  foundation of psychoanalysis, 74; scientific claims of, 2; scientific procedure
  within, 70
Psychopathology: Freud on origins/nature
  of, 5, 272–73; Klein's conception of,
  272; new nosological categories within,

206; as result of self-deception, 170, 252
Psychopathology of Everyday Life (Freud), 10, 217
Psychosis: compared to neurosis, 28–29, 31–34; development of, 30–31; narcissistic neuroses as, 243
Psychotic experience of reality, 6, 34

Question Concerning Technology, The (Heidegger), 78
Question of Lay Analysis, The (Freud), 242
"Question of a *Weltanschauung, The*" (Freud), 51

Racker, H., 237
Rank, Otto, 247
"Rat Man" (Ernst Lanzer) case: analysis of, 134, 209–10, 213–18; false success of, 210–11, 239; obsessions of, 219–23; resolution of, 224–30; surviving process notes of, 230–31; transference within, 221–23; unconscious plea for sympathy in, 150
Rational, 24
Realistic anxiety, 15
Realistic love: described, 43; genuine vs., 48–49; socially acceptable, 44–45
Realistic thinking, 26
Reality: ego and, 12, 28–29; escaped through phantasy, 53–54, 116, 131–32; experience of psychotic, 34–36; external, 9, 12; Freud's exploration of, 2–3, 6, 17–20, 53–54; idealizing to transform, 46; as interchangeable with truth, 5; psychical, 7–8; psychoanalysis to reveal, 5–6; psychosis as disavowal of, 31–32; repressive nature of, 14; strengthen ego to accept, 254; unfulfilled longings removed from, 179–80; using doubt to escape from, 227–28. *See also* Truth
"Reality and Actuality" (Freud), 124
Reality principle, 22, 24, 43
"Recommendations to Physicians Practicing Psycho-analysis" (Freud), 64, 135, 145–54, 171
Reich, Wilhelm, 208
"Remembering, Repeating, and Working-Through" (Freud), 135, 176
Repetition, 193–94, 201, 203

Representational theory of language, 60–61
Repression: childhood, 256; of disappointments, 241; of erotic longings, 34, 39, 47, 187; governed by ego, 203; neurosis as failed, 29; neurotic symptoms and sexual, 118; origins of, 18; vs. concealment, 64–68; of wishes, 130; within Oedipus complex, 29–30
Resistance: False Self's collaboration for, 255; as feature of obsessional neurosis, 226–27; free sessions and increased, 163–65; Freud's proposals regarding, 203–4; id, 258–59; interpretation of, 170–71; overcoming, 199–200, 248; to analysis, 42–43, 160, 181–82, 201; to personal analysis, 151–52; transference-love as, 40–41, 200; unresolvable, 257–58
Resistance analysis, 191
Revelations: counter-will and, 65; from analyst to patient, 152–53; of repressed wishes, 130; *techne* vs. *episteme*, 83; through technology, 82
Rickman, J., 237
Rycroft, Charles, 22–25, 55

Sanity, Madness, and the Family (Laing and Esterson), 124
Sartre, Jean-Paul, 51, 65–67, 195
Schilder, Paul, 56
Schizophrenia, 243–44
Schneider, Kirk, xxv
Schreber, Judge, 33
Science: criteria of truth in, 69–70, 74–75; as foundation of psychoanalysis, 88; Greek's approach to, 70–71; Newton's approach to, 71–73; technology epitomized by, 92
Scientific method, 1
Scientism, 4
Scopophilic urge, 68
Secondary gain, 203
Secondary thought process, 21–24, 253
Secrecy. *See* Concealment
Seduction theory, 7
Self-destructive behavior, 260–61, 270
Sexuality: Freud's conception of, 261–62; money and, 163–64; of Oedipus com-

Sexuality (*Continued*)
   plex, 16–18, 29–30; repression of, 118;
   within Rat Man case, 224–25
Socrates, 4, 187–88
Spinoza, Baruch, 51
Standard Edition (Freud), 133, 171, 192
Strachey, James, 11, 133–34, 175, 230,
   237, 253
Straus, Erwin, 56
Structural model: anxiety in terms of, 229;
   as challenge to Freud, 253–54; counter-
   will and, 21–22; neurosis within, 27; regarding unresolvable resistance, 257–58;
   subjectivity within, 75–76, 203
Studies in Hysteria (Freud), 133
Subjectivity: bias of, 73; of structural the-
   ory, 75–76, 203; within psychoanalysis,
   65
Suffering: conceptualizing nature of, 266;
   experience of, 261–63; as part of life,
   264–65; psychoanalysis and, 267–69; relationship with pleasure, 266–67
Sullivan, H. S., 165–66
Superego: assault on ego by, 17; function
   as conscience, 27; moral conflicts arbi-
   trated by, 229; resistance governed by,
   203
"Superego and Time" (Loewald), 201
Supine position, 165–66
Supportive treatment, 158
"Symposium" (Plato), 187

Techne, 82–83
Technical papers (Freud): "Analysis Terminable and Interminable," 162, 203, 245,
   247; described, xxv, 133–39; *Durcharbeitung,* 192; "The Dynamics of Transference," 135–36, 175–91; *Inhibitions,
   Symptoms and Anxiety,* 192; "Observations on Transference-Love," 37, 136,
   171, 175–91, 233; "On Psychotherapy,"
   134, 155–74; "Recommendations to
   Physicians Practicing Psycho-analysis,"
   64, 135, 145–54; "Remembering, Repeating, and Working-Through," 135,
   176
Technology: causality role within, 79–82;
   challenge of modern, 84–87; defining,

78–79; of psychoanalysis, 83–84; purpose of, 82, 90–91; truth and, 78–87
Thanatos, 261–62, 266–67
Therapeutic ambition: Freud's counsel
   against, 171, 255; lengthy treatment as
   violation of, 271; as source of countertransference, 149–50, 153–54
Thoughts: id capable of, 26; language as,
   61–62; process of primary/secondary,
   21–24, 253
Tillich, Paul, 51
Totem and Taboo (Freud), 8, 17, 228
Transcripts, 148
Transference: described, 225–26; positive
   vs. negative, 183–85; resolution of, 202;
   within Rat Man case, 221–22, 225–26
Transference-love: for analyst, 37, 178–82;
   of Dora to Freud, 116, 120, 122–23,
   127; Freud's technical papers on, 129,
   135–36, 175–91; of neurotics, 46–48;
   neutrality of analysts and, 171–74; patient's repression of, 39; positive vs. negative, 183–85; recognizing in patients,
   176–79; as repetitions, 194; as resistance, 40–41, 200; significance of concept, 189–91, 193; three forms of, 185–
   86; vs. real love, 40–44. *See also* Countertransference; Love
Transference neurosis: described, 196–97;
   within Rat Man case, 221–23, 225–26,
   231
"Transference Neurosis of the Rat Man,
   The" (Kanzer), 231
Trial analysis, 156
Trieb, 11
Truth: acceptance of, 200; disclosed
   through language, 62–64; as Dora case
   theme, 124–25; freedom to enjoy telling,
   226–27; Freud's lifetime search for, 52–
   53; from experience, 63, 77, 131–32;
   God and, 59; guilt through denial of,
   229; Heidegger's conception of, xxiv,
   57–65; historical, 125; as interchangeable with reality, 5; love of, 267; nature
   of, 1; phantasies as, 9; psychoanalysis
   and, 5–6, 88–92; quota of disclosure of,
   248–49; science and, 69–77; technology
   and, 78–87; un-truth compared to, 64–
   68. *See also* Reality

Truthful (psychical) reality. *See* Psychical reality

"Two Principles of Mental Functioning" (Freud), 22

Unamuno, Miguel de, 51
Unconscious: access to mind of, 2; acts of, 4; counter-will and, 9–11; delusions as door to, 36; ego development and, 13–14; expectations of love in, 178; free association to release, 166–70; Freud's theory of, 21–24; limiting disclosure of, 248–49; psychoanalysis aims to reveal, 5; purpose of anxiety, 15; recognizing concealed truth of, 64; source of guilt in, 217; unfulfilled longings withdrawn into, 179–80. *See also* Dream interpretation
"Unconscious, The" (Freud), 13
Unobjectionable (positive) transference, 185
Un-truth, 64–68. *See also* Truth

Ver Eecke, Wilfried, xxv
Virtue, 267
Vorstellen, 60

Weakened ego, 256
Weingarten, Randall, xxv
Westfall, Robert, xxv
What Is a Thing? (Heidegger), 70
" 'Wild' Psychoanalysis" (Freud), 134
Will, 10
Will, Otto Allen, Jr., xxv
Winnicott, D. W., 124, 255, 269
Wishes: hysterical as expression of, 130; phantasies from unfulfilled, 193; repetition of unfulfilled, 194–95; vs. intentions, 111n.
Wishful impulses, 11
Wishful (primary thought process) thinking, 6, 25–26
Wolf Man case: Freud's free treatment during, 164; length of treatment in, 270–71; stratagem to overcome resistance in, 248; successful termination in, 274
Working-through, 192–204
Wortis, Joseph, 160, 237